AF361431

ONE-SIDED ARGUMENTS

SUNY Series in Logic and Language
John T. Kearns, editor

ONE-SIDED ARGUMENTS

A Dialectical Analysis of Bias

Douglas Walton

State University of New York Press

Published by
State University of New York Press, Albany

© 1999 State University of New York

All rights reserved

Printed in the United States of America

*No part of this book may be used or reproduced in any manner
whatsoever without written permission. No part of this book may be stored
in a retrieval system or transmitted in any form or by any means including
electronic, elctrostatic, magnetic tape, mechanical, photocopying, recording,
or otherwise without the prior permission in writing of the publisher.*

*For information, address State University of New York Press
State University Plaza, Albany, New York 12246*

Production by Dana Foote
Marketing by Nancy Farrell

Library of Congress Cataloging-in-Publication Data

Walton, Douglas N.
*One-sided arguments : a dialectical analysis of bias / Douglas
Walton.*
p.   cm. — (SUNY series in logic and language)
Includes bibliographical references and index.
*ISBN 0–7914–4267–5 (alk. paper). — ISBN 0–7914–4268–3 (pbk. :
alk. paper)*
1.Reasoning.   2. Bias (Psychology)   I. Title.   II. Series.
BC177.W3255   1999
168—dc21   99–15100
CIP

10   9   8   7   6   5   4   3   2   1

For Karen, with love

Contents

CONTENTS

Contents

Acknowledgments

I would like to thank the Social Sciences and Humanities Research Council of Canada for support in the form of a research grant, and to thank specifically the following individuals for their help: Amy Merrett, for word-processing the text and figures of the manuscript; Victor Wilkes, for helping to collect materials that were used in the research; Alan Brinton, Erik Krabbe, Frans van Eemeren, and Rob Grootendorst, for discussions that provoked thoughts and suggested some of the subjects and ideas pursued in the book.

I would like to thank the editors of *Argumentation* for permission to reprint (in slightly altered form) section 1 of my paper, "Dialogue Theory for Critical Thinking," *Argumentation* 3 (1989):169–84, which appears in this book as chapter 1, section 10, and for permission to reprint "The Witch Hunt as a Structure of Argumentation," which appears, in slightly altered form, as chapter 9. Some of the work in this project was done at the University of Western Australia (UWA) where I was research associate from September 1996 to March 1997. I would like to thank the Department of Philosophy of the UWA for providing space, facilities, and support for my research work during that period. Some of the rewriting of the first draft was done while I was a Distinguished Visiting Research Associate at the Oregon Humanities Center. During this period, discussions with Don Levi and Paul Schollmeier at the Humanities Center were helpful. The final work on the book was done while I was Fulbright Scholar at Northwestern University in early 1999. I would like to thank the Foundation for Educational Exchange Between Canada and the United States of America and the Department of Communication Studies of Northwestern University for their support of my work during this period. I would like to thank Harry Simpson for help with the proofreading and Rita Campbell for preparation of the index.

Introduction

It has been a widely accepted presumption in the Western world for some time that one of the main benefits of a university education is learning an ability to detect bias in an argument, particularly bias of a dogmatic or rigid sort that interferes with critical thinking. At any rate, this assumption has been an important, even central feature of the way that methods of reasoning in the traditional disciplines in the humanities, social sciences, and natural sciences have been taught in the modern period. Recently, however, it has come under severe attack as itself being a sort of bias that is questionable and open to challenge.

The most serious challenge to the traditional academic disciplines in this period just before the millennium is the widespread acceptance, or at least tolerance, of the postmodernist view that there are no objective standards of rational argument. This view is taken to mean that all viewpoints, even the supposedly rational viewpoints of logic and scientific method, have a bias that reflects the advocacy of the interests of those who are members of certain groups, e.g., the traditional logicians or the established scientists, who promote that point of view and who stand to gain from promoting it. The conclusion drawn from this skeptical and relativistic premise is that it is perfectly acceptable for one to promote the point of view of the group to which one belongs. So, for example, if one happens to belong to a particular interest group that has been victimized, then it is all right, indeed it is necessary to take actions and adopt viewpoints that promote the interests of this group. And if these steps happen to clash with the views or standpoints of logical or scientific reasoning, or the views of any other competing group, then it is perfectly proper and acceptable for one to push ahead with the advocacy of one's own group, discounting opposing views as merely the biases of other interest groups.

Of course, because of its relativistic nature, it is difficult to define postmodernism in some clear, precise, or consistent definition. Simons and Billig (1995, p. 2) express this difficulty concisely: "Place two postmodernists in a room and they will inevitably come forth, not with three definitions (as in the usual joke), but with a treatise on the vacuousness of definitions." But whatever postmodernism is exactly, it certainly is against the idea of there being objective standards of reasoning, of the kind presupposed by the traditional disciplines in the humanities, social sciences, and natural sciences. The idea that bias could be defined and evaluated, in a nonbiased and academically useful way that would make it possible to detect and evaluate (from a detached, critical perspective) the bias in a given case of a text of discourse, is precisely what is rejected by the postmodernist view.

The difficulty in making an effective reply to this postmodernist challenge has been posed by the framework of the traditional logic, which views an argument as an impersonal kind of inference, deductive or inductive, from premises to a conclusion. In this framework, bias in reasoning (Evans 1989) is seen as an erroneous inference where standards of correct (valid) inference characteristic of deductive and inductive standards of logic fail to be met. This quite narrow conception of bias is satisfactory within its self-imposed limits of application. But, unfortunately, it does not apply in any useful way to many of the most common kinds of cases in everyday argumentation where bias in argument is alleged or is criticized as a serious problem or obstacle to critical thinking.

To confront the problem more directly, this book presents a dialectical analysis of bias, based on the idea that an argument is a sequence of reasoning used in a dialogue exchange between two parties. According to this analysis, bias in argument is to be identified and evaluated in relation to the context of use of an argument in such a dialogue framework. The idea of argument being dialectical (dialogue oriented) in nature was familiar to the ancient Greeks but has been lost sight of for two millennia. Thus when the idea of detecting bias in arguments as a task for logic began to trickle into the modern academic curriculum, the structures needed to conceptualize bias were not there.

The idea of detecting and identifying bias in arguments was introduced by Francis Bacon in the *Novum Organum* (1620) but was more sharply formulated by Arnauld in his *L'Art de Penser* (1662). Then it was put into the mainstream material of the logic curriculum by Isaac Watts in his doctrine of the prejudices of the mind in his *Logick* (1725). What has been conspicuously lacking is any serious underlying research that would offer a clear structural account of bias that could be applied usefully to judging cases of arguments in a text of discourse from a critical perspective.

This book leads the way toward filling this gap by providing useful and reproducible criteria for the identification, analysis, and evaluation of dialectical bias in argumentation. The goals of the project are (a) to provide a philosophical analysis of the concept of 'bias,' of a general and abstract sort, that will be useful in guiding research and the design of instructional materials in the areas of informal logic, argumentation theory, and critical thinking; (b) to provide indicators that will enable the identification of this type of bias in argumentation in a text of discourse in a given case; and (c) to study the evaluation of bias in such a case to give criteria to help in judging when such a bias is a problem, that is, is critically harmful so that the argumentation may be said to be faulty or defective because it contains an obstructive bias.

The specific purpose of part (a) of the project is to provide a definition of bias in argumentation that can be taken as a target concept to be identified in particular cases by various indicators of bias. The definition proposed is a dialectical one that involves the analysis of argumentation as a sequence of reasoning used in a context of conversation, determined by the given text of discourse in a particular case.

In attempting to define bias, it should be emphasized that we seek to define a concept of bias in argumentation that will be useful for purposes of normative evaluation of arguments. Textbooks in informal logic and critical thinking are always warning us that bias is a problem because it can, and often does, interfere with critical thinking. The modern textbooks seem to assume that, in particular, bias of which an arguer is not aware can pose problems in argumentation and lead to fallacies and other obstructions to communication. Thus, while we may not be able to avoid bias in argumentation, there seems to be a consensus of opinion in the modern textbooks that one of the most important skills of critical thinking is the ability to recognize bias in argumentation and to be able to deal in a critical manner with cases where bias is a problem.

However, it should be emphasized at the outset, that the kind of bias or slanting we seek to identify for use in a critical and dialectical analysis of argumentation is narrower than, and possibly quite different from, the kind of bias concept widely used in ethics, for example, gender bias, racial prejudice, employment bias, and so on, where bias appears to be, broadly speaking, a kind of unfairness or injustice. 'Bias' in this meaning, is something unethical or "bad," subject to condemnation in the sense that an action that is biased is morally wrong and a biased person is a bad person. We use words such as *bigotry* or *prejudice* to describe this type of bias.

Our sense of dialectical bias is narrower than this other sense in that it only refers to a certain kind of communicative bias in argumentation and not to ethical bias in persons, practices, social institutions, and so on. In the sense of the word into which we will be inquiring, bias is found in how arguments are presented, as they occur in a given text of discourse. For this purpose we are interested only in judging bias as bad, or a problem, as opposed to being harmless, in the sense that if it is a critical fault in argumentation that can interfere with the argument serving its proper or a useful function in discourse. In the dialectical sense, bias is bad not because it is ethically wrong or infringes anyone's rights as a citizen but because it is a critical fault—it opens an argument to criticism on the grounds that it falls short of some standard of rationality as a correct or well-reasoned argument used in a communicative exchange.

Prejudice, from a point of view of morality, seems to be a kind of attitude that is always negative or bad. However, the concept of bias in argumentation appropriate for informal logic is quite subtle in that (a) it seems to be something that we can never entirely escape or avoid, as human arguers, and (b) if you equate it with advocacy, partisanship, or point of view in argumentation, it may be, in many instances, a good thing.

Bias or dialectical slanting in argumentation, in the sense appropriate for our analysis, then, is not inherently bad, even in the critical sense of 'bad' referring to a criticizable, incorrect, or logically defective argument. Blair (1988, p. 94) very helpfully distinguishes between what he calls "good bias" and "bad bias" of this kind. Bias of a "good" or harmless kind is normal in partisan argumentation advocating a particular point of view. But according to Blair (1988, p. 95) bias is *bad* (in this sense of being critically bad in argumentation) when it exhibits closedmindedness, distortion, misinterpretation, or a lack of proper balance in argumentation. This does not mean necessarily that bias, in this dialectical sense, is morally bad, or that a biased argument indicates the arguer is a bad person, guilty of some moral transgression of good conduct. It only means that there is a certain quality or characteristic of bias or slanting in his or her argument that is worth drawing attention to, or alleging, as a source of potential problems in dealing with the argument from a critical perspective of good communication.

Of course, the logical and ethical concepts of bias are probably connected in various ways. But our project is not one of attempting to define ethical notions of justice or fairness generally. It is a much narrower and more specialized one of defining a sense of 'bias' or 'slanting' in argumentation that is appropriate for use in argumentation theory, as part of the larger project of devising practical methods for the normative analysis and evaluation of argumentation in everyday discourse.

The kind of dialectical bias we seek to identify is centered around the critical evaluation of argumentation, so it is concerned with the kind of case where bias or slanting becomes a problem, leading to errors, deceptions, or fallacies that need to be carefully identified as common faults, failings, or danger points in reasonable argumentation. As such, dialectical bias here is a normative concept, having to do with the evaluation or criticism of arguments as meeting or failing to meet standards of what constitutes an argument that is good or successful for some communicative purpose.

This book not only presents a general theory of the concept of dialectical bias in argumentation. It also sets out ten diagnostic indicators that can be used to determine whether dialectical bias exists in a particular case in an argument. The book also goes on to take up the problem of evaluating when and why such bias found in an argument can properly be described as being negative, in the sense of being harmful to the rational credibility of the argument, and open to criticism for being a defect, so that the argument is discounted.

However, the book argues that dialectical bias is quite normal in everyday conversational arguments and does not, by itself, constitute grounds for criticizing an argument as critically deficient or fallacious. It is argued that one-sided advocacy or partisanship in an argument is only a basis for negative criticism of the argument in some cases.

The analysis of this book is based on the relativistic premise that whenever an argument is advocated, that argument is based on and expresses the commitments and/or interests of the proponent who advocated it. Consequently, the book also accepts the somewhat postmodernistic thesis that dialectical bias is normal, not pathological, and it should not (necessarily) justify evaluating the argument as deficient or fallacious. But the analysis of dialectical bias presented in the book blocks the postmodernist conclusion so often drawn from this premise, namely, that you should therefore feel free to advocate the interest of your own group, because academic, logical, or scientific standards of rational argument are themselves biases that merely reflect the interests of those who stand to gain by them.

Chapter One
HISTORICAL BACKGROUND

The modern concern with detecting bias in arguments, as an aspect of critical thinking to be taught to university students, gradually seems to have become a significant part of the logic curriculum as late as the seventeenth and eighteenth centuries. The notion of bias being a distortion in scientific reasoning, produced by the human way of seeing things, was introduced as a prominent idea in Francis Bacon's *Novum Organum* (1620), and then it was incorporated as an important part of the methods of critical thinking in the *Port-Royal Logic* (1662). It seems then that this concern with identifying and evaluating bias made its way into the mainstream of the logic curriculum in the universities through the doctrine of the prejudices of the mind in the very popular textbook *Logick* (1772) written by Isaac Watts.

1. Plato and Aristotle on Dialectic

In the ancient world, nothing exactly corresponds to the concern of the modern teachers of logic to warn their students about bias in argument or to teach them how to detect bias as a logical skill. However, both Plato and Aristotle placed great emphasis on the method of reasoning they called "dialectic" (or "dialectical argument"), which could be roughly described as a reasoned, probing conversational question-reply exchange between two parties where the aim is to find the truth of some matter. Both Plato and Aristotle made a central point of contrasting this two-sided dialectical type of argument with the one-sided method of argument said to be practiced by the Sophists.

Both Plato and Aristotle saw philosophy as a search for truth and

1

knowledge that was a valuable end in itself. But their predecessors, the Sophists (Zeller 1931, p. 77), saw knowledge as valuable only insofar as it "formed a means to the control of life." To pursue this practical aim, the Sophists gave popular lectures, for which they charged admission fees, and in these lectures they stressed teaching practical skills of rhetoric and persuasion. Plato and Aristotle both criticized the Sophists generally for putting too exclusive an emphasis on skills of advocacy instead of teaching truth-seeking dialectic.

Both Plato and Aristotle placed an emphasis on dialectical argument as a sequence of exchanges between two parties where one examines the other through asking a series of challenging and probing questions to which the other must reply. Plato saw dialectic as his main method of seeking the truth, but his conception of what dialectic is changed during the stages of evolution of his philosophy. According to Robinson (1953, p. 70), "the word 'dialectic' had a strong tendency in Plato to mean 'the ideal method, *whatever that may be.*'" But one can get an idea of what Plato meant by looking at his works written in dialogue form.

Aristotle saw dialectical argument as a kind of question-reply dialogue that initially was based on opinions of the majority or the wise, as contrasted with demonstrative argument or proof based on premises known to be true. In *On Sophistical Refutations* (165b3–165b4), he writes, "Dialectical arguments are those which, starting from generally accepted opinions (*endoxa*), reason to establish a contradiction." The value of dialectic, according to Evans (1977, p. 32) is that because it starts from generally accepted opinions, and because its method of argument is that of question and answer, it is "able to debate *both* sides of the case," thereby serving a function of balancing one side against the other.

Both Plato and Aristotle recognized a negative counterpart to dialectic, *eristic* (contentious) dialogue where the participants both have the purely negative aim of defeating the other in argument by any means, foul or fair. Both Plato and Aristotle identified eristic dialogue as the method of the Sophists, professional debaters who as noted above took fees to train their students in the art of persuasion. Plato and Aristotle both convey a generally negative view of the Sophists, suggesting that their method was to use rhetorical persuasion or "slick salesmanship" with no regard for the truth of a matter. The terms *Sophist* and *Sophistical* took on this connotation in language, referring to something persuasive but inherently deceptive, based on verbal trickery or illusion, as opposed to truth or reliable reasoning.

For both Plato and Aristotle, eristic dialogue is a kind of negative counterpart of dialectical argument, a bad or degenerative type of dialogue into which a dialectical discussion can descend if the participants are not careful. Dialectical argument is a cooperative, two-sided truth-seeking art that requires a constructive and balanced attitude, whereas eristic dialogue is one-sided, quarrelsome, and antagonistic.

While there is opposition between the participants in dialectical argument, according to Robinson (1953, p. 85) the aim of dialectic for Plato is to discover the truth of a matter, and the participants must be "gentle and friendly with each other." By contrast, in eristic dialogue, the participants care nothing for the truth and exhibit a childish contentiousness.

We might make an allusion already to the modern language of normative pragmatics by saying that a collaborative critical discussion depends on the observance of principles of politeness and cooperation (Grice 1975; van Eemeren and Grootendorst 1984). It requires an attitude of being open to concession or even defeat in the face of a convincing argument that goes against one's position. Eristic dialogue, by contrast, according to the ancient conception of it, makes no concession to truth and always resorts to tactics that will give an appearance of winning the argument, avoiding any concession that might possibly lead to the defeat or weakening of one's position.

In Plato's dialogue *Euthydemus,* two Sophists, Euthydemus and Dionysodorus, are shown using their eristic skills to trap a young and innocent boy into absurd contradictions and paradoxes. We are shown that eristic dialogue uses antilogic, a kind of cavilling or "logic-chopping" that traps people into contradictions and falsehoods through the use of clever tricks—a kind of misuse of logic for bad purposes. We can see here a kind of fear that dialectical argument can "run wild"—it can be used for the wrong purposes and create all kinds of mischief. Thus eristic dialogue is something to be careful about, to be on your guard against as a dangerous possibility in any argument.

Aristotle followed Plato in characterizing eristic dialogue as involving a spurious and misleading kind of argumentation that "only apparently accords with the subject-matter and so is deceptive and unfair *(De Sophisticis Elenchis* 171b23). Like Plato, Aristotle saw eristic argumentation as inherently deceptive and contentious, because the goal is to defeat the other party by seeming to have the strongest argument.

Aristotle even went so far as to compare eristic argument with cheating in sports, writing that contentious reasoning is "an unfair kind of fighting in argument" used by "those who are bent on victory at all costs" and will stop at nothing to win *(De Sophisticis Elenchis).* This is quite an interesting remark, as noted in Walton (*Prag. Theory*, 1995, p. 270), given that the root meaning of the word *fallacy (fallacia)*, is the word *sphal*, meaning "waver and fall." This word was used by Homer, for example, to refer to tactics used in wrestling contests to cause an opponent to fall. It can also be used to mean "cause to fall by argument," referring to verbal tactics of argument. It seems then that there is a close conceptual link between the concept of eristic argument and the concept of fallacy. Eristic dialogue is associated with the use of unfair and deceptive Sophistical tactics by a participant in argument whose goal is to win by any means—a kind of verbal equivalent of resorting to techniques of "street fighting" in a competition where such tactics are illegal and unfair.

Aristotle introduced a further refinement into this classification by distinguishing between Sophistical argument and (purely) contentious argument. Both use the same kinds of arguments, and both aim at victory, but their goals are different. The quarrelsome (contentious) argument has "semblance of victory" as its motive, whereas the Sophistical argument has "semblance of wisdom" as its motive. For, as Aristotle defined it, "Sophistry is an appearance of wisdom without the reality *(De Sophisticis Elenchis* 171b36). Here, once again, Aristotle identifies Sophistical argument with the group of professional orators and teachers called "Sophists," writing, "The art of the Sophist is a money-making art which trades on apparent wisdom, and so Sophists aim at apparent proof" *(De Sophisticis Elenchis* 171b31). Aristotle took considerable pains then to warn of the dangers of one-sided persuasion. So it is reasonable to infer that the task of detecting and evaluating bias in arguments generally should have an important place in his dialectical conception of reasoned argument.

In the subsequent history of logic (Kneale and Kneale 1962; Hamblin 1970), dialectic fell into obscurity. An impersonal (nondialectical) approach to logic, based on Aristotle's theory of the syllogism, and subsequently on the propositional logic of the Stoics, took over as the exclusive and dominant theory. The idea of dialectical or two-sided argument fell into neglect and disuse for two thousand years. It took a long time for the idea of detecting and evaluating bias to gradually appear and grow in importance in the modern logic textbooks.

2. Twentieth-Century Logic Textbooks on Bias

When we look at the textbooks and manuals on informal logic that treat the concept of bias, from the turn of the century to the present, we see a remarkable variety of different views on what bias is. On the whole, they do not give any clear or precise logical definition of bias or prejudice but presume that it is something bad or harmful in logic that needs to be overcome or corrected and that it has a psychological nature.

Creighton (1904, p. 257) cites Bacon's doctrine of the idols of the cave or den (see the next section below) in characterizing bias: "Each individual, as he represents the matter, is shut up in his own cave or den; that is, he judges of things from his own individual point of view. In the first place, one's inclinations and passions, likes and dislikes, pervert one's judgment." Creighton thinks that it is difficult to free oneself from personal bias and national prejudices, but recognizing such bias is the first step to passing beyond it (p. 258).

Mander (1936, pp. 25–34) thinks of biases as groundless beliefs that become habitual after a while but that originate from self-interest, as propositions that are picked up from others or are held through sentimental associations. Although we tend to believe such opinions strongly (32), on this account, they are not based on justified grounds or good evidence.

Thouless (1936) sees prejudices "as obstacles in our minds that make us unwilling to think straight on certain subjects" (p. 213). He thinks that prejudices are hard to root out and that even those who have a "keen, logical intellect" and who reason very logically can be highly prejudiced in their arguments (p. 216). Prejudices, according to Thouless, are not based on good logical grounds, but on mental causes (p. 217): "When any of us hold the kind of opinions we have called 'prejudices,' we have a part of our minds in the same condition as that of the delusional system of the insane. We too reason to the best of our ability in defence of our prejudices, but these reasonings are not the real support for our opinions. These are based on other (often quite irrational) grounds." Huppé and Kaminsky (1957, p. 9) also see prejudices as mental obstacles to logical thinking, but they see them as arising from environmental and social influences. "*Prejudice.* To a large extent our ideas and beliefs are molded by biases and prejudices of which we may be wholly unconscious but which serve as obstacles to thought. Bacon's *Idols* (see Exercise 3) lists the major prejudices that prevent the use of thought. Because of family and friends we tend to believe some things more readily than others." Both these textbooks see the detection of prejudices in our thinking as an important task of informal logic.

Fearnside and Holther (1959) see a number of different fallacies as based on prejudice. They define prejudice very broadly as any opinion not held on reasonable grounds (p. 94):

Prejudice is an opinion held without reasonable grounds: it takes the form of a decided preference for something or aversion to it. One man may favor foreign aid, luxury taxes, or nonrepresentational art; another may firmly oppose the very same things. An appeal to prejudice shrewdly represents a position as coinciding with whichever bias the speaker supposes to prevail in his audience. Such an appeal is evidently different from an examination of the merits of a given proposal—or even of general tendencies and policies relating to the proposal.

Among the forms of prejudice Fearnside and Holther recognize are stereotyping, apriorism or "invincible ignorance" (p. 111), cultural bias (p. 117), and "lip service" (p. 104). Scriven (1976, pp. 230–236) emphasizes over-generalization in the form of stereotyping as the kind of bias that is an important obstacle to logical reasoning.

Beardsley (1966, pp. 197–219) defines the kind of bias that is important to analyze in logic as *slanting,* or suggesting conclusions indirectly, as opposed to asserting them explicitly in an argument. Thus Beardsley points out that many of the most powerful kinds of biases in an argument are somewhat concealed and need to be extracted from the context of conversation in which the argument was put forth.[1] Beardsley's treatment of bias is extensive and innovative, and a more lengthy account of it is given later in this chapter.

Little, Groarke, and Tindale (1989) treat bias and slanting as harmless and normal in some instances, but as a problem that can distort news reporting, which is supposed to be a kind of information-giving: "We are emotional as well as rational beings. Each of us has likes and dislikes, loves, loyalties, and commitments. To the extent that our reporting or our reasoning is *distorted* by such affections, we may justifiably be accused of being biased" (59). Because "it is the job of news reporters to report facts," too much bias or slanting in the arguments used in such a report is an obstacle to its supposed purpose (61). Little, Groarke, and Tindale see such bias as an important factor to be identified for purposes of critical thinking.

Bias also has been connected to several of the informal fallacies commonly treated by logic textbooks. Hurley (1991, 116) sees the circumstantial *ad hominem* argument as taking the form of the allegation that attempts to discredit someone by charging that they have a bias, or vested interest, for example, by being chairman of a big corporation. Walton (1990, 149–154) has cited this personal bias type of allegation as a distinctive form of *ad hominem* attack in argumentation that is sometimes justified and sometimes fallacious.

Bias also has been studied as a concept underlying many of the fallacies based on emotional appeals in Walton (*Place Emot.*, 1992). The finding advocated with respect to types of argumentation like the *ad populum, ad misericordiam, ad baculum,* and *ad hominem* in Walton (*Place Emot.*, 1992) is that they are not always fallacious, even when they are based on or connected to the notion of bias.

Detecting bias in argumentation, and evaluating it critically, seems to be an idea that came to be of importance to the discipline of logic in the seventeenth century. Before that time, there appeared to be little or no serious or systematic attention given to this task in the logic textbooks and manuals. Francis Bacon began to identify certain types of bias in human thinking in his *Novum Organum* (1620) that he saw as factors in distorting human reasoning. However, it was Arnauld, in the *Port-Royal Logic* (1662), who identified factors he called "self-love," "interest," and "passion," which nowadays we would call "biases," and showed how these factors lead to certain critical defects in reasoning he called "Sophisms." The link between bias and fallacies was now established, and in many of the current textbook treatments of fallacies, there is a presumption that fallacies can be explained as defects in reasoning by referring to some underlying concept of human bias.

3. Bacon on Idols of the Mind

Francis Bacon begins his *Novum Organum* by stating that knowledge comes to us from objects in nature, but that in order to understand this knowledge, we are always imposing our own theories on it, our "creations of the mind and hand" (p. 12). Our scientific theories are constructions built on our human ways of seeing things, and hence they contain a bias or distortion of nature (p. 12):

> IX. The sole cause and root of almost every defect in the sciences is this, that while we falsely admire and extol the powers of the human mind, we do not search for the real helps.
>
> X. The subtilty of nature is far beyond that of sense or of the understanding: so that the specious meditations, speculations, and theories of mankind are but a kind of insanity, only there is no one to stand by and observe it.

According to Bacon, when humans interpret what they see in nature, they create "idols" or "idle dogmas" (p. 16) that are different from "the real stamp and impression of created objects, as they are found in nature." These are "anticipations" that are "powerful in producing unanimity" because they are "of familiar occurrence" and "immediately hit the understanding and satisfy the imagination" (p. 17).

Bacon describes four types of idols or false appearances that are deeply rooted in the human mind. The *idols of the tribe* (p. 20) represent the way humans see everything according to a human standard. The *idols of the den* represent each person's way of interpreting nature according to his or her "own peculiar and singular disposition" (p. 21). The *idols of the market* arise from "bad and inapt formation of words" so that the mind is obstructed and confused (p. 21). The *idols of the theatre* are dogmas of philosophy and science that have "crept into man's minds" (p. 22).

Bacon seems to be saying that in our reasoning we are very much influenced by conventional ways of thinking. Human thinking, he writes, in the *Novum Organum* (p. 26) "resembles not a dry light, but admits a tincture of the will and passions . . . for a man always believes more readily that which he prefers." Thus the idols are natural biases that always influence and structure our reasoning about the world.

Bacon claims (p. 31) that the idols of the market are "the most troublesome of all" because "words formed in a popular sense" have "entwined themselves around our understanding and reasoning." Thus there is a verbal bias built into everyday reasoning. In "solemn disputes" learned philosophers try to contend with this problem by having "controversies about words and names," but such redefinitions cannot escape being themselves biased language "because they consist themselves of words."

According to Hamblin (1970, p. 144), the word *idol* (*eidolon*) literally means "*false appearance*," but in the seventeenth century it had connotations of "idolatry," or worship of false gods in a religious sense. Thus 'idol' seemed to have for Bacon a negative implication. In a passage in the *Novum Organum* quoted by Hamblin (1970, p. 45), Bacon describes the human understanding as a "false mirror" that "distorts and discolors the nature of things."

How the doctrine of the idols seems to have influenced logic, according to Hamblin (1970, p. 146) is by bringing it about, that from that point on, some part of the analysis of the concept of 'fallacy' began to involve an element of psychological factors.

Bacon did not offer any kind of logical structure or theory for the detection, avoidance, or evaluation of bias. Indeed, Bacon was a strong empiricist who was very skeptical about logic generally as an instrument for guiding scientific reasoning.

Nevertheless, through his doctrine of the idols, he did set in place a recognition of the concept of bias that appealed to many subsequent generations of logic teachers, who began to see the detection of bias as having some place in the teaching of logical skills.

The next step was the tying in of bias to the subject matter of informal fallacies by Antoine Arnauld in his *Port-Royal Logic.*

4. Arnauld on Sophisms of Self-Love, Interest, and Passion

Chapter 20 of the *Port-Royal Logic* (1662) is entitled "Of the Bad Reasonings Which are Common in Civil Life and in Ordinary Discourse."[2] In the first part of the chapter, there is a long section entitled, "Of the Sophisms of Self-Love, of Interest, and of Passion" (Baynes 1926, pp. 267–81). In this section, Arnauld develops the theme that there are three important "bonds" that "commonly attach" people to accept "one opinion rather than another"—self-love, interest, and passion. Arnauld calls these three bonds "Sophisms, meaning that they commonly cause us to draw conclusions that would not be justifiable on the weight of real evidence, which must be found in the thing itself, independently of our desires." It is not that self-love, interest, and passion are fallacious in themselves, according to the Port-Royal theory. The problem is that these three bonds lie at the basis of much of our fallacious reasoning in everyday discourse.

Arnauld does not use the word *bias,* but his three factors of self-love, interest and passion do comprise something that very likely would be equated with bias in argumentation in the current viewpoint of informal logic. It is these three factors, all aspects of what we would now call "bias," that swing an argument in a certain direction, commonly throwing it off the path of good reasoning. Arnauld writes of these three factors, "This is the weight which bears down the scale, and which decides us in the greater part of our doubts" (pp. 267–268). These three factors commonly influence the weight of presumption we put on an opinion. And, in many cases, that is as it should be. The problem is that in some cases, this bias is misleading. It causes us to rest a much greater weight of presumption on an opinion than is really warranted by the objective evidence in a case.

Arnauld draws a contrast (p. 268) between these three factors and objective evidence, or reasons the truth of which "must be found in the thing itself." Noting that it is normal and very natural for us to choose to hold as true that which is to our advantage, Arnauld (p. 268) questions the rationality of this practice.

Nevertheless, what can be more unreasonable than to take our interest as the motive for believing a thing? All that it can do, at most, is to lead us to consider with more attention the reasons which may enable us to discover the truth of that which we wish to be true; but it is only the truth which must be found in the thing itself, independently of our desires, which ought to convince us. I am of such a country; therefore I must believe that such a saint preached the gospel there. I am of such an order; therefore, I must believe that such a privilege is right. These are no reasons. Of whatever order, and of whatever country you may be, you ought to believe only what is true; and what you would have been disposed to believe, though you had been of another country, of another order, and of another profession.

We naturally tend to favor a view that seems to us to support our own interests, but the problem is that this common bias can influence us unduly in some cases in our reasoning.

Self-love has this same effect (Arnauld 1662, p. 272):

The mind of man is not only in love with itself, but it is also naturally jealous, envious of and ill-disposed towards others. It can scarcely bear that they should have any advantage, but desires it all for itself; and as it is an advantage to know the truth, and furnish men with new views, a secret desire arises to rob those who do this of the glory, which often leads men to combat, without reason, the opinions and inventions of others.

Self-love, or as social scientists might now call it, "self-esteem," is natural and normal, but when conjoined to reasoning, it can lead to bias or error. The "good opinion" people have of "their own insight leads them to consider all their thoughts as so clear and evident, that they imagine the whole world must accept them as soon as they are known." This bias toward one's own insights is a force with which to be reckoned in argumentation.

Passion is another factor that leads to a bias (p. 269), often resulting in Sophisms and delusions when it leads people to rash judgments.

If they love any one, he is free from every kind of defect. Everything which they desire is just and easy, everything which they do not desire is unjust and impossible, without their being able to assign any other reason for all these judgments than the passion itself which possesses them; so that, though they do not expressly realise to their mind this reasoning: I love him; therefore, he is the cleverest man in the world: I hate him; therefore, he is nobody;— they realise it to a great extent in their hearts; and therefore, we may call sophisms and delusions of the heart those kinds of errors which consist in transferring our passion to the objects of our passions, and in judging that they are what we will or desire that they should be.

Thus it is not that passion or emotion is wrong in itself. The problem is that it is responsible for a natural and normal bias that lies behind certain very attractive and common but Sophistical inferences, like the following pair, cited above.

> I love him (her).
> Therefore, he (she) is the cleverest person in the world.

> I hate him (her).
> Therefore, he (she) is a nobody.

Another of the several very nice examples of Sophistical reasoning presented by Arnauld (p. 270) is the following one (see also the examples cited in Hamblin 1970, p. 156).

> If this were so, I should not be a clever person.
> Now, I am a clever person.
> Therefore, it is not so.

The nice thing generally about the Port-Royal theory of bias is that it has a pronounced normative-critical element, because it shows how bias (in the form of self-love, interest, and passion) lies behind certain common types of reasoning that should be judged as faulty, erroneous, or Sophistical. Another nice thing is that this theory does not imply that bias in argumentation is always wrong or fallacious *per se*. It only becomes fault, from a critical or logical point of view, when too much weight is put on self-love, interest, or passion, with the result that there is a deviation from the correct reasoning that properly would be justified by the weight of the objective evidence (being convinced by the truth) in a case.

5. Watts on Prejudices of the Mind

Isaac Watts, in his very popular textbook *Logick* (1772) expanded the Port-Royal notion of bias in reasoning to a full-blown doctrine of *preju-*

dices of the mind in reasoning.[3] Watts laid out this doctrine in chapter 3 of his textbook, *The Springs of False Judgment, or the Doctrine of Prejudices* (pp. 186–231). Watts ventures well into psychological territory in this long chapter, making many generalizations that seem to be mentalistic and empirical in nature. For example, he develops an account of "tempers, humors, and peculiar turns of the mind" that are claimed to "have a great influence upon our judgment." Although this account was clearly based, in its general approach, on that of the Port-Royal Logic, it ventures well beyond that careful and rather circumspect theory.

Watts selects the word *prejudice* as the central term for his theory, and he intends it to have both the negative and the mentalistic sense that this word has in everyday language. But he also intends to use the word in a technical or scientific sense that is narrower than that of its usual meaning (pp. 186–187):

> Rash Judgments are called *Prejudices,* and so are the Springs of them. This Word in common Life signifies *an ill Opinion which we have conceived of some other Person,* or some *Injury done to him.* But when we use the Word in Matters of Science, it signifies *a Judgment that is formed concerning any Person or Thing before sufficient Examination;* and generally we suppose it to mean a *false Judgment* or *Mistake;* At least, it is an Opinion taken up without solid Reason for it, or an Assent given to a Proposition before we have just Evidence of the Truth of it, though the Thing itself may happen to be true.
>
> Sometimes these rash Judgments are called *Prepossessions;* whereby is meant, that some particular Opinion has possessed the Mind, and engaged the Assent, without sufficient Search or Evidence of the Truth of it.

The concept of 'prejudice' (or prepossession, or rash judgment) is meant to be mentalistic or psychological (it "possesses the mind") and also negative, in a critical sense—it is an opinion "taken up without solid reason for it," or on insufficient evidence. This implies that such prejudiced or prejudicial opinions are always wrong, faulty, or erroneous, from a logical or critical point of view. These prejudices are divided into four general types by Watts (p. 187)—prejudices arising from things, words, ourselves, or other persons.

According to Brinton (1995, p. 319), Watts' doctrine about prejudice is "most overtly a doctrine about sources of error." Brinton (p. 319) shows how, in Watts' view, the mind is seen as having "certain problematic doxastic tendencies" that lead thinking into error. It is these doxastic tendencies that Watts takes to constitute prejudices. So, for Watts, it is not principles or beliefs that are prejudices, but ways of thinking.

The doctrine of prejudices arising from things sounds very Baconian in spirit but develops some new ideas. One is a kind of prejudice called by Watts "mixture of different qualities in the same thing" (p. 191), which is reminiscent both of the *secundum quid* fallacy (or "neglecting qualifications"—see Walton, *Sec. Quid,* 1990) and also the modern psychological notion of the halo effect.

> When we have just Reason to admire a *Man* for his *Virtues,* we are sometimes inclined not only to neglect his *Weaknesses,* but even to put a good Colour upon them, and to think them amiable. When we read a *Book* that has many excellent Truths in it, and divine Sentiments, we are tempted to approve not only that whole Book, but even all the Writings of that Author. When a *Poet,* an *Orator,* or a *Painter,* has performed admirably in several illustrious Pieces, we sometimes also admire his very Errors, we mistake his Blunders for Beauties, and are so ignorantly fond as to copy after them. (191)

According to Watts (p. 192), "this Sort of Prejudice is relieved by learning to distinguish Things well, and not to *judge in the Lump.*" Many modern textbooks would treat this problem under the heading of the fallacy of "hasty generalization" (Walton, *Sec. Quid,* 1990).

It is interesting to see that Watts, like Arnauld, has a whole section on biased language, in Watts' case under the heading "Prejudices Arising from Words" (pp. 195–198). But it is in the much longer section on "Prejudices Arising from Ourselves" (pp. 198–214) that Watts introduces some new ideas.

There are four kinds of attitudes in argumentation that Watts calls "tempers, humors and peculiar turns of the mind—the credulous temper, the spirit of contradiction, the dogmatical humor and the skeptical humor" (pp. 208–209). These are interesting, because they do seem to articulate certain types of characteristic attitudes in argumentation that are key signs or indications of biased argument.

The *credulous person* gives assent too easily.

> The *credulous Man* is ready to receive every Thing for Truth, that has but a Shadow of Evidence: every new Book that he reads, and every ingenious Man with whom he converses, has Power enough to draw him into the Sentiments of the Speaker or Writer. He has so much Complaisance in him, or Weakness of Soul, that he is ready to

resign his own Opinion to the first Objection which he hears, and to receive any Sentiments of another that are asserted with a positive Air and much Assurance. (p. 208)

The *person of contradiction* is always ready to oppose and dispute the opinion of another person.

The *Man of Contradiction* is of a contrary Humour, for he stands ready to oppose every Thing that is said: He gives a slight Attention to the Reasons of other Men, from an inward scornful Presumption that they have no Strength in them. When he reads or hears a Discourse different from his own Sentiments, he does not give himself Leave to consider whether that Discourse may be true; but employs all his Powers immediately to confute it. (p. 208)

As Watts notes (p. 208), it is difficult for those of us who make a living by disputation not to fall into this prejudice. But it can lead a person to become "pedantick and hateful" (p. 209).

Persons of a dogmatical humor find it difficult to admit any mistake.

By what Means soever the *Dogmatist* came by his Opinions, whether by his Senses or by his Fancy, his Education or his own Reading, yet he believes them all with the same Assurance that he does a *mathematical Truth;* he has scarce any mere *Probabilities* that belong to him; every Thing with him is *certain* and *infallible;* every Punctilio in Religion is an Article of his Faith, and he answers all manner of Objections by a sovereign Contempt. (p. 210)

The contrary prejudice is that of the *skeptical person* (p. 210) who "believes nothing" and is "afraid to give assent to anything again," once he has found his opinions mistaken in the past.

Finally, there are the *"inconstant, fickle, changeable spirits"* (p. 211) who accept opinions they find agreeable at the time but later reverse their opinion or retract it when their human changes. What is lacking in this temper is *firmness of mind* (p. 211).

All these various "humors" and "tempers" are expressed by Watts in psychological terms. But they do have a critical-normative dimension. They all relate to what could be called the "fixation of commitment" in dialogue. Evaluating argumentation has to do with the incurring and retraction of commitment in dialogue, in the sense of Hamblin (1970,

263).[4] The problem Watts rightly perceives as important to the critical evaluation of argumentation is that sometimes arguers are too rash in taking on commitments too quickly or thoughtlessly, while in other cases, once a commitment is lodged in place, a person may be too slow or reluctant to retract it.

6. Bentham on Prejudices and Interests

Jeremy Bentham, in his *Handbook of Political Fallacies* (1824), cites several different types of bias in reasoning that, he thinks, lie behind fallacies used in political argumentation. Bentham (p. 229) cites four "causes of the utterance of these fallacies": (1) sinister interest, (2) interest-begotten prejudice, (3) authority-begotten prejudice, and (4) the need of self-defense against counterfallacies. The first three of these factors could be described as or identified with kinds of bias that occur in argumentation in political discourse.

The first factor, called "sinister interest" by Bentham, arises out of a conflict that always exists between the public and the private interests of a public servant (p. 229).

> His public interest is that which is constituted by the share he has in the happiness and well-being of the whole community. His private interest is made up of the share he has in the well-being of some portion of the community that is less than the major part. The smallest possible portion of public well-being which can constitute a man's private interest is that which composes his own personal or individual interest.

This kind of conflict of interest is normal and inevitable in politicians. Why would Bentham call it "sinister"? The answer is that because they have the common bond of this conflict of interests and because of the "general predominance of personal interest over every variety of more extensive interest" (p. 230), any group of public servants who have an interest in a system will band together and defend each others' interests (p. 231).

> As long as any man has the smallest particle of this sinister interest belonging to him, he will have a fellow-feeling for every other man who in the same situation has an interest of the same kind. Attack one of them, and you attack them all. In proportion as each

of them feels his share in this common concern is dear to him, he is prepared to defend every other confederate's share with no less alacrity than as if it were his own. But it is one of the characteristics of abuse, that it can only be defended by fallacy. It is, therefore, to the interest of all the confederates of abuse to give the most extensive currency to fallacies, not only those which may be serviceable to each individual, but also to those which may be generally useful. It is of the utmost importance to such persons to keep the human mind in such a state of imbecility that shall render it incapable of distinguishing truth from error.

This is quite a subtle and complex type of bias. It means that there is a tendency in an institution for the individuals in it to stick together and defend the bad aspects of it, as well as the good, because that is conducive to the sinister interests of each of the members of the group. We could call this a type of institutional bias.

Bentham's second type of bias, called "interest-begotten prejudice," appears simpler and more straightforward. According to Bentham, "every act of the intellectual faculty" is "directly or indirectly" produced by "interest" (p. 235). However, Bentham adds that such interests are generally not perceptible, because it is usually not very profitable, flattering, or interesting for a person to delve into these personal motives for thinking or arguing the way she does (p. 236). Such self-probes tend to be unattractive and even painful to people, Bentham thinks (p. 237).

Bentham is putting forward the thesis here that all our thinking and reasoning is biased, in the sense of being produced by an interest of some sort, even though this prejudice is normally "secret" or concealed. However, Bentham does not seem to think there is anything bad about this type of bias, or that the existence of it, in itself, is a sufficient reason to condemn reasoning as fallacious or faulty.

The third type of bias, called "authority-begotten prejudice" by Bentham (pp. 238–239), consists in the taking of an opinion on the trust of some other person, instead of examining the evidence oneself. Bentham sees this type of prejudice as not being universally bad or erroneous—although "pernicious" in some cases, "it has its root in sheer necessity" (p. 238). Where it does become fallacious, according to Bentham (p. 239), is in the kind of case where "it becomes constitutive of a mass of authority rooted in sinister interest." The danger, Bentham thinks, comes about when the authority is institutionalized in a group, in a certain way, so that promoting a particular view too strongly is in the sinister interest of the member of the group who advocates this view.[5]

7. Kant on Prejudices and Provisional Judgments

Kant, in his *Introduction to Logic* (1800; trans. 1885),[6] defined prejudices in terms of what he called "provisional judgments" (p. 64): "A provisional judgment is one by which I represent to myself that there are more reasons *for* the truth of a thing than *against* it; [249] but that these reasons are not sufficient for a definitive judgment by which I should decide positively for its truth. Provisional judgment, therefore, is that which is consciously problematical." What Kant calls "provisional judgments" are very similar to what are called "presumptions" in Walton (1992, pp. 278–281). These are propositions that are accepted tentatively, for practical reasons, by agreement of all parties in a dialogue, even though there is insufficient evidence to prove or disprove them. Presumptions are subject to retraction should evidence against them arise in the subsequent dialogue (meaning they are *defeasible*).

According to Kant, presumptions are very useful and even necessary in thinking and inquiry (p. 65), even though they can be problematic. "Provisional judgments are very necessary—nay, indispensable for the employment of the understanding in all meditation and inquiry; [250] for they serve to guide the understanding in its inquiries, and to supply it with various means thereto." The problematic part arises where a defeasible presumption is taken in an absolute way. Kant (pp. 65–66) defines *prejudices* as provisional judgments that are taken as principles, or judgments that are absolutely true, without qualification.

> Prejudices must be distinguished from provisional judgments. Prejudices are provisional judgments that are *adopted as principles*. Every prejudice is to be viewed as a principle of erroneous judgments, and from prejudices arise not prejudices, but erroneous judgments. We must, therefore, distinguish from the prejudice itself the false cognition that arises from the prejudice. Thus, for instance, the significance of dreams is in itself not a prejudice, but an error that arises from the assumed general rule—that what sometimes happens always happens, or is always to be regarded as true. And this principle, to which the significance of dreams is to be referred, is a prejudice.

Kant goes on to say that prejudices can even be based on true provisional judgments. However, what is "not right" is when these provisional judgments are taken as principles, instead of recognizing that they are only tentative, subject to further testing and reflection (p. 66). Thus in the dreams case above, inferring that the dream has some significance would not, in itself, be prejudice. But inferring that what occurred in the dream must have really happened would be an erroneous kind of inference based on a prejudice.

This view of prejudice as a kind of absolutization of a defeasible presumption is very similar to the analysis of the *secundum quid* fallacy given in Walton (1990b; 1992, pp. 282–284). And it could be identified as a form of bias or an aspect of bias in argumentation. It represents the kind of phenomenon in argumentation often identified with the dogmatic attitude, where an arguer improperly absolutizes the principle or general warrant behind an inference.

Kant claims that the three chief sources of prejudice are imitation, custom, and inclination, and he classifies many kinds of common prejudices under these headings (pp. 66–71). One can easily see how these different prejudices could be seen to underlie several of the different types of erroneous inferences classified as informal fallacies by the logic textbooks.

One is the tendency "to take as true what others allege as true" (p. 66) based on the prejudice "what everyone does is right." This kind of erroneous reasoning is associated with informal fallacy of the *argumentum ad populum.*

Another is called by Kant (p. 68) the "prejudice of personal authority":

> When, in matters that depend on experience and testimony, we build our knowledge on the authority of other persons, we are not thereby involved in any prejudice; for in things of this sort, since we cannot ourselves experience everything, or embrace everything with our own understanding, personal authority must be the foundation of our judgments. But when we make the authority of others the ground of our assent with respect to rational cognitions, then we accept these cognitions from mere prejudice.

This draws an inference based on prejudice. This interpretation of the prejudice of personal authority is associated with the informal fallacy of the *argumentum ad verecundiam.*

Kant is taking quite an intelligent approach to the kind of reasoning associated with these two traditional fallacies. First, he is saying that they are not always fallacious kinds of reasoning. Drawing on popular opinion or on appeal to expert opinion, according to Kant, is, in itself, a reasonable and useful kind of presumptive inference to make. It is not always fallacious. But it becomes fallacious, in Kant's view when it is based on the prejudice that what popular opinion or an authority says or does is always right.

One twentieth-century textbook treatment of bias has gone into much more depth than usual on the concept of 'bias' and is worth examining at length.

8. Beardsley on Suggestion and Slanting

Beardsley (1966, pp. 197–219) treated bias in his innovative informal logic textbook *Thinking Straight,* under the heading "Suggestion and Slanting" (p. 197). His point of view was that bias in argumentation, of the kind we need to detect in critical thinking, comes from suggestions not explicitly stated in argument but which arise indirectly by innuendo or presumption. This seems to be one aspect of bias that is very important in the evaluation of argumentation, and *slant* is a good word for it.

Beardsley (p. 198) drew a contrast between explicitly asserting a statement and saying something that shows you believe it by suggestion.

> *Case* 1.1: For example, you can say, in a flat tone of voice: "The Republican candidate for mayor has refused to appoint a Human Relations Committee." If you stress the word "Republican," you manage to say something more: namely, that perhaps the Democratic candidate has not refused to appoint such a committee. If you stress the word "appoint," you suggest that, if elected, he probably will be willing to cooperate with such a committee if someone else sets it up. The difference in what is conveyed by the three assertions is not a difference in what they state, but in what they suggest.

Beardsley adds (p. 198) that there are speech conventions in a natural language that lead to expectations that lead us to make presumptions about what we would normally take as being suggested or implied by what someone says.

> *Case* 1.2: Bob passed Roger, a colleague in the philosophy department, in the hallway, and commented, "You look very thoughtful today." Mary, another colleague passing by commented, "You mean normally he does not look thoughtful?"

Here the suggestion that someone who is a philosopher would not normally look thoughtful is somewhat insulting. Hence the interest in Mary's having pointed it out.

In the light of recent developments, we would analyze this type of drawing out a suggestion as a species of implicature, as studied by Grice (1975). In case 1.2, the implicature upon which the suggestion rests is that if a person is identified or remarked upon as having a changeable kind of property on a particular day, then it is worth drawing attention to by stating it, because he does not normally exhibit this property (on other days).

Beardsley gives another good example to show that, in some cases, such an implicature is drawn by suggestion from what is not said (p. 199).

> *Case* 1.3: **Reporter:** "Is the World's Fair going to show a profit this year?"
>
> **World's Fair President Robert Moses:** "The contribution of this Fair to our times and our city in the end will be measured not by the clicking of turnstiles, but by the effect it has had on thinking people of all ages."

According to Beardsley (p. 199), the *Time* magazine article in which this exchange appeared drew the implicature, "Freely translated, Moses was admitting that the Fair would never make any money."

The tricky aspect of this type of slanting by suggestion is that one has to judge the explicit language in a discourse in light of how it was used in context. It is certain normal expectations and conventions of language use that enable us to draw out the suggestion by implicature. Hence this kind of bias tends to be not easy or straightforward to detect.

Nevertheless, Beardsley's approach gives an important clue on how to rethink the notion of bias so that it can be analyzed critically. The three cases studied by Beardsley all indicate that bias is a function of how the argument in the given case is being used to contribute to the goals of a conversational dialogue between two parties. As Grice indicated in his study of conversational implicature, figuring out what one is meant to infer as a conclusion in such a case involves knowledge of the conversational context, the type of dialogue to which the argument was meant to be a contribution.

We return to this conversationally contextual way of thinking about bias below. As indicated above, however, it seems that the alternative approach of viewing prejudice as something psychological or "in the mind" has been the prevalent conception of bias.

9. Psychologism in Logic

One interesting thing about the Port-Royal approach was that it introduced a psychological or mentalistic element into logic by using such ideas as self-love, interest, and passion to explain why certain types of arguments are fallacious. This approach of evaluating forms of argument in logic with reference to psychological factors is called "psychologism" and has been strongly condemned in modern logic, since it separated, as a discipline, from psychology. The basis for the condemnation is that when one evaluates an argument in logic as correct or incorrect, valid or invalid, one should do so by abstract and general normative criteria and not by the intentions or psychological states of the arguer. This latter aspect is seen as an empirical matter, outside the scope of logic as a discipline.

The condemnation of psychologism was, on the whole, a good thing for the development of logic as a field that was able to make progress by restricting the discipline to a normative and critical task of evaluating arguments as correct or incorrect, rather than trying to address empirical questions.

However, when it comes to the analysis of informal fallacies, exclusion of all psychologism in a very rigid way can be counterproductive. For fallacies are an applied branch of logic. One has to understand how they work as tactics of deceptive argumentation that are commonly effective in fooling people and tripping them up.

At any rate, in studying fallacies, and in informal logic generally, the question of psychologism is a controversial issue. And it especially comes to the fore in any attempt to study the concept of 'bias' in argumentation. It becomes worrisome to logicians if this psychologistic aspect tends to become too intrusive, by resting the basis of evaluation of arguments on psychological factors that cannot be exactly defined by structures of the kind recognized in logic.

This danger became evident early on, in the treatment of bias given in the influential textbook *Logick* (1772), written by Isaac Watts. In this treatment, the more careful and modest account given by Arnauld turned into a very definitely psychologistic theory of "prejudices of the mind" in reasoning. Watts even went so far as to identify different tendencies or "humors" that characterize different types of psychological biases in different types of thinkers.

This notion that prejudice can be found at the roots of many of the most important informal fallacies was taken up by Bentham, who used it in his *Handbook of Political Fallacies* (1824) to expose some kinds of bias in political argumentation. From that point onward, the idea of human prejudice as being an important underlying concept for informal logic took root. And we see it fully illustrated in the many appeals to bias and prejudice in the recent textbooks and manuals on critical thinking.

Taking a step back from this trend toward an explicitly psychologistic account of prejudice as a factor in logic, Kant, in his little-known monograph *Introduction to Logic* (1880), defined a narrower and more structured concept that is quite different from any of the other accounts. Kant based his notion of prejudice on a concept of 'provisional judgment' that is more logical than psychological in nature and seems comparable to the notion of default reasoning that has played such a large role in recent developments in computer science.

Paying no attention to Kant's idea, the textbooks on informal logic seem to have based their ideas of bias more on Watts' interpretation, which sees prejudice as a mentalistic tendency or emotion that should be restrained or controlled by logic.

One problem with this seventeenth-century notion of bias is that it seems to be based on the Cartesian idea that bias is the human will, passions, or inclinations that outrun the intellect.[7] Bacon, as we noted, cites human thinking as having "tincture of the will and passions." Arnauld too cited passion and emotion as springs of prejudice. And Watts, even more so, bases his account of prejudice on human motives, tendencies, and humors. This Cartesian notion seems to go back to the Platonic distrust of the emotions, the spirited parts of the soul, as unruly forces that tend to drive the intellect away from the sober and narrow path of reason. Prejudice, by these lights, is seen as the emotional part of the mind that is always struggling with, or even antithetical to, the reasoning or calculative part of the mind.

This kind of folk psychology, whatever its merits, is not a very useful basis for defining a concept of prejudice that is useful for purposes of logical analysis of argumentation. However, it is hard for us to resist the appealing idea that prejudice is a monster lurking within us, causing us to do all kinds of bad things, that can be tamed or rendered less harmful only by learning to recognize it in ourselves, and we can overcome it by being more open-minded, better critical thinkers, and so on. If we could only root out our psychological prejudices, the story goes, we would all become reasonable people, get along together, stop behaving irrationally, and so forth. That seems to be the program. However, this is not the program we will pursue here. Not only does this psychologistic notion of prejudice show no prospect of being definable in any way that would be useful for logic, as a tool for the critical evaluation of argumentation but, even worse, it seems to be based on an ill-considered and deeply erroneous view that arguments based on emotions are inherently unreasonable, defective, or fallacious.

10. Normative Reconstruction of Argumentation

We can see from this chapter that informal logic as a discipline has taken on, as part of its modern task, teaching its students to develop or enhance their ability to detect bias in an argument and to cultivate a critical detachment to avoid being too heavily partisan to attain a balanced, critical perspective in argument. But how are these goals to be facilitated?

The basic ability required can be made sense of only in relation to the ancient dialectical notion that every argument has two sides to be considered, the *pro* and *con* of argument. Hence what is needed is the reintroduction of the concept of dialogue as a framework of rational two-sided argument. But what does this mean in the context of modern logic? What is a dialogue? How can it be regulated or structured? And how could dialogue as a normative and theoretical tool be applied to the particulars of a given argument that is being subjected to criticism?

Broad models of reasoned dialogue that look like they should be applicable to argument analysis in critical thinking recently have been advanced, notably by Hamblin (1970), Rescher (1977), Hintikka (1979), and Barth and Krabbe (1982). But each of these models of dialogue has different goals and different rules. Each seems to represent a different conception of how dialogue should be structured as a model of reasoned argumentation and how strictly the rules should be formulated and applied to the practices of argumentation.

What is needed is a more general outline of the structure of reasoned dialogue, a dialogue theory for argument analysis. What is most important, is to see how such a theory could be applied effectively to the work of critical analysis of argumentative texts of discourse. For that is the stuff and substance of critical thinking as a working discipline. Here we turn (in the next chapter) to the pluralistic conception of different types of dialogue proposed in Walton (1995; Walton and Krabbe, 1995).

However, the immediate problem is that the textbooks have not been able to give any widely accepted definition of what they mean by 'bias,' 'slant,' 'prejudice,' and other terms used in this connection. Why is this so? Perhaps it is because bias is a dialectical notion, depending on the purpose of the type of discourse in a given case of argumentation. The logic textbooks still tend to be more familiar with the dominant traditional approach that sees an argument as a designated set of propositions—a set of premises and a conclusion—and this approach abstracts from how that argument is used or presented in a context of conversational discourse.[8] However, now that certain types of conversation or dialogue as contexts of argumentation have been identified (Walton 1989a; 1990d; *Plaus.* 1992b; 1995; Walton and Krabbe 1995) and their structure has been analyzed, we can also begin to identify and analyze dialectical bias in argumentation.

The dialectical theory of argument presupposes abstract, normative models of dialogue that should present a relatively simple but precise set of rules and procedures representing how reasoned dialogue ought to be. This abstract conception of dialogue is, of necessity, an idealization, but one that should be capable of being used to model a given, particular text of discourse and thereby aid in arriving at an analysis of whether the particular argument can be reasonably judged to be open to criticism in certain respects. Complementing this theoretical point of view, dialogues also can be studied in a practical or empirical manner, where actual parliamentary debates, courtroom trials, and other texts of argumentative discourse are examined (Hamblin 1970, p. 256). However, it is in the union between the theoretical and the practical points of view that real progress can be made in evaluating the justifiability of criticisms of bias in critical thinking.

It is important to recognize that in studying bias, the informal fallacies, and other types of important argument criticisms, we are making normative judgments about whether the argument in question is good or bad, reasonable or unreasonable, open to criticism or not.[9] These are value judgments, but they can be backed up by precise, theoretical conceptions of what a good dialectical argument ought to look like, as used in a particular context of dialogue. Yet these value judgments need to be backed up by evidence from the given, particular text of discourse of the argument being put under scrutiny, interpretation, and criticism. There is actual evidence of various sorts that can be brought to bear in argument criticism.

The job of critical analysis of an argument begins with the presumption that there is a given text of discourse. This text may be some ink marks on a piece of paper, or it could be a taped transcript of a speech or debate. Before the would-be critic can get down to the job of making or evaluating some specific criticism of the argument, he must answer the question What is the argument? Characteristically, this question turns out to be nontrivial, for several reasons. One is that an argument is rarely stated in a completely explicit form. Another is that the context of dialogue may be an important factor in making a reasoned determination of whether or not an argument should be judged open to criticism.[10]

What the critic must do then is to assemble the given evidence in the text and work up a reconstruction of the argument he sets out to criticize. The basic questions of any reconstruction are the following: What are the premises? What is the conclusion? If there are several stages in the sequence of argumentation, how are the premises and conclusions linked together? If there are several conclusions, what is the ultimate (global) conclusion to be proved by the proponent of the argument? Who is the proponent? What is his position on the issue? Who is his opponent, and what is the opponent's thesis? What is the issue? What type of argument is it supposed to be (inductive, deductive, etc.)? What is the burden of proof? What type of dialogue is it? These are the sorts of dialectical questions a critic must ask in order to work up a reconstruction of an argument, prior to the job of assessing the strength or weakness of the argument.

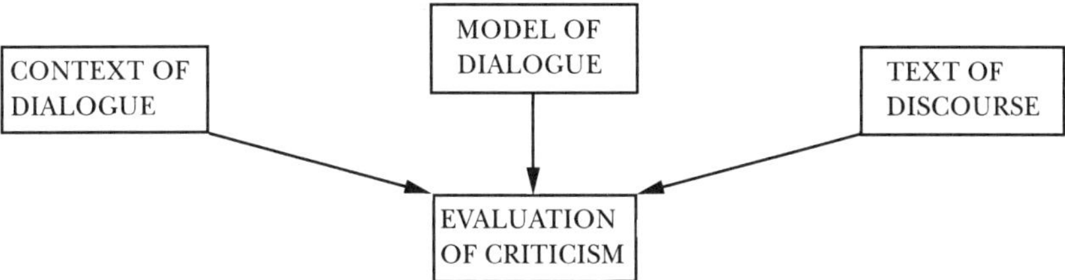

Figure 1.1. Evidence for Argument Evaluation

The assessment of an argument as open to criticism, or defensible from criticism, involves a normative evaluation but one that should be based on three sources of objective evidence. First, the given text of argumentative discourse furnishes verifiable evidence of an arguer's commitments. Second, the context of dialogue provides scripts of information in the form of plausible presumptions and inferences. Third, the abstract model of dialogue provides a coherent system of argument rules, conventions, and procedures that can be matched to a type of dialogue from the evidence given by the text and context.

The basic problem with the traditional treatment of criticizing bias, and other faults of argument in informal logic, was that "one-liner" examples were given a superficial and often substantially incorrect analysis because the three lines of evidence above were largely ignored. The new dialectical approach requires looking at each particular example as an extended sequence of argumentation that needs to be appreciated in its proper context as a type of dialogue with goals and standards of argument that need to be articulated. We now turn to an analysis of these types of dialogue.

Notes

1. See, for example, Beardsley (1966, pp. 202ff.).

2. The interest and importance of this chapter of the *Port-Royal Logic* was drawn to my attention by Alan Brinton's lecture, "Sophisms of Self-Love, of Interest, and of Passion," given at the University of Winnipeg, February 5, 1993.

3. The importance of Watts was brought to my attention by Alan Brinton, in his paper, "The *Logick* of Isaac Watts," in (Walton and Brinton, 1997, pp. 84–98).

4. These ideas will be developed further in chapter 2.

5. There is a link between this type of bias and the traditional fallacy of the *argumentum ad verecundiam.*

6. According to Abbott (1985, Prefatory Note), this work was first published in 1800.

7. See Brinton, op. cit., note 3.

8. Walton (1990).

9. Hamblin (1970).

10. Numerous cases of this sort are cited in Walton (1995).

CHAPTER TWO

DIALECTICAL PRELIMINARIES

This chapter is a brief outline of and introduction to the main dialectical structures that are useful for the analysis and evaluation of arguments. Six so-called types of dialogue are defined. Each type of dialogue represents a conventional context of conversation in which arguments are used for a purpose. But each type of dialogue is also a normative structure, meaning that it has a conventionalized goal defining how the argument ought to be used.

We begin by giving a pragmatic definition of the concept of an argument and then fill out the detailed implementation of this definition by defining each of the types of dialogue as goal-directed types of conversational exchanges in which two or more parties participate by engaging in argument with each other. The outline in this chapter is based on the classification of types of dialogue in Walton (1995, chapter 4) and the analysis of the concept of argument in Walton (1996a) but is specifically designed to be used as a framework to define the concept of bias.

1. Reasoning and Argument

In this book, we define the word *argument* in terms of reasoning, and *reasoning* in terms of inference. Let us begin with the concept of an 'inference'. An *inference* is a set of propositions, one of which is designated a conclusion (end point) and the others are designated as premises (start points). The inference "goes" from the premises to the conclusion. Evidence that an inference exists in a text of discourse is indicated by the so-called indicator words—*thus, therefore, so, on this basis,* and so on. *Reasoning* is a sequence of propositions and, more particularly, is a sequence of inferences linked together such that the conclusion of one inference also functions as a premise in the next inference in the chain.[1]

27

Then an *argument* is defined as a sequence of reasoning, a network of propositions in which some propositions, functioning as conclusions, are inferred from others, functioning as premises by means of inferences. But that is not all there is to defining an argument. An argument is a sequence of reasoning, but it is a sequence of reasoning that can have different uses or functions. It can be used in a hypothetical way, or it can be used in a probative way to prove or refute the conclusion.[2]

The third characteristic of an argument is that it is used to resolve some uncertainty or unsettledness that exists in a particular case. This unsettledness could be a conflict of opinions or a conflict of interests, or it could be the lack of a decisive proof of some claim that is not known to be true and needs to be established. It could be a situation that demands some sort of choice on a prudent course of action, or it could be a lack of information. It could be an antagonism between two parties that have a grievance against each other that is felt but has not yet been precisely articulated. This unsettledness means that there is a lack of agreement between two parties or that two different points of view are possible with respect to a particular proposition. The perception is that this particular proposition is an "issue."

Then an argument is different from an explanation. In an explanation, it is assumed that the proposition to be explained is settled. The purpose is not to settle it but to throw some light on it or show why it is true.[3] In contrast, in the case of an argument, there is an unsettled issue, or so it is perceived by two sides who have different points of view so that the issue is open to contention, and there is some need, or would be some usefulness to attempt to settle it by supporting the point of view on either side as a claim made by one side against the other.

Reasoning occurs in explanations as well as arguments, and in many cases, the same indicator words such as *because, so, consequently,* and *so forth,* are used to link the inferences together in a sequence of reasoning that makes up the explanation or the argument.[4] To determine in a particular case whether a sequence of reasoning is an explanation or an argument, we have to ask what the purpose of the reasoning is. We have to ask how the reasoning is being used. Is it being used to give reasons or considerations in favor of or against a particular proposition that is unsettled? If so, it is an argument. Is it being used to throw light on a proposition that is accepted as a fact by both parties but is not well understood by one or both parties? In that case, the reasoning is an explanation as opposed to an argument.

So there are really two aspects to an argument. One aspect is that it is a set of propositions chained together in the form of a sequence of reasoning. And, as we look at each inferent step in the chain of reasoning, we can classify it as a deductive argument, an inductive argument, or a presumptive argument. Our clues to this are both the context and the indicator words of how the argument is being used. But an argument also has a second aspect in addition to being a sequence of reasoning. It is reasoning that is used for the purpose of resolving some uncertainty, instability, or unsettled issue. The second aspect is the dialectical aspect of argumentation. It is the question of how an argument is being used to contribute to a goal of dialogue where a dialogue is a conventionalized type of conversational exchange between two or more parties.

Typically then, when we evaluate arguments, we do so from two points of view. First, we can evaluate an argument as a specific localized inference made up of some small set of propositions, and then we can evaluate this argument by deductive, inductive, or presumptive standards with respect to the question of whether it is a valid or correct inference. But then we also raise the larger dialectical question of how that inference is being used as part of the chain of reasoning in a wider sequence of dialogue. Typically, this second dialectical question relates to factors that are important when it comes to detecting and evaluating bias. Judging bias in an argument very much requires looking at the more localized inference in light of how it should be meant to be a contribution in a wider context of dialogue.

2. Persuasion Dialogue

The purpose of a persuasion dialogue is to test out the strongest arguments on both sides of a particular proposition. There are two sides in the sense that the one party is committed to the proposition, while the other side is uncommitted or may even be committed to the negation of it. Each side tries to persuade the other side to change its commitment.[5]

The persuasion dialogue has this collective goal, as a conventional type of dialogue. But within the dialogue, each participant has a particular goal. The goal of the proponent is to persuade the respondent that a certain proposition called the "proponent's thesis" is true. The role of the respondent is to doubt that the thesis is true and to raise critical questions concerning it. A central notion in the persuasion dialogue is that of commitment. In virtue of their moves in the sequence of dialogue, the two participants will become committed to various propositions, and, at certain points, it is also possible for them to retract commitment to certain propositions.[6] What is meant by the term *persuasion* is that the proponent has an obligation to prove a proposition to the other party, and such a proof is carried out by inferring that proposition from propositions that are commitments of the other party. What is characteristic of the argumentation in a persuasion dialogue is that a participant argues for a particular proposition by making inferences from the concessions or commitments of the other participant. Obviously, persuasion dialogue essentially involves a kind of empathy.[7] In order to make one's arguments successful, one has to base them on premises that are acceptable to the other side. This means that one has to have the capability of understanding what the other side is prepared to accept as premises. In a successful persuasion dialogue, there has to be a genuine interaction between the arguments of the two sides. They must engage with each other, in certain respects specified below.

In the persuasion dialogue, the two parties are opposed to each other in a certain technical sense of the term *opposition*. There are two types of opposition. In a persuasion dialogue where there is strong opposition, the thesis to be proved by the one party is the opposite or negation of the thesis of the other party. In a persuasion dialogue where there is weak opposition, the first party—the proponent—has a particular proposition or thesis to be proved while the second party does not have the same positive type of burden of proof. The objective of the second party is merely to raise doubts or ask critical questions concerning the thesis of the first party, and, if good enough critical questions can be asked so that the proponent cannot successfully prove her thesis, then the respondent's argumentation is successful in the dialogue and he proves his case.

The type of dialogue called the "critical discussion" in van Eemeren and Grootendorst (1984) is a subspecies of the persuasion dialogue. The goal of a critical discussion is to resolve a conflict of opinions.[8] Van Eemeren and Grootendorst (1984) describe four stages of critical discussion: the *opening stage,* the *confrontation stage,* the *argumentation stage,* and the *closing stage.* Van Eemeren and Grootendorst (1987) give ten rules for the conduct of a critical discussion. According to van Eemeren and Grootendorst, there are different types of critical discussions depending on the nature of the initial conflict from which the dialogue starts. A single conflict has to do with only one expressed opinion or thesis, whereas multiple conflicts have to do with more than one question at issue. In a simple dispute, only one positive or negative position is taken, whereas in a compound dispute or conflict one participant takes a positive and the other a negative attitude toward the thesis at issue. Looking at the account of critical discussion given by van Eemeren and Grootendorst

(1984; 1992), we can see that it is a special type of persuasion dialogue characterized by its goal of resolution of conflicts by verbal means by the four stages through which it goes and various rules of conduct on the argumentation of the participants. In particular, the ten rules for the conduct of argumentation by van Eemeren and Grootendorst (1987) guarantee that the critical discussion represents a fairly high standard of normative rationality of argumentation.

Persuasion dialogue is a more general type of dialogue. Its main characteristic is that, in order to successfully prove something or put forward a good argument, one has to be able to derive the conclusion by means of acceptable types of inferences from premises to which the other party is committed. So the essential characteristic of persuasion dialogue is that argumentation, by its very nature, is always directed toward the commitments of the other party and tries to steer those commitments toward one's own conclusion. Persuasion dialogue is a generic type of dialogue defined by the concept of commitment and by the use of commitment and, in particular, the other party's commitment to prove one's own conclusions in argumentation. The critical discussion, as presented by van Eemeren and Grootendorst, is more specific in the sense that there are a number of rules regarding relevance and other matters concerning how the participants must put forward their arguments. Thus, the critical discussion is a special type of persuasion dialogue.

When characterizing the critical discussion generally, we need to be careful to distinguish between individual goals of the participants and the collective goal of the dialogue as a conventional type of conversational activity. The goal of the critical discussion, generally, according to van Eemeren and Grootendorst, is to resolve a conflict of opinions by rational means. And each participant in a critical discussion has his or her individual goal. The goal of the one party is to prove that her thesis is right, that is, that a particular proposition designated as her thesis in the discussion is true. The goal of the other party is to raise sufficient doubts against this contention so that the burden of proof of the first party is not successfully fulfilled, where in the other type of conflict, the burden of proof is symmetrical and both parties have an obligation to prove their respective theses. According to van Eemeren and Grootendorst (1984, p. 89), a *point of view* is a proposition taken together with an attitude—either pro or contra—with respect to that proposition. Thus, we can distinguish between two types of conflicts that define the two types of critical discussion. In the one type, the respondent merely has critical doubts about the thesis of the other party; whereas in the other type, the respondent has a contra attitude, which is not just a suspended point of view but is definitely a contrary point of view. These matters of burden of proof are set during the confrontation stage of the dialogue, and partly also during the opening stage so that, from the beginning, it is made clear what the obligation of each party in the dialogue is supposed to be. This obligation defines whether or not any argumentation in the dialogue should be judged as normatively successful.

A persuasion dialogue is won or lost on a balance-of-considerations basis. The conflict of opinions is resolved when the sequence of argumentation as a whole reveals that the one side has made out a stronger case for its thesis than the other side. In order for the dialogue to be successful in revealing this outcome, the sequence of argumentation in the dialogue must exhibit five positive characteristics. Each of these characteristics is revealed in the argument itself—by an arguer's performance—but the performance reveals an attitude on the part of the arguer. As mentioned above, it is crucial that the argument on the one side must really interact with the argument on the other side—a genuine communicative interaction is necessary. When these five characteristics are achieved, the result is called a *balanced* (genuinely two-sided and interactive) *argument*.

1. *Flexible Commitment.* An arguer generally must stick to her commitments, but she must also be ready to retract them (in the appropriate circumstances).
2. *Empathy.* An arguer must base her arguments on the commitments of the other party, portraying these commitments accurately, perceptively, and fairly.
3. *Open-mindedness.* An arguer must be willing to consider the arguments of the opposed point of view and weigh them on their merits, instead of just rejecting them out of hand.
4. *Critical Doubt.* In considering objections to her own arguments, an arguer must be able to suspend her own commitments (hypothetically).
5. *Evidence Sensitivity.* An arguer must react by retracting or modifying commitments when confronted by an argument based on evidence of the type generally appropriate for the type of dialogue.

A participant who is genuinely taking part in a persuasion dialogue will exhibit all five of these attitudes at appropriate points in the sequence of her argumentation.

3. Commitment and Maieutic Insight

What is most important in all persuasion dialogue is that there needs to be some method of keeping track of the commitments of each participant at each move during the sequence of the dialogue. The device of a *commitment store* or *commitment set*, invented by Hamblin (1970, p. 257), is the best technique for this purpose. Right at the beginning of any persuasion dialogue, both participants will be committed to certain propositions in virtue of their initial obligations in the dialogue, but as the persuasion dialogue proceeds and the participants make moves, commitments will be inserted into or deleted from their commitment sets.

According to Hamblin (1970, p. 263), a commitment store can be thought of as a set of propositions written down on a piece of paper or a blackboard. In real life, of course, it is very often subject to dispute just what a participant is committed to in virtue of what is known of his or her previous argumentation in a dialogue. People may simply forget what they said before, and they may dispute about whether so-and-so actually said this or is committed to it or not. But a persuasion dialogue is a normative model of how argumentation ought to be carried out, ideally, and in this ideal model, both participants will keep track of their commitments, so that, whenever one party makes any kind of move or puts forward an argumentation or asks a question, for example, the appropriate propositions will be inserted into his commitment set, or, if it is appropriate, certain propositions will be deleted from that commitment set. Then the idea is that some record will be maintained of what each participant's moves were in the dialogue and that, at the same time, a record will be kept of how those moves affected the participant's commitment set at any given point.

This process of addition and deletion of movements is defined by the kind of move made in a dialogue. For example, when a participant makes an assertion, saying, "I assert proposition A," then proposition A goes into her commitment set. If a participant makes a retraction, saying, "I no longer want to be committed to proposition A," then proposition A is removed from the commitment store. So for any type of move there will be rules defining how that type of move affects a participant's commitment set.[9]

Hamblin thought of commitment stores as being open to inspection; that is, they represent propositions that are clearly on view to all participants in a dialogue.[10] None of the propositions is masked or concealed to any of the participants. This represents a kind of normative ideal of rational argumentation. However, in realistic conversational exchanges where argumentation occurs, commitment may not always be this clear. Participants may forget what they said previously. They may deliberately lie about what they said, or they may commit fallacies that are tactics to deceive people about those things to which what they or others are really committed.

In Walton (1985), a distinction was made between explicit or what are called "light-side" commitments and nonexplicit or "dark-side" commitments. Light-side commitments are those of the kind considered by Hamblin that are clearly known to the participants and are on full view to all the participants. One can determine whether or not something is a light-side commitment simply by looking into the participant's commitment store and determining whether a particular proposition is there or not. However, dark-side commitments have not been explicitly conceded and can be inferred only indirectly from a person's argumentation or from the text of discourse that we have, which records the record of their argumentation. The dark-side commitment represents the underlying position of the participant.[11]

One very important side benefit of the persuasion dialogue is the *maieutic function* of bringing a participant's dark-side commitments to light during the course of the dialogue. The word *maieutic* comes from the Greek word *maieutikos,* meaning "skill in midwifery" and refers to the skill of a philosopher such as Socrates in being able to bring new ideas to birth through verbal argumentation with another party. The maieutic function of dialogue is the enabling of a participant to express dark-side commitments in a more explicit and careful way so that they become light-side commitments.[12] Although the purpose of a critical discussion and of persuasion dialogue generally is to resolve a conflict of opinions, in many cases the dialogue turns out to be very beneficial even though the original conflict is not resolved. In such a case, even though the dialogue does not lead to agreement, it may nevertheless generate quite a bit of significant understanding on both sides because both sides have modified their commitments significantly enough during the course of the dialogue that a maieutic function has been fulfilled.

Maieutic insight or increased understanding of one's commitments in arguments is a very valuable gain. It is not a kind of knowledge, but it is a kind of insight into one's own or another's point of view that can be very valuable in preparing the way for knowledge. The advance consists in a negative clearing away of dogmatic preconceptions, biases, and fallacies that can remove obstacles to the advancement of knowledge.

The dialogue on tipping in Walton (1992b, pp. 7–12) is an illustration of a persuasion dialogue where maieutic benefits are illustrated. In this dialogue, the two participants, Helen and Bob, had a conflict of opinions concerning the practice of tipping. Bob was generally in favor of tipping as a practice that should be retained. Helen disagreed. She argued for the proposition that tipping is generally a bad practice and one that it would be best to eliminate. Bob begins the dialogue by arguing that tipping is a good thing because it rewards excellence of service. Helen uses the counterargument that tipping tends to become an expected practice after a while, so a tip is expected even for mediocre service. This is a counterargument to Bob's initial argument. She goes on to give further arguments against tipping as a practice by citing many examples of how tipping can lead to misunderstanding and bad consequences. Bob counters her arguments by contending that there are also good effects of tipping that outweigh the bad consequences. As the dialogue continues, Bob and Helen examine many of the most powerful arguments on both sides of the issue, and they question and criticize each other's arguments.

In the end, neither side is defeated, although both sides are thoroughly criticized by the probing questions and objections of the other side. At the end of the dialogue, one does not get the impression that there is a winner or a loser or that the argument of the one side has definitely been refuted. Nevertheless, one does get the impression that both participants and anyone else who listens to or reads the dialogue learns quite a bit about the pros and cons of the argumentation on tipping and would judge that the exercise is somewhat insightful and worthwhile. Of course, some positivistic commentators will always say that such an exercise is always a waste of time unless the issue is definitely resolved one way or the other by overwhelming evidence or by appeal to some definite facts that may prove the one side or the other. But most of us would probably disagree with this interpretation, at least in the case of the dialogue on tipping, because it does seem that we learn something worthwhile from the dialogue even though the original conflict of opinions was not resolved decisively one way or the other. The real benefit of such a persuasion dialogue is that the deeper positions on both sides are revealed through the course of the dispute so that the covered, unexpressed presumptions on both sides are made more explicit and are articulated and refined in such a way that we can better understand the arguments for and against them.

This maieutic benefit could not be achieved unless the argumentation in the dialogue was balanced, in the sense defined above. Unless the argumentation exhibits the five characteristics of a balanced dialogue exchange—flexible commitment, empathy, open-mindedness, critical doubt, and evidence sensitivity—no real gain in maieutic insight will be achieved by either side. Instead of moving forward to clear the way of misconceptions and weakly supported arguments, the sequence of argument, if it does not exhibit these five characteristics, will simply be an unconnected sequence of advocacy arguments on both sides, without any genuine interaction between the two sides having taken place. Two one-sided arguments do not necessarily add up to a balanced, two-sided exchange of the kind required for a productive persuasion dialogue.

4. Negotiation Dialogue

Negotiation dialogue arises from a conflict of interest between two parties concerning some goods or services that are in short supply. By making concessions to each other, the participants could make a deal that would benefit both, even though it would involve some losses for both parties. Thus, the type of argumentation involved in a negotiation could be called "bargaining" or "making a package deal." The goal of each participant is to get the best out of it for his own interests, but collectively, the goal of the argument is to make a deal that will distribute the goods to give significant benefits to both parties.[13]

Thus, negotiation is a very different type of dialogue from persuasion dialogue in principle and also in its general methods. In a persuasion dialogue, the goal is to prove or to give reasons to accept a particular proposition as true or false by giving evidence for that proposition or against it. However, a negotiation has very little to do, at least directly, with the truth or falsity of a proposition or with trying to prove something true. In negotiation, it is not commitment to the truth of a proposition that is at stake, but it is some kind of goods, interests, or economic resources. The goal of a participant in a negotiation is to maximize her share of these goods or interests by verbal means of making concessions to and securing agreements from the other party. In a negotiation, each side tries to get what matters to her most and to trade off concessions that are less important to her.

Walton and McKersie (1965) distinguish four subtypes of negotiation dialogue. In *distributive bargaining*, the goal of the one party is in a *basic conflict* or zero-sum game with that of the other party. As they put it (p. 4): "One person's gain is a loss to the other." By contrast, in *integrative bargaining*, there is a problem instead of a basic conflict and the interests of both parties can be integrated to some degree in solving this problem together. In the third type of negotiation dialogue, *attitudinal structuring*, the issue concerns relationships between participants, attitudes such as friendliness, hostility, trust, respect, or motivation. This type of dialogue is not so much about economic interests, at least directly, but more about personalities and relationships. In *intraorganizational bargaining*, the goal is to bring the expectations of one side into alignment. For example, in labor negotiations, the local and the international union may get together and try to agree on their objectives. This type of negotiation has the goal of working toward broad agreement on objectives where both parties are on the same side, basically, even though they have particular differences of interest on how to achieve their larger objectives.

One striking contrast between the critical-discussion type of dialogue and the negotiation type concerns the concept of a 'threat.' According to Walton and McKersie (1965, p. 50), the threat can be, in some instances, a legitimate part of the argumentation in a negotiation. A threat here is seen as a kind of strategy to secure commitment in the sense of getting the other party to pledge itself to a course of action. Donohue (1981, p. 279) agrees by writing that 'promises' and 'threats' are among the core concepts of bargaining theory. However, (p. 279) Donohue concedes that a threat is a high-risk tactic because it is often viewed as a kind of ultimatum by the other party.

Threats count as being legitimate tactics, generally, in negotiation, that can be used by participants to achieve legitimate goals successfully. Contrast this with the case of the critical discussion where, generally, a threat is immediately perceived as being normatively inappropriate and even outrageous. If we are having a philosophy seminar and discussing the truth and falsity of some particular proposition that is at issue, and, suddenly, I stand up and threaten you, saying that if you do not agree with my point of view, I will have a large man named Bruno, who is also in the seminar, forcefully eject you from the room and punish you, this would be regarded as highly inappropriate—a kind of interruption that immediately would be perceived as illegitimate and contrary to the aims of the dialogue. Threats are highly inappropriate in any kind of persuasion dialogue because it is very important that participants not be prevented from expressing a point of view as fully and freely as possible in order to articulate their dark-side commitments and come up with the strongest arguments that they can find for or against a position. Thus, in this sort of context, threatening somebody is inappropriate because it gives no evidence to support or refute a conclusion, and its only function could be to distract us from this goal of the critical discussion or to try to prevent somebody, by irrelevant or inappropriate means, from pursuing the goals of the discussion.

However, in a negotiation, things are different. Threats are normally part of a negotiation. In negotiation, overt or direct threats are generally regarded as inappropriate or not acceptable, but indirect or covert threats generally are regarded as part of the bargaining process. For example, in union management negotiations, threats of this sort are quite common. For instance, the union leader, who represents the bargaining unit, may suggest to the management negotiators that if they do not agree to a particular proposition, then there is a great danger that the workers will go on strike. This argument is put in the form of a warning, on the surface at any rate, but everyone in the negotiation may perceive quite correctly that it is really meant to be a covert or indirect threat. That is, the union negotiator is saying that if the management does not agree to some recommendation being put forward, then the union leader will see to it that an action is taken that will be punitive or will be against the interests of management. Everyone may be quite clearly aware that this is a threat; nevertheless, it may be acceptable as an argument that is part of the bargaining process.

Negotiation does not require the same characteristics of balanced argumentation as persuasion dialogue. For negotiation is based on personal interest (and financial gain, in most cases) rather than on an attempt to get at the truth of some contested proposition. However, negotiation does involve elements of flexibility and empathy. A good negotiator has to find out what is really important to the other party and what is less important to him and make concessions and trade-offs based on this judgment. A good negotiator also has to be willing to give up things that are less important to herself, in exchange for concessions from the other party.

However, negotiation is based on a party's interests, and the goal is to maximize those interests, even if this means being illogical or committing fallacies, as such matters would be judged in a persuasion dialogue.

5. Inquiry

The goal of the inquiry, as a type of dialogue, is to establish or prove a particular proposition or, alternatively, show that it cannot be proved given the present state of knowledge. The inquiry is defined as an essentially *cumulative* type of dialogue, meaning that the whole intent of the inquiry is to eliminate the possibility or likelihood of retraction of commitments.[14] In a critical discussion, retraction is freely permitted, though it is under some constraints, whereas, in the inquiry, retraction is generally frowned upon and the whole design is to minimize the need for retractions of propositions once the inquiry has actually established its conclusions. Cumulativeness means that the inquiry is essentially a hierarchical type of structure of argumentation where the premises are supposed to be established and then the conclusion proved from these premises.

In epistemology, this type of philosophical point of view is called "foundationalism." However, ordinary examples of the inquiry in daily life also can be given. An example would be an inquiry into an air disaster where, for reasons of safety, it may be very important to determine, as definitely as possible on the available evidence, exactly what happened to cause the disaster. In order to do this, there may even be an undertaking to have an official government inquiry. In such an inquiry, considerable care is taken to interview experts and collect as much circumstantial evidence as is available so that a conclusive and exhaustive examination of all the available evidence can be given. Then, in a later stage of the inquiry, this evidence is used to derive certain conclusions concerning what happened. In the case of an airline disaster, the purposes may be to satisfy the families of the victims, to settle lawsuits, or simply to determine the cause of the accident as conclusively as possible in order to prevent possible future accidents of this type from occurring.

Each specific type of inquiry such as a coroner's inquiry or an inquiry into an air disaster has its own methods and standards of proof. What is characteristic of the inquiry, generally, is the attempt to amass complete evidence on the issue of the inquiry so that a conclusive determination can be made that is not subject to retraction or questioning.

The first stage is the opening of the inquiry. Once an inquiry has been launched, the next stage is the collection of data. At this stage, experts will be interviewed, and arguments and testimony from various witnesses will be taken. Once all these data are collected in the form of verbal and written testimony and reports of various kinds, the next stage is a discussion stage where there is an attempt to reach an agreement on what conclusions can be drawn from the evidence concerning the issue of the inquiry. The final stages will be the writing up of some sort of report or document that outlines the results of the inquiry and the presentation of the conclusions at which the participants in the inquiry ultimately arrived.

Along with cumulativeness, another important property of the argumentation in an inquiry is *evidential priority*, meaning that the premises of an argument are better established than the conclusion they are supposedly being used to prove. In an inquiry, the conclusion to be proved is initially more doubtful than the premises of the argument, so that when the premises are brought forward, they are used to remove this doubt from the conclusion and to establish it as something that can be accepted according to the standards of proof required by the inquiry. In other words, argumentation in an inquiry is very directional, and circular argumentation is regarded as highly inappropriate in an inquiry (Walton, 1990a). Evidential priority is in sharp conflict with circularity of argumentation and tends to exclude circular argumentation.

Of course, it is always an interesting question whether scientific reasoning takes the form of an inquiry or whether it is more like a persuasion dialogue. According to the foundationalist point of view, scientific argumentation is like an inquiry, whereas, according to the currently more popular sociological explanations of how scientific reasoning takes place, it seems to be more like a persuasion dialogue. Amongst the philosophers, we can see quite clearly that Descartes was very much a champion of the inquiry as a model of reasoning, both in philosophy and in science. His method of doubt proposed beginning with premises that are absolutely indubitable and then reasoning from these to establish conclusions.

What we mean by the inquiry as a type of dialogue is very similar to what Aristotle in *The Posterior Analytics* called a "demonstration." In *The Posterior Analytics* (72b25), Aristotle writes that demonstration must be based on premises "prior to and better known than the conclusion." Aristotle then immediately draws the inference (72b27) that circular demonstration is not possible. In other words, a demonstration, in Aristotle's sense, has evidential priority in that the premises are the evidential basis for knowing that the conclusion is true. Hence, evidentially they are prior to the conclusion so that, arguing from the conclusion back to the premises, by means of circular reasoning, would not be an acceptable demonstration.[15]

Perhaps the best example of the type of cumulative reasoning characteristic of the inquiry as argumentation is Euclidian geometry. In Euclidian geometry, the axioms and theorems are numbered so that, as Mackenzie (1980) shows, circular reasoning is not tolerated. In order to qualify as a proof in Euclidian geometry, an argument must go from earlier numbered theorems or from earlier numbered axioms to a conclusion that has a later number. Thus, it is clear that in this structure of argumentation, evidential priority is applicable and circular arguments are not acceptable as proofs within the context of the inquiry.

The inquiry differs from persuasion dialogue in that it does not start from a conflict of opinions generally but from an open problem or a situation where something is not known to be true but is only suspected to be true or where there is some evidence for it, but not sufficient evidence to determine conclusively whether it is true or false. The problem in the inquiry is that we need to know with a high degree of certainty or confidence that once we have marshaled all the available evidence, we can derive the conclusion that some proposition is either definitely known to be true or false or, conversely, that there is not enough evidence to show one way or the other if it is true or false. Even establishing this negative result could be a useful outcome of an inquiry, for at least it would satisfy the concerned parties that the question has been looked into thoroughly and exhaustively and a serious attempt has been made to collect and evaluate all the available evidence in a thorough and objective manner.

Balanced argument is very important in an inquiry, just as it is in a persuasion dialogue. All five characteristics of a balanced argument are very important in an inquiry, but two characteristics of this kind are especially important. First, evidence sensitivity is very important. There must be some agreement at the outset of the inquiry on what is to count as evidence, and then at the argumentation stage, a participant must drop a hypothesis if this evidence falsifies it. The other characteristic that is very important in an inquiry is that evidence must be accumulated carefully and stored as the inquiry proceeds. At the concluding stage of the inquiry, the outcome must be decided on a basis of all the evidence that has been collected. The conclusion must not be based on a partial or incomplete set of facts. It must be based on the whole evidential picture or body of knowledge that has been gathered.

6. Deliberation

Deliberation is a type of dialogue that is often confused with persuasion dialogue or critical discussion, but what is distinctively different about deliberation as a type of dialogue is that it is directed toward finding a course of action. Deliberation always asks what is the most prudent thing to do in a particular situation where an individual or group is faced with a need to make a choice or to proceed with some practical problem that demands action or settling on some sort of policy for a practical course of action.

The main kind of reasoning that is characteristic of argumentation in deliberation is practical reasoning, which is a kind of means-end reasoning. According to the account given in Walton (1990c), practical reasoning is goal directed and concludes in an imperative to action based on a structure of argument called the "practical inference scheme." In the simplest type of case, the practical inference scheme is based on a goal premise and a means premise. The goal stipulates the agent's goal or intention, as far as this can be determined in a given situation. The means premise is based on the agent's knowledge or information as known in a given situation, furnishing the agent with some line of action that could contribute to or fulfill the goal given the resources available. These two premises function together to lead toward a conclusion describing a practical course of action for the agent based on the assumptions made in the premises.

Then the goal of deliberation is to reach a conclusion on how to proceed or act prudently in a particular situation, given that one has certain goals or that one can determine generally what one's goals are relative to that situation.

Aristotle described deliberation very clearly as a type of argument in the *Nicomachean Ethics* (book 6, chapter 9). According to Aristotle (1142b), it is characteristic of deliberation that we deliberate about things that are are within our power to change. Aristotle writes (1142b13) that deliberation is a kind of correctness of thinking and that excellence in deliberation involves reasoning.

Then deliberation can be described as a normative framework of dialogue in which argumentation takes place. This argumentation can be evaluated as successful or not from a normative point of view, to the extent that it contributes to the goals of deliberation. But, within the argumentation itself, there is a sequence of reasoning, and, characteristically in deliberation, this kind of reasoning is practical reasoning.

The question of retraction of commitment is very important to understanding the nature of deliberation, because deliberation is characteristically carried out on the basis of incomplete information. That is, typically in deliberation, we are in a practical situation where an inquiry is not appropriate as a method of solving the problem because we do not have enough time for practical reasoning to engage in a scientific type of inquiry that would collect all the available data. By that time, the window of opportunity would be gone. So, characteristically then, in deliberation, the particular circumstances of the agent's given situation yields a kind of information that is constantly subject to change and updating. Thus, the conclusion of a sequence of practical reasoning in deliberation is generally a tentative presumption, a defeasible proposition that is subject to retraction if new information comes in requiring a revision of the sequence of practical reasoning.[16] Hence, in deliberation, it is useful to be much more flexible in one's argumentation than would be characteristic of the inquiry.

In deliberation, it is important to be open to new information and not to be too dogmatic or too fixed in one's conclusions. What is important in deliberation is good judgment in weighing presumptions in a balance of considerations, in a situation where hard knowledge that would definitively resolve the issue one way or the other is lacking. The inquiry involves striving for high standards of proof in order to avoid the possibility of retraction if possible. However, if deliberation strives for standards that are too high or become too conservative, it runs the risk of losing its flexibility and openness to the changing parameters of realistic circumstances.

It may sound strange at first to describe deliberation as a type of dialogue, for it often seems to us that much ordinary deliberation is of a solitary kind where someone is mulling over a problem and trying to arrive at a personal decision on what course of action to take. However, even solitary deliberation of this type can be described as a kind of inner dialogue with oneself where one provisionally adopts a point of view and then plays devil's advocate by looking at the arguments or critical questions that might be applied to that point of view and count against it.

Closure of deliberation often is dictated by practical considerations because there may not be enough time to acquire a sufficient body of knowledge by conducting an inquiry to resolve the question conclusively one way or the other. But, even so, action of some sort tends to be necessary in a deliberation because doing nothing at all is in effect a form of action that has practical consequences.

Deliberation essentially has to do with an open-ended future. An agent has to try to visualize what are the possible or likely consequences of the courses of action that are available. Of course, it is impossible ever to predict what will happen in the future, so that deliberation typically involves intelligent speculation and guesswork about the plausible consequences of courses of action that one might adopt. Thus, deliberation involves the formation of plans and policies based on contingencies.

Deliberation always involves a process of adjustment between one's general goals and the particular circumstances that dictate what is possible in a given situation. Thus, practical reasoning in deliberation always involves meshing together different propositions that represent possible courses of action at different levels of abstraction. For example, one's general goal may be to save money or accumulate enough money for retirement, but how does one do that in a particular situation given the fluctuations in the economy, the stock market, and other available investments? Deliberation always seeks out a course of action by practical reasoning that would satisfy one's general goals in relation to the means available in one's given circumstances.

Balanced argumentation is important in a deliberation because an intelligent and reasoned practical deliberation needs to take into account all the pros and cons of a possible course of action that are likely to have significant consequences. Not only that, deliberation is like persuasion dialogue in that a mere listing of all the arguments on both sides is not nearly as productive and useful as an interaction of these arguments revealing the weaker parts of both. The best kind of deliberation is an interactive dialogue that has qualities of balanced argument comparable to that of a persuasion dialogue.

7. *Information-Seeking Dialogue*

The purpose of the information-seeking dialogue is to transmit information from one party to another. The aim of the one party is to seek information, while the aim of the other party is to give that information to the first party. Hence, you could also call this type of dialogue an "information-giving" type of dialogue, but it is an asymmetrical type of dialogue because the goals of the two parties are quite different. In this respect, it is different from the inquiry where the participants all are equally ignorant in the sense that they lack some kind of knowledge or proof of a proposition. In the information-seeking type of dialogue, however, one party has this knowledge or information and the other party is trying to get it.

The one party who could be called the "information-seeker," asks questions put to the other party, who could be called the "source" or "the informant." In the dialogue, the information seeker asks "why" questions, which are requests for explanations, and also asks "yes-no" questions and questions asking how or where something happened. The answerer is obliged to be as helpful as possible in giving clear explanations and in answering questions as directly and informatively as possible.

One particularly important subtype of information-seeking dialogue is the *expert consultation* dialogue where the one party is an expert in some particular field or domain of knowledge and the other party is seeking advice from that expert on how to solve a problem or pursue a course of action.

In some cases, the interviewing party is not so much seeking advice on a practical course of action as seeking information, that is, trying to determine whether or not a particular proposition is true.

An example of the expert consultation type of dialogue would be the kind of case where one goes to a financial adviser who is an expert on investments for advice on investments. The problem here—as is typical with cases of the expert consultation dialogue—is that the financial situation tends to be very complex and it may be difficult for the person seeking advice to ask the right questions. Thus, in order to make this type of dialogue successful, both parties have an obligation. The expert has an obligation to put the technical information in as clear a manner as possible so that it will be understandable by the questioner, and the questioner has the obligation to ask probing questions and to ask for explanations of technical terms or complex concepts that he may not understand very well.

It is always difficult for an expert to explain technical questions in a domain of knowledge in a way that is clearly intelligible to a layperson who lacks the special knowledge used in that field. Therefore, there are communication problems inherent in the expert consultation type of dialogue. The questioner has to tread a delicate line between respecting the expertise of the other party while, at the same time, asking critical questions that will enable him to gain a sufficiently clear grasp of what he needs to know in order to pursue an intelligent course of action with respect to the problem he confronts.

An example of information-seeking dialogue that is not of the expert consultation type would be the kind of case where a person asks a pedestrian on the street for directions on how to get to the train station. The person being questioned here is not necessarily an expert such as an architect or cartographer or someone who has some kind of specialized knowledge of the city streets. But on the presumption that this person has lived in the city for some time and is familiar with the streets, she could be a helpful source of information because she is presumably in a position to know how to get to the train station.

Another somewhat different type of information-seeking dialogue is the *media interview*. Consider, for example, the type of celebrity interview carried out by Barbara Walters on the television program "20/20." The interview here arises out of interest in the personal character or deeper commitments of the person being interviewed. A good interview takes place when the respondent feels comfortable and replies in a revealing sort of way to probing questions asked by the interviewer so that the outcome will be information that will be of interest to the viewing audience.

Another type of information-seeking dialogue that is now very familiar to academic researchers is the process of searching through a computerized database to elicit information about a specific topic. Such a database could be a collection of authors' titles and abstracts of books and articles in a particular field. The searcher can then put in key words asking for listings of titles or abstracts that contain one or more of these key words. This process can be described as a kind of dialogue exchange between the information seeker and the computerized database.

The information-seeking type of dialogue does not require balance in the same way as the persuasion dialogue, because it (information-seeking dialogue) is asymmetrical. Different attitudes for the proponent (information seeker, questioner) are required than for the respondent (information provider, answerer). The proponent must ask questions that really do seek out the information wanted, and this task does require some qualities of empathy and flexibility comparable to the characteristics of a balanced argument in a persuasion dialogue. Similarly, the respondent must try to convey this information clearly, honestly, but in a judicious way that balances the various factors needed to sum up what is likely to be a complex set of facts that is hard to summarize. As with the persuasion dialogue, there needs to be genuine interaction in the question-reply exchanges.

8. Eristic Dialogue

A type of dialogue, which we will call "the quarrel," arises out of hidden conflicts, grievances, or antagonisms that are under the surface. When a quarrel does arise, it tends to erupt suddenly, and then these perceived harms, slights, or grievances are brought to the surface in a very fast and reflexive way that, typically, makes the quarrel violate the normal maxims of politeness of everyday conversation. Typically, a quarrel is very emotional and intense, and even profane, in a way that would be highly inappropriate for conducting ordinary conversational transactions. The reason for this is that the smooth functioning of social—and especially business—concerns require the overlooking of small differences or disagreements, so that it is generally very helpful not to dwell on minor complaints or grievances in order to make for more smoothness of collaborative efforts in arriving at constructive agreements in daily life. However, occasionally, it is very useful for such grievances to be brought to the surface, and this is the function of the quarrel. The chief goal of the quarrel is to bring about a catharsis whereby these hidden conflicts are brought out into the open and acknowledged by both parties. Each party then acknowledges that he can now see that this is a serious concern to the other party.[17]

The quarrel commonly is taken to be a very negative kind of dialogue, and most people seem to have the preconception that the quarrel generates more heat than light, so to speak, and that it is completely inimical to logical reasoning of any sort. While it is true that the quarrel is no friend of logical reasoning, this type of dialogue can have important benefits. That is to say, we are adopting a thesis here that, in some instances, it is possible to have what we could call a "good" quarrel.[18] This type of good quarrel occurs where, through the argumentation exchange, hidden grudges or antagonisms are brought out and acknowledged as important problems by both parties. Each party acknowledges to the other party that there were certain grievances or problems that he or she did not perceive as being serious before but now recognizes as being important to the other party. In a good quarrel, each party resolves to try to overcome this grievance or deal with this complaint in the future by being more sensitive to it. Thus, ideally, the closing stage of the quarrel is not necessarily the complete resolution of the conflict but nevertheless an acknowledgment that it exists and an expression of willingness by both parties to be more sensitive to this problem or conflict or to be more aware of it in the future.

The quarrel is a very emotional and intuitive type of dialogue. Both parties tend to lash out in argumentation against the other party without thinking about it first. It is not a very calculated type of argumentation, although it can be in some cases. The goal of each party individually, in the quarrel, can be described as a verbal "hitting out" at the other party. It is a very adversarial, even antagonistic, type of dialogue where each party focuses on directly attacking the other person.

The initial situation of the quarrel is a feeling of truculence or resentment by one or both parties at some hidden injury that is very important to this person but that is under the surface and has not previously been stated in a very overt way. So once this feeling is first expressed, there is a strong reaction to it by the other party and it is like a volcano erupting—all sorts of hidden feelings then pour out in the exchange. Typically, the event that instigates the quarrel is some small dispute or grievance that really has nothing to do with the underlying grievances that surface during the quarrel. For example, the event that provokes a domestic dispute may be some small bone of contention such as who is supposed to take out the garbage on a particular day. Now this grievance or antagonism or dispute may, in itself, be relatively trivial, but it may trigger underlying grievances or feelings that then pour out of both parties during the exchange of the quarrel. And once these deeper feelings come out, there is often very little relevance of the argumentation to the subject that provoked the quarrel in the first place. As the participants start seriously getting into the quarrel, they may argue about finances or jealousy, for example, which really has very little to do with the garbage issue.

This irrelevance of argumentation—that is, skipping from one topic to another—is very characteristic of the quarrel. So we can contrast the quarrel and the persuasion type of dialogue on this account because the relevance of argumentation is very important in the persuasion type of dialogue. It is very important for the successful resolution of a conflict of opinions by rational means that each argument be relevant to the topic at issue, and relevant to the other arguments used to bear on that topic which is the issue of the dispute. But, in the quarrel, typically, the argument jumps all over the place. It goes from one thing to another that is apparently unrelated to it but is connected only in the sense that it is somehow important as a grievance or hurt feeling of the other party.

Ad hominem argument is strongly associated with the quarrel as a type of dialogue and is often a key indicator of a shift from another type of dialogue to a quarrel. In a quarrel, the one party attacks the other party personally for some fault or some alleged personal failure or breach of good conduct. So the party who is attacked is charged of being guilty of committing some culpable action or some breach of ethics. This type of exchange could be called "counterblaming."

The quarrel is a subtype of a more general type of dialogue called "eristic dialogue" (from the Greek word *eris* for "strife"). Eristic dialogue is highly adversarial and could even be described as a kind of verbal combat where each party tries to win out over the other by any means in order to humiliate the other party and show that one is superior to the other party.[19]

The quarrel is not completely antagonistic, however; the participants do follow certain rules. For example, they take turns, and it is necessary for the participants to take turns in order for them to have a quarrel and to have a successful quarrel. It is true that they use aggressive and fallacious arguments very often in a quarrel, which makes it almost seem like a kind of anarchy, but there is a certain kind of order to a quarrel.

Aristotle, in *On Sophistical Refutations,* described eristic dialogue as comparable to unfair fighting or cheating in sports to win a victory at any cost (171b24). Aristotle distinguished a particular subtype of quarreling which he identified with Sophistry, a kind of staged intellectual quarrelsome exchange where the participants use clever arguments to try to defeat each other in order to impress an audience with their intellectual powers. In this Sophistical type of exchange, the participants use all kinds of fallacious arguments that are nevertheless very clever and will impress an audience.

Both the quarrel and the Sophistical type of dialogue are classified as eristic dialogues because the goal is to defeat the other party at all costs, and there is very little or no real regard for the truth of the matter.

Parties often portray themselves as engaging in a kind of critical discussion where they are very concerned with logical reasoning, relevance, and truth, in the quarrel, but this is often really a pose. Their underlying or real interest is in attacking the other party and trying to make the other party appear guilty for some unethical conduct.

Generally, in a quarrel, the elements of balanced argumentation that are characteristic of the other types of dialogue are only present at a very minimal level. All the other types of dialogue require at least that the participant be honest and sincere and try to follow the Gricean collaborative maxim of contributing what is required at the appropriate stage of the dialogue.[20] All of the other types of dialogue require that a participant's arguments reflect an attitude of being balanced and open to giving up an argument if it is shown to be weak or refuted. But in eristic dialogue, the presumption is the opposite. Each participant presumes that the other party is dishonest and has a bad character for veracity and is generally trying to cheat and unfairly defeat the opposed party. The main goal of each participant is to prove this, that is, to show that the other party is lying or cheating or who is otherwise not as honest or sincere as the other person in the dialogue.

A closed attitude is typical of the eristic type of dialogue, as expressed by the principle If you are not for us, you are against us. This is the very antithesis of the kind of openness required in a critical discussion where participants have to base their arguments on commitments of the other party, which means that there must be a kind of empathic awareness of what the other party is willing to accept or is committed to, and there must also be an openness to defeat or willingness to give up one's argument if the other party shows that the opposing argument is based on better evidence. In the eristic type of dialogue, none of this applies. The attitudes of the participants are essentially closed in the sense that, even if presented with a strong argument based on very good evidence that opposed their own position, they will not give up that position. They will still dig in deeper and maintain that position even more vehemently in the face of the objections.

In eristic dialogue, instead of making an effort to determine what the commitments of the other party really are, the participants try to give a distorted picture of the commitments of the other party in order to make that other party appear to be stupid and irrational. So, in the eristic dialogue, it is always dichotomized as a case of "us against them," and neither party is willing to concede defeat against the superior argument. The other party is always labeled as a terrorist, fanatic, prejudiced, and so on, by a negative system of terminology that makes her arguments always appear to be biased and unbelievable so that they can be holistically rejected and ridiculed. Essentially then, the characteristics of a balanced argument required for persuasion dialogue are not required, or even normally present, in argumentation in eristic dialogue.

A classical example of the Sophistical subspecies of the eristic type of dialogue is the series of exchanges between the two Sophists, in the Platonic dialogue *Euthydemus,* who use all kinds of tricky and clever arguments to try to get the best of each other. Tricky and deceptive moves are typical of eristic dialogue. The aim of each party is to make one's opponent appear stupid or somehow illogical or silly.

9. Mixed Dialogues

The basic six types of dialogue are *persuasion, negotiation, inquiry, deliberation, information-seeking,* and *eristic.*[21] But there are many familiar types of conversational exchanges where argumentation occurs that does not fit exactly into one of these basic types. In many cases, we have a mixed type of dialogue, which is a composite of two or more other types of dialogue.

A good example here is the *forensic debate.* The forensic debate has certain elements of the persuasion dialogue. But in other respects, it is more like an eristic type of dialogue because there is a judge or audience, and sometimes that judge or audience will be persuaded or convinced by personal attacks or other kinds of fallacious moves that would be inappropriate in a critical discussion. So, in many ways, the debate has what could be called a "bear pit" or antagonistic aspect that is characteristic of eristic dialogue. It is a kind of free-market situation, a survival-of-the-fittest arena where there is a contest to see who can put forth the strongest arguments or, at least, the arguments that would be most successful in persuading the audience or the judges of the debate. These successful arguments may not necessarily be the most logical or rational arguments from the point of view of a critical discussion.[22]

Nevertheless, the debate is a noble institution that has, in the past, often rightly been extolled by orators and commentators. As such, it does have some aspects of the persuasion type of dialogue. So we classify the debate as a "mixed" type of dialogue that combines elements of both the persuasion dialogue and the eristic dialogue.

Another thing about the debate that is quite interesting is that, in a particular case, certain conventional rules will be stipulated. That is, ground rules will be laid down in a particular debate so that the judges will have criteria that are agreed to in advance by the participants that will determine (among other things) which side wins and which side loses the debate. These rules are part of the *speech event,* the cultural or organizational, structured setting in which the argument takes place. For example, in a parliamentary debate, there will be parliamentary rules of order. Or in argumentation in a legal trial, there are legal rules of procedure and rules of evidence that all parties are bound to follow.

One important factor is that, in evaluating a particular case where a debate has occurred, one cannot use just the normative models of the persuasion dialogue and the eristic dialogue to judge the arguments. One has to judge them also in relation to the particular rules set down as part of the particular framework for that given debate. This aspect of specific rules, conventionalized to a particular situation, is the speech event.

A good example here would be the legal argumentation in a criminal trial. A criminal trial presumably has some elements of persuasion dialogue, and it also has some elements of eristics. But, over and above that, there are certain rules laid down for that argumentation by the rules of evidence and also by the rules appropriate for that particular trial. These rules will be enforced and adjudicated by the judge. This means that when we come to evaluate an argument in a legal trial, it would not be completely appropriate to see it as being just an argument that took place in a critical discussion, which could be evaluated purely by the normative requirements for a critical discussion. It might be interesting and valuable to look at it from that point of view, but it also might be important to recognize, in some cases, that the argumentation is governed by the legal rules as set in a particular jurisdiction as applied to that case. Therefore, to get a full evaluation and analysis of that argument, one would have to look at it not only from the normative structure of dialogue that would apply but also as a particular speech event where the participants would be constrained by particular rules that would govern what they can say and the sorts of argumentative moves they can make.

So, when one looks at argumentation in everyday conversation and comes to analyze or evaluate the argument and judge whether it commits a fallacy or whether or not the argumentation in it is reasonable, one has to judge it from the point of view of some normative model of dialogue, for example—from the point of view of a critical discussion—and then evaluate it insofar as the argumentation meets the normative requirements of the critical discussion or not. But, in reality, it may not be this simple, and one may have to look at the dialogue as a mixed type of dialogue to begin with, taking into account the particulars of the speech event as appropriate for that particular text of discourse.

Another kind of example here would be a meeting of the library committee at a university, which sets a topic on the agenda, let us say the topic of when the library should close on Sundays. Some people may argue that the library should stay open later so students can have a place to study, while others might argue against this, saying that it would cost more money and there are not sufficient students using the facility to justify it.

In such a case, at a meeting of the library committee, there will be a chairman of the meeting, who will have the job of enforcing the rules of order governing the discussion, so that both sides have a reasonable chance to make their arguments heard. But the conduct of the meeting will also be bound by practical constraints. For example, it may be limited to a certain time. So, in this kind of case, whether or not a particular argument is relevant or whether or not a particular question is judged as legitimate may depend very much on the particulars of the speech event.[23]

Another interesting case in point is the kind of political dialogue that would typically take place, for example, in a congressional or parliamentary debate. At first it might seem that this is a type of persuasion dialogue or critical discussion. But, upon closer examination, one can see that it often involves very strong elements of deliberation. For example, the purpose of a particular debate may be to discuss a particular bill upon which the participants are then going to vote, and the aim of the discussion is to judge whether this bill makes a legislative recommendation that would be a good policy for the country to follow in the future. This very much makes the dialogue seem as though it would be a kind of deliberation. However, it has often been emphasized by the Western ideal of democratic politics that political dialogue, ideally, should be a kind of critical discussion that meets standards of rational argumentation appropriate for exploring the issues on both sides in a reasonable way and looking at the best arguments on both sides of an issue. So it would seem that political dialogue is often a mixture of the deliberation and the persuasion types of dialogue.[24]

But if we look at it a little more closely, we can see that negotiation is inherently involved in all political dialogue because there are always interests at stake and parties that have something to gain and lose. So it is not possible to exclude negotiation from this type of dialogue as being at least one element of it. Sometimes the inquiry too can be involved indirectly in political dialogue where experts are brought in—for example, scientific experts—in order to give input to a congress or legislature on important facts that may be highly relevant to determining the outcome of a political discussion. For example, on questions of the environment, experts on pollution, biologists, or other scientific experts may be brought in to give information about the consequences of certain possible courses of action and about the effects on the environment of actions that are taking place.

However, it is generally possible to see that eristic dialogue is very much a part of political debate. Commentators on political debate often observe that it is a very adversarial type of exchange in which parties attack each other, and the dialogue is very much an open forum where this type of eristic dialogue has a function. For example, the *ad hominem* argument, in principle, at least to some extent, is regarded as a legitimate type of argumentation in politics.[25] The problem is that most of us cannot always fully understand all the issues. We just do not have time to go into all the issues and information that would affect government policies. Hence, we elect representatives, trusting that they will support our interests and will behave in an honest way as government functionaries. Thus, it is inevitable that personality should play a role in this. We tend to pick political leaders based on our assessments of their character, their character for veracity in particular, based on the media reports we have of their conduct. There is nothing inherently illegitimate about this; it is an appropriate part of the political system. But, by the same token, it is therefore also a legitimate kind of argumentation, in some cases, for politicians to attack other politicians using *ad hominem* arguments by questioning the honesty and the character of their opponents. This is regarded as a legitimately acceptable type of political argumentation.

Of course, the problem is where to draw the line because if this type of *ad hominem* argument is carried too far, then it becomes an obstacle to discussion of what are presumably more important affairs of state that need deliberation.[26] Nevertheless, it is hard to exclude eristic dialogue as a legitimate part of political debate; therefore, generally, we can see that political debate is a mixture of all these different kinds of dialogues. This poses a critical problem because if an argument occurs in a text of discourse in a political debate, and it contains some sort of fault that we judge to be a defect or fallacy, let us say from the point of view of a critical discussion containing an *ad hominem* attack, then should we judge that this *ad hominem* argument is fallacious? Well, perhaps we could judge that it is fallacious on the assumption that the type of dialogue involved is that of a critical discussion. But, if it is a political debate, can we say that? Would it not be equally justified to say that the political debate involves elements of the negotiation, the deliberation, the eristic dialogue, or perhaps even elements of the inquiry or information-seeking type of dialogue are partly involved as well. The bottom line then is that in a case of political debate, the best one might be able to do is to arrive at a conditional judgment on the evaluation of the given argument, saying that, for example, it is a fallacious *ad hominem* argument from the point of view of a critical discussion, so that if this case of a political debate is supposed to be a critical discussion, then the *ad hominem* argument would fall short of the normative standards appropriate for argumentation in that type of discussion.

But we still have this separate question of identifying the type of dialogue. Is it a critical discussion, or is it some other type of dialogue? Or is it a mixed type of dialogue, which would, of course, be characteristic of political dialogue, so that it involves several distinct types of dialogue in its contextual makeup? With political dialogue in particular, one always needs to take great care to make the requisite qualifications, so that one does not operate on the naive assumption that the debate is supposed to conform to the normative requirements of a critical discussion and that is the end of the matter. This would be an overly naive evaluation of many a political debate because, as we have seen, a political debate typically, and even characteristically, involves very strong elements of the negotiation as well as the eristic type of dialogue. Moreover, a given case of political debate has to be analyzed carefully in relation to the particular requirements of the speech event. For example, if it occurred as part of a parliamentary debate, then there would be rules of order governing that debate, and it might be very helpful to take those rules of order into account in judging whether a particular argument, in the context of the debate, commits some fallacy or some logical error of reasoning.[27]

10. Dialectical Shifts

A *dialectical shift* is a change during a sequence of argumentation from one type of dialogue to another.[28] For example, a group of executives may be having a business meeting, but then they may adjourn the meeting temporarily for a break and have a discussion on sports and some other topics. But during this interval, the argumentation in the business meeting may be continued by some participants.[29] So here the same line of argumentation was continued, but the context of it changed. In the first instance, it was in a structured meeting with a chairman where the executives were deciding on certain issues, but after the break, it occurred in the context of a casual conversation where some remarks were being made or arguments put forward with the dialogue structure of the argumentation being quite different. In this kind of case, one can see that the shift involved an agreement to end the meeting, and therefore there was a very sharp and definite transition from the one context of dialogue to the other, and it would be apparent to all the participants that the shift had occurred.

In other cases, the shift can also be quite abrupt and definite but may not be the result of an agreement by the participants. For example, two neighbors may be having a conversation about some topic of concern when, all of a sudden, two dogs start fighting in the one neighbor's yard and the discussion turns to the practical question of what they should do about this situation. Here the line of argumentation has changed abruptly. At first, they might have been having some sort of critical discussion about some general issue, but then, once the problem of the dogs intruded, they began engaging in a deliberation on how to deal with this or what to do.

Another very common type of case would be where two people are having a critical discussion about some general issue and then one party attacks the other using an *ad hominem* argument and the other replies with a *tu quoque* (you too) type of *ad hominem* attack. In such a case, it is unfortunately quite common for the critical discussion to degenerate into a quarrel as the personal attacks become more heated, and each party is so upset by being personally attacked by the other side that she becomes more emotional and more adversarial in her attacks. This is a kind of gradual shift from a persuasion dialogue to a quarrel. It may have started out as a persuasion dialogue with some elements of the quarrel, but during a sequence of personal attacks, the dialogue may gradually slide toward more and more of an eristic exchange until, in the end, it may be very clearly a quarrel that is taking place.

Another familiar type of case here is the shift in union management negotiations to the quarrel, where the one side begins to demonize the other side through the use of *ad hominem* attacks portraying the other side as being unreliable and untrustworthy and trying to exploit its opponents by unfair means.[30] Unfortunately, when this kind of shift to the quarrel occurs, it can block the progress of negotiations so completely and so irrevocably that the company goes bankrupt before the negotiation can arrive at an outcome that is satisfactory to both sides. This is a highly negative kind of shift, from the point of view of successful or constructive argumentation.

Some dialectical shifts are positive or constructive in nature. For example, a divorcing couple may shift from quarreling to a negotiation dialogue, bargaining with each other over child custody.[31] However, it may be even better if the dialogue shifts to a critical discussion on the question of which party is better equipped to care for the children. This is a more impersonal or dispassionate kind of issue because it involves looking at evidence to judge whether an opinion is supported by that evidence. In this kind of case, there were two dialectical shifts, but it may be that the shifting was not a bad thing, and it may have helped the argumentation to deal with communication.

However, some dialectical shifts are problematic and even have a negative impact on argumentation. If the dialogue was supposed to be a critical discussion, in a philosophy seminar, for example, and one side keeps quarreling and engaging in eristic dialogue, then this shift could be very destructive and inappropriate—a kind of illicit, negative shift.

From a normative point of view of evaluating argumentation, a lot depends on the type of dialogue in which the participants were supposed to be engaged at the outset. Any shift away from this type of dialogue to another type is likely to mean that the goals of the original type of dialogue will not be realized by the conversation.

Shifts are especially problematic where they are concealed or where deception is involved. In fact, it is exactly in this sort of case that bias in argumentation tends to be a problem. A party who is supposed to be engaged in persuasion dialogue may be covertly bargaining to support his own interests that are at stake. If the other party sees evidence of this, and especially if the first party tried to conceal his financial interests, then the other party may accuse him of biased argumentation. Indeed, this is a key type of situation in which bias is perceived as negative in argumentation, as something for which a partner in argumentation should be criticized, as having a defective argument.

The most important thing is that if an arguer is supposed to be engaging in a type of dialogue such as a persuasion dialogue (or inquiry or deliberation) where requirements for balanced argumentation are in place, then there is an expectation (presumption) that this arguer has the attitudes of flexible commitment, empathy, open-mindedness, critical doubt, and evidence sensitivity. This presumption gives the arguer a certain credibility—it is presumed that her arguments in the dialogue are based on the evidence presented on both sides of the issue. This presumption alone gives the arguer's thesis a certain weight or standing as a plausible presumption. But if we find that this argument is not balanced (two-sided) but is purely one-sided, there is a lowering of expectations. In such a case, where we have grounds for suspecting bias, the arguer herself is accorded less credibility and the plausibility value of her argument is adjusted downward. Her argument was one-sided, but should be balanced, we find. Therefore, we accord it less plausibility as an argument because we perceive it as biased. It is this kind of shift that is at the basis of bias.

Notes

1. Walton (1990; 1992b, chapter 6).
2. Walton (1992b, chapter 5; 1996a).
3. Govier (1987, chapter 8).
4. Walton (1996a).
5. Walton (1989a, 11–19.
6. Hamblin (1970, p. 257), and Walton and Krabbe (1995).
7. Walton (1989a, p. 12).
8. See also van Eemeren and Grootendorst (1992).
9. Walton and Krabbe (1995).
10. Hamblin (1971, 136).
11. See also Walton (1992b, 102–103).
12. Walton (1992c, 22–23).
13. Walton (1989a, 7).
14. Woods and Walton (1978; 1982).
15. Walton (1990a, 13–15).
16. Walton (1990c, chapter 9).
17. Walton (1992b, chapter 4).
18. Walton and Krabbe (1995).
19. Walton (1992b, chapter 4).
20. Grice (1975).
21. Walton and Krabbe (forthcoming).
22. Woods and Walton (1982, chapter 1).
23. Walton (1989a, pp. 71–75).
24. See Walton (1989a, chapter 10).
25. Ibid., chapter 5.
26. Walton (1989a, chapter 6).
27. Walton (1990a).

28. Walton (1992d).
29. Ibid., p. 137.
30. For a detailed outline of such a case, see Walton (1992b, pp. 147–150).
31. See Walton (1992d, p. 139).

Chapter Three
THE THEORY OF BIAS

The purpose of this chapter is to offer a general, abstract theory of the concept of bias in argument that is useful for evaluating arguments. Then once this target concept has been articulated clearly, chapter 4 goes on to give a set of indicators that can be used to detect whether bias is present in a given case of argumentation.

In this chapter, the concept of 'bias' is distinguished from a number of related concepts to which it appears to be similar—point of view, commitment, and position in argumentation. Bias also is contrasted with a number of concepts to which it appears to be opposed—objectivity, neutrality, fairmindedness, impartiality, and critical doubt. Bias in argumentation, in the sense we will advocate here as central for informal logic, will be defined in terms of the concept of 'balance' in a dialogue exchange of arguments.[1]

Bias, in this sense could be called "dialectical bias," meaning that an argument is to be judged as biased or not in relation to the standards appropriate for the kind of conversational exchange in which it was supposed to have been put forward. Dialectical bias has to do with the use of an argument in a context of dialogue.[2] As such, it is not primarily or essentially an ethical failure or a legal transgression or a psychological characteristic but a judgment of an argument to meet normative standards appropriate for a verbal exchange when speech partners reason together. It is a characteristic of reasoning used in an argument exchange. This concept is a logical meaning of 'bias', at least in the broad sense of logic meaning "informal logic," or the study and evaluation of arguments as used in a given case of a natural language conversational exchange of viewpoints.

Some critics will maintain that this attempted definition of 'bias' is

59

itself biased. And, of course, this criticism is justified, to some extent. For this attempt at definition will reflect the dialectical viewpoint on argument outlined in chapter 2. For example, these critics might allege that studying the empirical psychology of bias, or righting the wrongs of racial or other kinds of prejudice, is much more important than any narrowly logical or dialectical conception of bias. These critics are entitled to their viewpoint, but it will be contended here that our analysis of dialectical bias in argumentation does not contain the kind of bias that is a bad or harmful bias, in the sense to be analyzed. The dialectical viewpoint advocated as best for informal logic will be defended on grounds of its practical usefulness as well as its theoretical clarity and consistency.

1. Initial Perceptions of Bias

When we first consider the concept of bias in an abstract or general way, there are several paradigms we are likely to have in mind. One is the idea of a balance, like the statue of the blindfolded woman holding a balance, or set of scales, often found displayed at the entrance to a law court building. By this picture of it, bias is contrasted with a balance between arguments on both sides of a disputed issue.

Another thing many of us might associate with bias is closedmindedness. The image we may have here is that of the enthusiast for a "cause," the evangelical or fanatical arguer whose commitment is unalterably fixed to the view of one side that there is no real openness to the arguments of the other side.[3]

Both closedminded and unbalanced argumentation may seem like bad or inappropriate kinds of bias to have, but perhaps not all bias is of a bad sort. For example, it could be quite all right for a scientist to be biased or predisposed favorably toward an untested hypothesis that she has devised. But it is quite another thing if the scientist still persists with the hypothesis even after it clearly has been falsified by evidence as the result of an experiment. Here what was initially an acceptable kind of bias became, at a later point, an inappropriate kind of insensitivity to evidence.

Another kind of bias most of us recognize easily is "my-side" bias, where an arguer is a strong advocate of a particular group, interest, or point of view.[4] Unlike the closedmindedness type of bias, advocacy or partisanship does not seem to be an inherently inappropriate type of bias, provided an arguer can deal with it or keep it in perspective. But the problem is that, in many instances, it does seem to become negative or harmful. What seems to be wrong is not just having a personal point of view but exhibiting a failure to restrain or moderate that point of view appropriately in the context of a dialogue exchange.

A judge or mediator in a dispute is supposed to be unbiased, in the sense of not favoring or advocating one side or the other's argumentation. In fact, such an individual is a human being and therefore will have a point of view on any issue involving values and issues of political or social controversy.[5] Thus, to say that a judge or mediator is not biased should mean that the person can suspend his or her personal point of view and not let it interfere with the resolution or judging of the dispute.

A party could be said to be neutral with respect to a dispute or conflict if he or she does not favor the opinion on the one side over that on the other.[6] However, it is possible for an individual to be nonneutral, yet to be impartial enough to be free of bias or at least bias in the "bad" sense in which it is a problem or obstacle.

Thus, we can see that there are different kinds of bias or absence or freedom from bias and that bias is not always contrasted with strict neutrality in argumentation.

Garver (1993) agrees that neutrality is not the opposite of the kind of bias important for critical thinking. According to Garver (p. 54), it is much better to conceive of bias along the lines of orchestration of plural points of view—rather than along the lines of being opposed to the conception of a disembodied mind. Garver also recommends (p. 50) that bias "be identified by the kinds of arguments invoked to establish and defeat charges of bias, and the kinds of correctives that can be employed to remove it." It is this defeasible notion of bias in argument that is pluralistic in nature, as opposed to postulating one ideal "right," neutral point of view that is the object of our investigation.

Bias also seems to be tied to one's role in an argument. We expect a mediator or judge to be unbiased to a much higher standard than we expect of a participant advocating one side of a contested dispute. For such a participant, we expect an advocacy or bias in favor of his or her own side. This could be called "partisanship." It also could be called a "bias" but is not necessarily a bad, unexpected, or inappropriate kind of bias. However, it could become bad, or pathological, if carried to excess, as in cases of closedmindedness or zealotry.

We often hear of cases of bias in journalism, news reporting, and the media, generally. But standards here vary, depending on the type of "story" involved. News reporting, on a show like "60 Minutes" for example, is supposed to be "objective," to report all the facts in a balanced way. Even so, such reports often will have a "spin" and definitely advocate a particular conclusion or point of view. By contrast, in a frankly advocacy format, like an "opinion" page of a newspaper or magazine, the standards are quite different. One expects to see a partisan argument selectively in favor of one side or point of view. Sometimes newspapers will even balance off a column expressing one point of view on a controversial issue with another column representing the opposed viewpoint. What would be an unacceptably biased argument in the one format could be quite acceptable (not perceived as exhibiting a "bad" bias) in the other format.

Hence, it seems that bias (or at least our perceptions of how acceptable or unacceptable it is), is a function of the avowed or supposed purpose of a discourse. This has posed a difficulty because it suggests that evidence for or against a charge of bias is contextual, that is, not explicitly identifiable in an argument itself as a set of premises and a conclusion. Logic, in the past, has not had the resources to deal with contextual factors. But in chapter 2, six normative contexts of dialogue were identified.

In logic, the kind of case we are primarily concerned with, when it comes to identifying and evaluating bias, is in a given argument. An argument in persuasion dialogue, typically, as defined in chapter 2, functions as a set of propositions (premises and a conclusion) put forward in such a way that the conclusion is a claim or contention in a context of a disagreement or a conflict of opinions with an opposed or doubting point of view.[7] In such a case, we do not expect the proponent of the argument to be neutral. We expect him or her to have a bias, to be an advocate for his or her point of view. The kind of bias we need to be particularly careful to recognize and identify, for purposes of logic and critical thinking, is the kind that interferes with the resolution of a dispute by reasoned argumentation. This can occur where a bias is too strongly fixed in place so that there is no real exchange of viewpoints, especially if the bias is concealed to one or both parties. It is these cases of excessive and deceptive bias that are associated with fallacies and logical faults of good reasoning. It will be our contention that this problematic type of bias occurs in cases of persuasion dialogue where the requirements for balanced argument are not fulfilled.

2. Objectivity, Neutrality, and Impartiality

People often speak in such a way as to imply that any bias is inherently bad or problematic, from a logical point of view, and that our goal in informal logic should be to eliminate bias in argumentation. This type of standard is often spoken of as "objectivity" or "neutrality." But bias is not the same thing as absence of neutrality or objectivity.

Neutrality is a kind of suspension of commitment where an individual does not accept the argument of one side or the other. Objectivity, similarly, implies a kind of removal from advocacy of either side of a conflict of opinions, where one's personal point of view is entirely removed or expunged. Impartiality also implies taking neither one side (part) nor the other in a dispute or conflict of opinions.

However, there may be distinctions to be made between impartiality and objectivity and between these concepts and that of neutrality. Perelman and Olbrechts-Tyteca (1969, p. 60) cite such differences by contrasting argumentation in a scientific inquiry with the type of case where members of a group are deliberating on a course of action that will affect them personally, whatever they decide to do.

> Contrary to what happens in science, where all that is necessary for the solution of a problem is knowledge of the techniques that enable the solution to be reached, interference in a controversy whose outcome will affect a specific group may be made only by one who is a member of, or closely bound up with, the group in question. Where an opinion influences action, objectivity is no longer sufficient, unless one means by objectivity the viewpoint of a wider group embracing both the opponents and the "neutral." The latter is qualified to judge not because he is neutral—anyone can reproach him with this neutrality in the name of common principles of right or justice—but because he is impartial: being *impartial* is not being *objective,* it consists of belonging to the same group as those one is judging, without having previously decided in favor of any one of them.

This suggests that in a scientific inquiry, objectivity is easier to define—it is simply knowledge and employment of the accepted techniques in the given field that are used to solve recognized problems. In other more personalized types of dialogue containing argumentation, however, the situation is more complicated. There are really three standards here that need to be distinguished, which could be categorized as follows.

1. *Neutrality.*
   This means not having any position or opinion, on one side or the other. This is the position of an "outsider" or "spectator" who has no commitment on the issue, *pro* or *contra.*

2. *Impartiality.*
This means having a (tentative) position or opinion for one side, but not in such a fixed way that a definite decision has been made that one opinion is right and the other is wrong.

3. *Fairmindedness.*
This means having a definite opinion or position for one side or the other but being able to suspend this commitment temporarily, so that one gives full consideration to the argumentation on both (or all) sides.

The actual terms one uses here may be somewhat arbitrary. Perelman and Olbrechts-Tyteca would perhaps call 2 and 3 two different types of impartiality. However, it is useful to distinguish these three standards, each of which represents a kind of absence (negation) of bias.

To put this another way, we could say that there are three types of absence of bias: (1) lack of any commitment, either way, on an issue, (2) lack of fixed commitment—that is, one has commitment, but it is open to doubt or suspension; and (3) the ability to suspend commitment and consider both sides of an issue.

The kind of bias one wants to study, analyze, and identify for purposes of informal logic is definitely not the first type, at least generally. For most of the cases we deal with in informal logic are arguments on common public controversies concerning conflicts of values upon which generally everyone may be expected to have some opinion or position— often a very strong opinion, one way or the other. Neutrality as a goal would be far too high a standard to be appropriate for critical thinking, in most typical cases of argumentation with which we are concerned.

The other two types of absence of bias could be categorized in terms of the characteristics of a balanced argument given in chapter 2 as follows. Impartiality seems to combine flexible commitment and critical doubt. Fairmindedness seems to combine elements of flexible commitment, critical doubt, and open-mindedness. Both are compatible with commitment, and therefore neither represents a complete absence of bias, going by the standard of (1). Neutrality, in contrast, is not compatible with commitment.

Van Eemeren and Grootendorst (1984, p. 79) define what amounts to neutrality (the *zero* point of view) in a critical discussion, in terms of an arguer's attitude toward an expressed opinion.

If we abbreviate the *expressed opinion* in respect of which language users adopt an attitude as *O*, it is then possible to identify three possible *attitudes to O:* a *positive* point of view, a *negative* point of view, and a *zero* point of view. In our example the first language user takes a positive attitude to *O,* the second a negative and the third a zero attitude. We shall abbreviate the three possible attitudes as follows:

(a) *positive point of view:* +/*O*
(b) *negative point of view:* -/*O*
(c) *zero point of view:* 0/*O*

If a language user advances a positive point of view in respect of *O,* then he is further *positively committed to O* and if he advances a negative point of view he is *negatively committed to O* (unless he revokes his positive or negative point of view). A language user adopting a zero attitude to O is *not committed to O either positively or negatively.*

Here it is quite clear that neutrality or the *zero* point of view is defined as absence of commitment—not being committed to an opinion either positively or negatively.

Neutrality, however, as noted in Walton (1991, p. 15) is too high a standard to define a concept of bias to be appropriate for informal logic generally: "This [standard] seems far too strong, for it condemns all advocacy arguments of any sort as biased, no matter how well justified, appropriate, and reasonable." Van Eemeren and Grootendorst, who see the critical discussion as an interaction of two points of view, also no doubt would agree that neutrality, defined as the zero point of view, is not a normative requirement for argumentation in a critical discussion. In a critical discussion, or any other type of persuasion dialogue, an arguer is not expected to be neutral.

3. Point of View and Commitment

The concept of 'bias' needs to be distinguished from two other related concepts that are also very important in argumentation theory—'point of view' and 'commitment'. This can be done best using an example, and the best one for this purpose is the dialogue on tipping in Walton (1992b, pp. 7–11). This dialogue is a persuasion dialogue between Helen and Bob on the practice of tipping for certain services—for example, tipping taxi drivers or waiters and waitresses in restaurants.

In the dialogue on tipping, Bob argues for the thesis that tipping is a good practice that should be retained. Helen argues for the proposition that tipping is a bad practice that should be eliminated. At the beginning, both participants agreed that this is what each of them would argue for in the dialogue.

According to van Eemeren and Grootendorst (1984, p. 79), a *point of view* in a critical discussion is made up of two things, an *expressed opinion* that is a proposition and an *attitude* toward that proposition. The three possible attitudes, as noted above, are a positive point of view, a negative point of view, and a zero point of view, which is neither positive nor negative.

In the dialogue on tipping, Bob has a positive point of view toward tipping, and Helen has a negative point of view.

The concept of 'commitment' in dialogue is closely related to point of view. Clearly, in view of their respective points of view, Bob is committed to tipping as a good practice, and Helen is not only uncommitted to tipping as a good practice, she is committed against it. Van Eemeren and Grootendorst (1984, p. 79) make this connection explicitly when they write that if a language user advances a positive point of view in respect of a proposition, then he is positively committed to that proposition. If a language user "advances a negative point of view, he is negatively committed" to the proposition in that point of view (p. 79). And, finally, a language user who adopts a zero attitude is not committed to the proposition in that attitude "either positively or negatively" (see above). So point of view in a critical discussion not only defines but also influences an arguer's commitment in that discussion.

Commitment is the basic concept in the structures of formal dialectic designed by Hamblin (1970; 1971), as noted in chapter 2. Hamblin had the idea that all the participants in argument in a dialogue would have a kind of log or repository that would keep track of all their commitments as the dialogue proceeds. Hamblin thought of such a *commitment store*, as he called it, along the lines of a blackboard list of propositions or a computer memory, where a set of propositions is recorded, or can be erased, as noted in chapter 2. At certain types of moves in a dialogue, like making an assertion, for example, a proposition would be added to a participant's commitment store. At certain other kinds of moves, for example, a retraction, a proposition would be deleted from that participant's commitment store. Hamblin generally presumed that these commitment stores would be in plain view for all participants, so that everyone would know what was in her own commitment store as well as in those of the other participants in the dialogue. But as noted in chapter 2, this notion more recently has been extended to take into account commitments not known to participants in a dialogue.

Adopting the Hamblin model, we can distinguish between commitment and point of view as follows. Point of view refers to two components—first, the proposition that the participant is supposed to argue globally for or against in a dialogue, and, second, the participant's attitude (positive, negative, or zero) toward that proposition.

Commitment is different from point of view because sometimes a participant in argumentation will adopt or take on a commitment that does not necessarily reflect his point of view. For example, in the dialogue on tipping (p. 9), Helen argues that in a foreign country it is easy to make mistakes and tip too much or too little. Bob replies: "I admit that there are problems of knowing customs in foreign countries. But that is a general problem with all traveling." Here Bob is making a concession to Helen's point of view, and he is committing himself to the existence of problems of knowing customs in foreign countries. But his commitment to this proposition is not part of his point of view.

In general, then, it seems that if a proposition is part of one's point of view in a dialogue, then one is committed to that proposition. But the converse is not necessarily true. One can be committed to a proposition in a dialogue, even if that proposition is not a part of one's point of view in the dialogue.

The difference, it seems, is that point of view is defined by the agreement one (presumably) has made at the opening or confrontation stage of a dialogue to defend or oppose a particular proposition. This defines the global issue of a dialogue, and it defines the initial and general commitment in the dialogue because it stipulates, or defines generally, the stance one is committed to taking.

However, as the dialogue proceeds through its sequence of exchanges of argumentation, particular moves one makes will define one's commitment in a much more detailed and specific way. One will build up a log of commitments in one's commitment store, reflecting what one has actually gone on record as saying in the dialogue exchanges. Not all these propositions may reflect, or be part of one's underlying point of view, but they very definitely determine to what one is committed.

The concepts of 'commitment' and 'point of view' are clearly very close to the concept of bias in argumentation and are important parts of it. But is either of them the same thing as bias? Certainly, a bias is based on a specific commitment to something, and a revealing of commitment to an identifiable position is often an important sign or piece of evidence that a bias exists in an argument.

But it seems that bias is not the same thing as commitment. To bring out the difference, we turn to the concept of 'position' in argumentation, which is defined in terms of commitment.

4. Position Revealed by Argumentation

When a sequence of argumentation in dialogue has proceeded for some time, it may be possible to define or recognize a certain pattern or shape in an arguer's commitment store. This is called an arguer's "position" in the sense of Walton (1985), meaning that an arguer's set of commitments in a dialogue may form into an organized whole, in relation to the point of view she has defended in the dialogue.

In the dialogue on tipping, once the argumentation was finished, it not only threw light on the issue of tipping, but it also revealed quite a bit about the underlying positions of Helen and Bob (Walton 1992b, p. 16). As the dialogue proceeded, it revealed that Bob and Helen argued from two distinctly different positions. Both consistently argued that when something was good, it was because it promoted or arose from a free market economy, unhampered by government restrictions. Helen's arguments were based consistently on the generally opposed position that financial standards should be set in a fair manner by government regulations on the workplace. These differing positions were more broad than their two differences of point of view on the issue of tipping. Even though the dialogue did not resolve the original conflict of opinions on tipping, it nevertheless seemed to have a definite value, both to the participants and to onlookers, in that it revealed these underlying positions and how they related to the argumentation on both sides of the issue of tipping. This revealing of underlying positions is the "maieutic function" of dialogue.

A technical problem in defining the concept of an arguer's position is that the previously mentioned assumption of Hamblin, that all commitments in a dialogue are clearly on view to all participants, is an idealization of rational argument that is commonly not characteristic of argumentation in everyday conversational exchanges.

Hence the complication was introduced (Walton 1984; 1985; 1992b) of dividing a participant's commitment store into two sides—a *light side*, where all the propositions are clearly on view and a *dark side*, where a set of propositions is partially obscured to view, and can only be conjectured by presumption or guesswork, from what was said in a dialogue. This distinction has been further developed in Walton and Krabbe (1995), where the concept of 'commitment' is studied in technical detail in different types of dialogue.

Some of the problems inherent in defining an arguer's commitment in a given case are that commitments can be logically inconsistent with each other, can conflict in other ways, or can change and evolve over the course of a dialogue. In some cases, it can be difficult, problematic, or even impossible to determine what an arguer's position really is, going by the available evidence of how this person has argued on different occasions.

An interesting illustrative case of this sort was a newspaper article (York 1994) in which questions were raised about the position of Lloyd Axworthy, a politician who had been given responsibility for restructuring social programs in Canada in 1994. Mr. Axworthy had long been known as a left-wing liberal but was now advocating job creation by reduction of social programs, of a kind that usually has been associated with a right-wing political position.

Case 3.1: Somewhere deep inside the soul of Lloyd Axworthy, there are still the traces of the angry young man from the working-class streets of Winnipeg's gritty North End.

You can sometimes hear faint echoes of it in his speeches, when he attacks the unfairness of child poverty or denounces business people "in the three-piece suits" who want to slash the social safety net.

But the crusades of Mr. Axworthy's younger days are long over. His fierce idealism may have begun to fade in 1988, when he lost the battle against Bay Street on the U.S. free-trade deal, or in 1990, when he realized that his left-wing reputation had killed his dream of seeking the Liberal leadership.

Today, at 54, he seems to accept the business-minded realities of the Liberal Party of the 1990s. As Human Resources Minister, with a $70-billion budget and one of the most powerful cabinet jobs in Ottawa, he has become a tax-cutting friend of the business community.

Some observers were shocked when he imposed a $5.5-billion cut in unemployment-insurance benefits. They were even more astonished when he used the savings to pay for a reduction in payroll taxes—and when he insisted that a tax rollback was the best way to create jobs.

In the old days, as a cabinet minister in the Pierre Trudeau era, Mr. Axworthy spent massive sums of money on urban renewal projects in Winnipeg's inner-city core. It was an expression of his belief in "direct job creation."

But the old tax-and-spend philosophy has disappeared. Mr. Axworthy has been reborn as a fiscally conscious moderate who talks of the need to "reward effort"

> among the unemployed. When he spoke to a class of high-school students in Ottawa recently, he sternly warned them not to "bum around" on welfare.

As a result of Mr. Axworthy's recent political stands and arguments, critics began to raise questions about whether his political position was consistent. One critic wrote, "This guy is a chameleon," adding that he was "mystified" by this "shift in the party's policies" (*York*, 1994, p. 2). Mr. Axworthy defended the shift, saying that the "precepts of traditional Liberalism had to be updated" and that now you have to "spend smarter" and "make better use of resources" (p. 2). An ally of Mr. Axworthy's was quoted as saying that it was a "pragmatic thing"—either he had to "move to the right, or he had no political future" (p. 2).

In this kind of case, the critics are trying to determine what this individual's position really is, especially now that it seems to have changed significantly. The general problem in this kind of case is that of retraction of earlier commitments and moving to a different position. In principle, such a shift is often quite acceptable in argumentation. But in political debate, if critics think the change is more due to self-interest than to a thoughtful, reasoned change of underlying convictions, they will attack it as showing hypocrisy. Many case studies of this sort of attack, often associated with the *ad hominem* argument, can be found in Walton (1985).

The perception in this kind of case is the opposite of the kind of perception associated with bias. An arguer who sticks too rigidly to his position will be perceived as having a bias in his argumentation. In this case, it is just the opposite. The arguer is being criticized for appearing to depart too much from an earlier position.

Bias is not just having a particular position, commitment, or point of view in argumentation. It also relates to how that point of view is defended in that argumentation. To have a position is one thing, but to defend it by putting forward positive argumentation meant to support it is the kind of identifying factor of bias. The term *bias* becomes especially appropriate if such pro-argumentation for a point of view is perceived as too strong, too closed, showing a loss of balance in allowing for critical doubt and openness to the criticisms of the other side.

5. Fairmindedness in Critical Thinking

As part of his program to advocate "strong" critical thinking as a vehicle to teach the use of reasoning skills in education, Richard Paul has emphasized a quality he calls "fairmindedness," defined in Paul, Binker, and Charbonneau (1986, p. 7) as follows.

> To think critically about issues we must be able to consider the strengths and weaknesses of opposing points of view. Since critical thinkers value fairmindedness, they feel that it is especially important that they entertain positions with which they disagree. They realize that it is unfair either to judge the ideas of another until they fully understand them, or act on their own beliefs without giving due consideration to relevant criticisms. The process of considering an opposing point of view aids critical thinkers in recognizing the logical components of their beliefs (e.g. key concepts, assumptions, implications, etc.) and puts them in a better position to amend those beliefs.

So defined, fairmindedness comprises a number of aspects. One seems to be the ability to suspend one's own beliefs or opinions (critical doubt) and to empathize with or enter into those of an opposed point of view (empathy). Another seems to be the ability to give "due consideration" to criticisms or arguments from an opposed viewpoint (open-mindedness). Still another is to desist from judging another viewpoint before fully understanding it. This aspect also would come under our category of "empathy" in the list of characteristics of a balanced argument (chapter 2). This last aspect, in particular, would seem to rule out strawman fallacies committed by rushing in too quickly to criticize or attack an oversimplified or inadequate representation of an opponent's real position or point of view in argumentation.

Paul (1990), as a basic part of his program for critical thinking, contrasts fairminded critical thinkers with both uncritical thinkers and closedminded critical thinkers. Fisher (1991b, p. 31) summarizes Paul's general view of this distinction succinctly.

> Uncritical thinkers are simply poor at reasoning things through (and would be expected to score relatively poorly on any well-designed test of critical thinking). Closedminded critical thinkers (often called *weak* critical thinkers by Paul) are good at reasoning up to a point (they are "clever in argument" and would be expected to score relatively well on existing tests of critical thinking). However, they use this skill narrowly, in particular they use it only in pursuit of their own interests and in defence of their own point of view *and they do not question these.*

Fairminded critical thinkers, on the other hand, are skillful in argument (and would score well on standard tests) but they apply that skill just as readily when their own beliefs are challenged or when their own interests are at risk. That is to say, even when their own position is threatened, fairminded critical thinkers will take seriously viewpoints and perspectives *other than their own* and will argue as sympathetically, and as powerfully as possible, *from those other perspectives,* when weighing the pros and cons in the case.

In this view, fairmindedness is more than just the ability to argue well by defending your own point of view skillfully or criticizing an opposed point of view with clever arguments that tell against it. It is the ability to argue both sympathetically and powerfully from the perspective of that opposed point of view. Both open-mindedness and evidence sensitivity are very important aspects of fairmindedness.

To operationalize this concept, Paul has even proposed a test for fairmindedness, taking the following form (Paul, Glaser, and Bowen, unpublished).

Step 1:   Present the student with two opposite (contradictory) beliefs and ask which one he or she considers more justified or correct.

Step 2:   Ask the student to identify, out of a given set, the best reason for accepting the belief and also the best reason for accepting the opposite belief.

In judging the outcome of the test, to score high on fairmindedness, the student must pick the strongest reasons for the belief he does not hold. "Strongest" here is interpreted to mean "easiest to defend before an open-minded audience of reasonable people." Although this audience factor has been criticized by Fisher (1991b, p. 34) as not free of difficulties, in general Paul's test gives one a relatively clear and precise idea of what the quality of fairmindedness comes down to, in operational terms.

Paul's test, in the preamble given to it, identifies clearly that what is being tested for is the ability to argue not just from one's personal point of view but also from a wider viewpoint of defending that position before a wider audience of persons whom one would suppose to be "reasonable" (Paul, Glaser, and Bowen, p. xx).

The "fairness" of mind that is being tested here is that achieved by individuals who have developed some ability to distinguish strongly relevant from weakly relevant and irrelevant reasons and considerations within the context of empathically entering into the points of view of those who hold beliefs they do not themselves hold. As part of this capacity, a fairminded person must be able to tell the difference between a reason that will seem best only to a narrow circle of believers (who often share a variety of questionable if not biased assumptions) from a wide circle of rational persons who will be moved most by reasons that are least dependent on assumptions as questionable as the belief itself.

So defined, fairmindedness is a fairly clear, but also fairly complex concept. It involves the ability to deal with points of view opposed to one's own, to pick out the most strongly relevant arguments for such a point of view and to make this judgment in light of the knowledge and expectations of a wider audience than just the "narrow circle of believers" supporting one's own point of view.

Fairmindedness is a skill or attitude that is reflected in the performance of an arguer's handling an opposed point of view during a dialogue exchange of points of view. It seems to involve the empathic ability to enter into an opposed arguer's point of view, and then to judge what would be the best arguments to support it, according to the standards of a general audience who, presumably, may not be strongly committed either way.

Paul's notion of fairmindedness requires all five characteristics of a balanced argument outlined in chapter 2, to some degree. But it especially centers on a variant of the characteristic of evidence sensitivity, while including empathy and critical doubt as parts of fairmindedness. The notion of evidence sensitivity to which Paul appeals is a special one, however. The fairminded arguer must be able to "tell the difference between the reason that seems best only to a narrow circle of believers" and the reason that will move a "wide circle of rational persons." This idea seems comparable to Perelman's notion of the universal audience (Perelman and Olbrechts-Tyteca 1969, pp. 34–35).

In short, then, Paul's notion of fairmindedness contains most (or perhaps all) of our characteristics of a balanced argument. But it also appeals to the additional idea of the wide and narrow circle of believers and therefore goes in a somewhat different direction from the theory of bias developed in this chapter.

6. Critical Doubt

The ability to have critical doubts about one's opinions by temporarily suspending one's commitment and looking at the matter from a questioning or skeptical point of view is closely related to the concept of bias. A biased argument—at least where bias is a problem or obstacle for good reasoning—is one where commitment is too strongly fixed to a point of view, so that genuine critical doubts are not expressed or even seriously entertained. Critical doubt seems to require temporary suspension of one's advocacy for one's own point of view in argumentation. And it is precisely the inability to do this that characterizes biased argumentation.

This aspect of bias is different from (and is just one aspect of) lack of balance or failure to weigh the arguments fairly on both sides of an issue. The problem with failure of critical doubt in an argument is a lack of openness to the doubts expressed by the uncommitted and a failure to suspend or restrain temporarily the *pro* attitude for one's point of view, to really acknowledge its potential weaknesses or critical shortcomings. This specific problem is the absence of critical doubt.

But what is critical doubt? Critical doubt with respect to an opinion *O* is not the same as having a negative point of view with respect to *O*. Nor is it the same as being neutral with respect to *O*, that is, having what Van Eemeren and Grootendorst (1984, p. 71) call the "zero point of view." For to express critical doubt about a proposition *A* does not bring with it a burden of proof in respect to *A* or for that matter in respect to the negation of *A*. Nor does it appear to require abstention from commitment to *A* or not-*A* in the way that neutrality does.

Van Eemeren and Grootendorst appear to agree with this account, for they define critical doubt (1984, p. 81) as a kind of iterated attitude— an attitude about an attitude in a dispute where two parties are engaged in argumentation with each other:

> It is important to realize that the doubt expressed by a language user in a dispute does not bear directly on the expressed opinion but on the *point of view or attitude* expressed by another language user in *respect of* the expressed opinion. Perhaps it is also important here to observe once more that expressing doubt, while it may *accompany* the adoption of the opposite attitude, is *not identical* to propounding the opposite point of view.

According to the account given by van Eemeren and Grootendorst, two parties who are engaged in resolving a conflict of opinions in a critical discussion each has a point of view (standpoint). A standpoint consists of a specific proposition, or thesis, and an attitude (positive, negative, or zero) toward this proposition. In their view, critical doubt does not bear (directly) on the proposition but on the attitude expressed by an arguer with respect to that opinion or proposition. Critical doubt then is an attitude toward an attitude.[8]

This way of defining the term *critical doubt* is somewhat subtle and complex. It means that if we are talking about critical doubt expressed in argumentation, it is implied that there is one arguer who has a particular attitude or point of view, that there is a secondary arguer who has another attitude or point of view, and that the one has a particular attitude toward the attitude of the other.

This way of defining critical doubt introduces a new dimension into the concept of bias. Somehow bias is a maladjustment of this nestling of attitudes, one into the other, in argumentation. But what kind of misalignment of attitudes occurs here that is characteristic of the negative kind of bias that is a problem in critical thinking? We introduce the following hypothesis.

On just about any issue of a critical discussion in everyday conversation, like issues on ethics or public policy, there will be an existing bias to one side or the other. But this may not be a problem, provided there is critical doubt with respect to the point of view that one favors.

Critical doubt is possible in such a case because one can suspend temporarily one's antipathy toward the *contra* attitude expressed by the other side. But what is even more significant, with respect to bias, critical doubt is possible because one can suspend temporarily one's own *pro* attitude toward the positive point of view of one's own side. This is a reflexive act of self-doubt, in the sense of requiring a suspension of commitment to one's own commitment toward the opinion one is advocating.

To carry out such an act of suspension of commitment, one must put oneself in the position of someone who has doubts about one's own point of view. By raising questions where one's own defence of one's position is weakest, one can discover where the strongest arguments against this position are, in a given context of dispute. This can be a very valuable skill in a critical discussion.

If bias exists in a critical discussion, that is normal and is not a problem. But it becomes a problem where the second-order bias—the bias in favor of that bias, so to speak—is too strong and does not permit critical doubt. The problem here with the biased argument is that it may be so strongly biased that it does not permit the temporary or hypothetical suspension of commitment needed to judge itself critically.

This iterated way of defining critical doubt is a subtle idea. You could say that it requires an arguer to balance two roles delicately, at the same time. Sometimes what is needed is to push forward by positively advocating one's point of view as forcefully as possible. Yet, at other points, what is needed is an attitude of critical doubt that means critically questioning the weakest links or gaps in one's position, as advocated to that point in a dialogue.

The kind of skills required to balance such a dual role in persuasion dialogue are ones of empathy, flexibility, critical doubt, evidence sensitivity, and open-mindedness. The problem of bias here resides with the dogmatic or inflexible kind of argumentation where there is an inability to suspend commitment, even temporarily or hypothetically, in order to open up one's arguments to an opposed lien of argument. In short, bias is a failure of critical doubt, and also a failure of the other four requirements to be met in a dialogue where these requirements matter.

7. Bias as One-Sided Argument

All the considerations above lead toward a new way of defining bias in argument as a dialectical concept. According to this new theory, a biased argument can be defined simply as a one-sided argument—an argument that lacks the balance necessary for it to be two-sided.

The dialectical theory of bias is based on the idea, expressed in chapter 2, that an argument has two sides. The normative models of dialogue outlined in chapter 2 are based on the idea that each type of dialogue has two sides. Argumentation in a persuasion dialogue, in particular, is resolved on a balance of considerations. In a good persuasion dialogue, as the sequence of argumentation proceeds, there is supposed to be a genuine exchange of views. The other side's arguments are taken seriously, and are taken account of, in improving one's own arguments. A growing body of evidence is considered and weighed at each move. As an argument goes along, and shows increased maieutic insight, it reacts to and benefits from the arguments on both sides.

A *one-sided argument* continually engages in pro-argumentation for the position supported and continually rejects the arguments of the opposed side in a dialogue. A *two-sided* (*balanced*) argument considers all arguments on both sides of a dialogue. A balanced argument weighs each argument against the arguments that have been opposed to it. A balanced argument considers all the other arguments that have been opposed to it in a dialogue and reaches a summary judgment on which side (as a whole) has the stronger case. A balanced argument advocates as conclusion the thesis of the side that has proved to have the stronger case (on a balance of considerations).

A one-sided argument amounts to pure advocacy of a proposition without taking into account the arguments against it. *Partisanship* is another word for the same idea. The one-sided argument never makes any real concessions to the other side.

Advocacy may now be more carefully defined as argumentation that is put forward to defend, justify, or promote one's own side of a dispute where there is some contested claim at issue. That is, in such a case, there will be two sides to the dispute. *Advocacy* means putting forward argumentation to support one's own side, as opposed to taking a balanced approach that would consider or support the arguments on both sides. It is a kind of exclusivity or one-sidedness.

The concept of 'pro-argumentation' defined by van Eemeren and Grootendorst is a very good account of advocacy in a critical discussion. Advocacy in a critical discussion can be defined as pro-argumentation put forward by a participant. Here we mean that advocacy is pro-argumentation for the speaker's own point of view. It is necessary to add, by way of clarification, that this also includes contra-argumentation against the (opposed) point of view of the other side.

Van Eemeren and Grootendorst (1984, pp. 43–44) put forward five conditions defining *pro-argumentation:*

1. The speaker has advanced an opinion O.
2. The speaker has put forward a series of assertions, $S_1, S_2, \ldots, S_n$.
3. Advancing $S_1, S_2, \ldots, S_n$ counts as an attempt by the speaker to convince the hearer O is acceptable.
4. The speaker believes the hearer does not already accept O, but will accept $S_1, S_2, \ldots, S_n$ as justification for O.
5. The speaker believes that O and $S_1, S_2, \ldots S_n$ are acceptable, and that $S_1, S_2, \ldots S_n$ justify O.

A comparable, negative set of conditions is given (p. 45) for *contra-argumentation.* The duality of this set of conditions reflects the view of the Amsterdam School that the purpose of argumentation is both the justification and the refutation of opinions, as noted above. The set of conditions for contra-argumentation is identical to the set above, except that the speaker believes that O is unacceptable (as opposed to acceptable) and she is advancing $S_1, S_2, \ldots, S_n$ to refute O to the listener's satisfaction (instead of using them to justify O).

By double negation, contra-argumentation against the other (opposed) side in a critical discussion turns out to be equivalent to pro-argumentation for one's own side.

This definition of advocacy can be generalized to the other types of dialogue. In a negotiation dialogue, instead of a conflict of opinions, there is a conflict of interests. So advocacy in this type of dialogue is promoting one's own interests. That is, advocacy occurs in argumentation by a speaker where that speaker's argumentation is an attempt to get the other party to make concessions that support the speaker's interests that are at stake in the negotiation. It is the same thing, pro-argumentation, but pro-argumentation takes a different form in the negotiation type of dialogue than it has in a critical discussion.

It is more difficult to define advocacy in the inquiry because the inquiry is not a symmetrical type of dialogue, with contested argumentation on two opposed sides. The inquiry is an attempt to prove something that has not been proved or disproved in the past. Advocacy does not have any central place in this type of dialogue, in contrast to the critical discussion and the negotiation. The aim of the inquiry is to avoid advocacy and to just collect all the facts, so that this buildup of knowledge will prove or disprove the proposition that is the subject of the inquiry.

There can be advocacy involved in an inquiry, where witnesses are asked to testify and give their point of view, for example. But this advocacy is never taken at face value, so to speak, as part of the argumentation. It is always weighed on its merits and put together with other collected information, as part of the data in the inquiry.

You could say there is a kind of advocacy in an inquiry because eventually the inquiry does come to a conclusion and declares a finding. But it is not really appropriate to call this kind of backing to support a conclusion, as the outcome of an inquiry, a kind of "advocacy." The participants in the inquiry are backing their conclusion, so in this sense they are "advocating" it. But it is misleading to call this a kind of "advocacy," at least without careful qualifications, because it suggests the more usual types of advocacy that we typically associate with the persuasion dialogue or the negotiation dialogue.

Advocacy is easily defined as pro-argumentation in the deliberation, however. Here it is an opinion that is advanced and supported by a speaker, like the case of advocacy in the critical discussion. However, in deliberation, the opinion is that a certain course of action is prudent. The speaker argues to the other party that he would be wise to choose this course of action, based on his (the other party's) goals. This is what is called "advocacy" in a deliberation.

Advocacy in the eristic type of dialogue is the most noticeable because in a quarrel, most of the argumentation is highly adversarial in nature. Thus pro-argumentation by any arguer is a very prominent, even dominant aspect. So much so, indeed, that it may seem plausible initially to define advocacy generally as quarrelsome argumentation. However, advocacy is not exclusive to the quarrel. It is also present in other types of dialogue.

So far then, the proposed theory of bias in argument is very simple. Bias is simply defined as a one-sided argument that advocates a particular proposition but fails to be balanced. And this theory will be shown to provide a satisfactory definition of bias in argument. But detecting whether an argument contains bias is not really this simple. Although advocacy can be defined in an abstract and context-free manner, judging whether or where it exists in a specific case of argumentation is very much a contextual task.

8. How Is Bias Detected in an Argument?

Each of us has a personal point of view influenced by our background, habits, and knowledge. Thus, you could say that every person who enters into an argument on any subject he or she is concerned about will have a bias in his or her argumentation on that subject. This kind of bias, or personal point of view, is well described by Little, Wilson, and Moore (1955, 261).

> Far more than most of us realize, the answers we get in our thinking are influenced by subjective factors—factors residing in the subject who does the viewing rather than in the object viewed. Our value judgments determine which objects and activities we seek and which we avoid. Habits and knowledge acquired from past experience determine the methods by which we satisfy our needs. The needs, value judgments, and past experience of the individual form a complex point of view from which he sees all new experience.

This personal point of view is what makes us human, and it is a kind of bias that is not problematic in argumentation, at least as a starting point or initial position. If an arguer defends this position during the course of a critical discussion, using carefully reasoned evidence to support it, the developed position will appear less like a bias and more like a defended and articulated position.

The most important benefit of a critical discussion is the articulation of the initial, implicit position or personal point of view of a participant, as the dialogue progresses. This was called the "maieutic function of dialogue" in chapter 2, defined as the revealing of an arguer's implicit (unarticulated) commitment in a dialogue by clarifying it in the face of probing objections and clarifications by an able opponent in argumentation. (Walton, 1991; 1992; Walton and Krabbe, 1995). In a successful critical discussion, by virtue of this function, what began as a bias can become an explicit position, revealing the reasoning behind an arguer's position on the issue of the discussion.

However, much depends on the nature of the argumentation used during the course of the discussion. This initial bias or personal point of view can remain a harmless or even positive factor in the argumentation, or it can become problematic, turning into a "bad" bias. It depends on how an arguer reacts to critical and opposed arguments to his point of view, during the dialogue. The more he shields off his position by deflecting legitimate criticisms and hardening his position, instead of altering or retracting it where necessary, the initial bias becomes a warping and distorting of the development of that point of view. This is where the fallacies come in and the critical discussion is hindered from moving forward toward its goals and benefits. The maieutic function fails to be carried out because of a lack of balance in the argument.

The initial bias may just be "there," unexamined critically, a matter of unreflective habits and customs, or the background of the individual. But in a successful critical discussion this set of initial commitments should be refined and deepened by its testing in reasoned argument. Parts of it may have to be given up or retracted, and other parts may be modified and restated. However, if an arguer cleaves too arbitrarily or dogmatically to that initial point of view, without modifying it in appropriate ways, in the face of criticisms, a harmful kind of bias or warping sets in. This is described by Little, Wilson, and Moore (1955, p. 261): "Every time we dodge a relevant fact or accept falsehood for fact, we warp our point of view. And a warped point of view distorts one's concept of reality just as flaws in a lens distort the image. A warped point of view is the source of much human folly." The problem then is not just bias, commitment, or having a personal point of view *per se*. It is what one does with that initial commitment during the course of a dialogue such as a critical discussion that is supposed to test out that view by subjecting it to interaction with a different point of view. As the dialogue proceeds, cumulative evidence of the bad sort of bias can accumulate, as closedminded moves are made during the sequence of argumentation.

This means that a criticism of bias in argumentation is best judged in a context of dialogue, in light of the contribution of an argument to a particular stage of the dialogue. If the past record of the conversation is available for inspection, it may show many indicators of biased argumentation at different stages in the evolution of the argument.[9] None of these indicators is likely to be conclusive, by itself. Yet when you look at the total body of evidence in the text of discourse of the argument, a clear pattern of biased argumentation may emerge.

Thus bias in argumentation is not just commitment, position, or point of view, but relates to how these things are put forward or revealed by a sequence of argumentation, indicating a lack of balance in the argumentation as the dialogue progresses. Hence, to properly judge whether an argument is biased or not, one needs to look at the given text of discourse (in context) to get a global picture of how the argument was used in the context of dialogue.

9. When Is Bias Harmful?

The term *bias* has negative implications of a certain sort that are more marked than those of *advocacy*. The basis of this disparity is to be found in the distinction of Blair (1988) between *good bias* and *bad bias*. The latter is the sort of bias that interferes with good argumentation in a way that results in deficiencies of critical reasoning. Good or harmless bias is a normal part of everyday argumentation. It is to be expected, and is not, in itself, an obstacle to sound critical reasoning.

Bad bias can be defined as "pure (one-sided) advocacy" in a situation where such unbalanced advocacy is normatively inappropriate in argumentation. Bad bias occurs in a dialogue situation where an arguer is supposed to be balanced on a disputed issue.

An example from Jacobs, Jackson, Hallmark, Hall, and Stearns (1987, 292) is the situation of a divorce mediator, who is not supposed to take sides. In other words, the mediator is failing in his or her job if he or she actively enters into the dispute, arguing for one side or the other. Here bias, or advocacy for one side, is bad bias because of the situation— the type of dialogue involved and the supposed role or function of the mediator in that dialogue.

However, good (or at least nonbad) bias occurs in a situation where advocacy is that in which a participant is supposed to be engaging. For example, when you go into a showroom to look at new cars, you expect that the salesman will try to sell you a car. The salesman may engage in frankly advocate argumentation. But there is nothing wrong with that, in itself. It exhibits a bias, so to speak, but it is not a bad bias. We know that positive advocacy is the salesman's role or function in the verbal exchange. We expect this bias and are aware of it because we know that the salesman makes his living by selling these cars.

Bias is often quite harmless when it is fully evident to everyone. If advocacy is what one expects, then the bias in the argument is not deceptive. Bias most often becomes a problem, from a logical point of view, when there has been a shift from one type of dialogue to another. However, the evidence here is contextual. It is not in the argument itself, or the performance of arguing for a point of view, but in the purpose of the discourse in which the argument is embedded. So identification of the type of conversational exchange of which an argument is supposed to be a part and dialectical shifts from one type of dialogue to another are important parts of the evidential picture of identifying and evaluating bias, according to the theory of bias presented here.

We now turn to our explanation, on the new theory, of the difference between bias that is appropriate (or, at any rate, harmless) and bias that is inappropriate, that is, bias that is judged to be bad, meaning that it reflects negatively on an argument's worth or plausibility. If an argument is supposed to be one-sided, then bias is not a problem. Bias, in the form of pro-argumentation and commitment to a conclusion, is normal and expected. Therefore, if the argument is seen as biased by an observer, it will not be devalued or discounted, for that reason. However, if an argument is supposed to be two-sided, but in reality turns out to be one-sided, showing a lack of balance, then that is good reason for devaluating it, in the sense of reducing the weight of plausibility accorded to it as an argument.

The phenomenon of bias arises because some arguments can increase their weight of plausibility by posing as being two-sided, when in reality they are one-sided (as revealed by the performance in the sequence of dialogue exchanges). In such a case, deceptive bias exists, because of the mismatch between the expectations set in place by the type of dialogue, requiring balanced argumentation, and the actual performance in the given case, revealing a pattern of one-sided argumentation. It is precisely in this kind of case that the bias revealed in the argument should be cited as a bad or inappropriate bias and the value of the argument reduced.

According to the theory of bias presented here, a biased argument exhibits bad bias when it is one-sided in a way that is not appropriate for a context of dialogue. Thus, what remains to be determined is when bias, in the form of advocacy, can be judged to be a bad kind of bias that reduces the credibility that should be accorded to an argument.

In the classic case, presented in Walton (1989a p. 149), Wilma and Bob are engaged in a critical discussion on the issue of the harmfulness of acid rain. Wilma keeps arguing that acid rain is really not harmful, or as harmful as Bob and others claim. But as Bob reveals, Wilma's argumentation is biased, as shown by her admitting the fact that she is on the board of directors of a coal company (and she concealed this from the audience of the debate). In this case, it is not simply Wilma's advocacy of the one side of the disputed issue that Bob uses as the criterion for judging her argumentation biased. It is also something else, a connection she has that is a fact external to the conduct of the argumentation in the dialogue itself.

Here Wilma's bias is not subject to criticism just on the grounds of her advocacy or taking a positive point of view in favor of one side on a disputed issue where there are two sides. Wilma is frankly an advocate for one side. But that is proper for her role in the critical discussion and is not, by itself, what makes us judge that she exhibits a bad bias.

The real reason that Wilma's bias in this case is perceived as being of the negative or harmful sort is that Bob has a reason for suspecting that Wilma is not really engaged in an open critical discussion at all. Covertly, he suspects, she is engaged in a negotiation type of dialogue where she is pushing for her own special interest for financial gain. That is, she is not really accepting or rejecting the arguments under discussion on their merits or on the basis of the evidence for or against them. Really, he suspects, she has made up her mind beforehand and is only making a pretense of considering the arguments on the evidence given. Really, the evidence suggests that she never was prepared to accept defeat if her arguments turned out to be refuted by evidence presented in the critical discussion.

Then in this case, there was a dialectical shift, as Bob saw it. Wilma was supposed to be taking part in a critical discussion. But, covertly, she was really engaged in a sort of negotiation or bargaining dialogue where the rules are quite different. One-sided advocacy in a negotiation dialogue can mean pushing ahead with arguments that can be used to pressure or sway the other side to make concessions, in a way that would be entirely inappropriate and fallacious in a critical discussion.

The problem exhibited here generally is that advocacy is all right in a critical discussion. There is nothing wrong with it, *per se,* that interferes with the progress of the dialogue or is a critical failure. Yet, as shown by this case, bias certainly can be a problem in a critical discussion. And a criticism by one side, claiming that the argumentation of the other side is biased, can have merit and can thereby lead the audience to lower the credibility it gives to the argument. So bias, or at least bad bias, cannot simply be defined as advocacy in a critical discussion. There is more to it than that.

What is shown is that bad bias is not simply advocacy, but advocacy of a kind that is inappropriate in a certain type of conversational exchange of argumentation. A kind of argumentation that is appropriate in a negotiation or bargaining type of exchange may be quite inappropriate and correctly judged as biased in the context of a critical discussion.[10] But if the dialogue was supposed to be a critical discussion at the outset, and the participants agreed to that, and that is what the audience was led to expect, then the argumentation in that case should be judged by standards appropriate for that of a critical discussion.

Now a critical discussion does require an arguer to be an advocate of the point of view she has expressed as her opinion on the issue. But here we are thinking of advocacy in a sense appropriate for a critical discussion. By these standards, it would not be regarded as a kind of appropriate advocacy for an arguer to try to get the other party to make concessions by offering him financial incentives or by threatening him with sanctions, penalties, or bad consequences, if he fails to "make a deal." This kind of advocacy, in a critical discussion, is the wrong kind and is a type of argumentation that properly would be evaluated as biased, in the sense of bad bias, or even as being fallacious. For example, the *ad baculum* fallacy would be cited in the case of a threat being used.

10. Aspects of the New Theory

We came to the conclusion that the best way to define bias is simply as one-sided advocacy for a point of view in a dialogue. This account is compatible with the important ideas that bias is not necessarily a bad thing and that bias is generally present in all human argumentation. However, it is also important to recognize that bias can be bad or negative, from a logical point of view, in some cases. The harm arises, for example, in the case of a critical discussion, because the argumentation on both sides needs to really interact with that of the other side. If it is just a show of real interaction with the point of view of the other side, the maieutic function will not be carried out and the clash of viewpoints will not really be tested out by the strongest relevant arguments on both sides. Thus, the critical discussion will fail to resolve the conflict of opinions by rational means, and the advocacy on both sides, even if strongly expressed, will not throw any real light (maieutic insight) on the issue.

This way of defining bias in terms of one-sided advocacy fits in nicely in the normative framework of argumentation called the "critical discussion" by van Eemeren and Grootendorst (1984; 1992). In a critical discussion, there is a conflict of opinions on some issue—that is, with respect to a particular proposition or "thesis"—one side accepts the proposition, and the other side either rejects it or doubts it. Hence, in a critical discussion, it is normal and appropriate for an arguer to advocate her own point of view by arguing for her own thesis and by arguing against the (opposed) point of view of the other side. Advocacy, in this context, is not bad bias. It is a kind of bias that is an expected part of the normative framework of dialogue. One is supposed to argue, as strongly as one can, in favor of one's own point of view.

In a critical discussion (van Eemeren and Grootendorst 1984), a participant has a particular proposition or thesis to be argued for, and she will have a positive point of view toward that thesis and a negative point of view to opposed argumentation. As the argumentation in the dialogue proceeds, whenever that participant indicates commitment to a proposition, that proposition is inserted into her commitment set (Hamblin 1970; 1971). If a participant retracts a commitment, the corresponding proposition is deleted from his commitment set (Walton and Krabbe 1995).

One way to define bias in argumentation is to make it equivalent to having a point of view. Another way is to make it equivalent to commitment. Having a zero point of view, in the sense of van Eemeren and Grootendorst (1984, 79) is what we called "neutrality" above. Neutrality might be thought to be the same as absence of bias.

But if we wish to define bias in a way to make it the opposite of the quality Paul (1990) calls fairmindedness in argument, we will have to go beyond either of these two more narrow definitions.

A third way to define bias is to identify it with the arguer's *position* in a dialogue, defined after the fashion of Walton (1985) as the total of an arguer's commitments at any particular point during the argumentation stage of a dialogue. A relatively stable position in an argument has a certain consistency and coherence in a dialogue, so it can be given a general characterization, for example, "communist," "conservative," "atheist," and so on, depending on the issue.

Position is an even better way to define bias in argumentation than the first two options, but it is still not adequate to the concept of bias opposed to Paul's sense of fairmindedness. For this concept has to do with how an individual performs in argumentation in identifying best reasons for accepting an opposed point of view.

For purposes of informal logic, we do not judge bias by the psychological states of an arguer. We need to judge the bias in an argument by the given text of discourse in a case as evidence of the performance of certain skills. Point of view, commitment, and position (once identified) are important pieces of evidence in a given case but do not represent the whole picture of bias.

The ability to exercise critical doubt is also a very important part of bias. Critical doubt is a kind of attitude about one's own attitude in argumentation. Bias, of the kind with which we are concerned becomes a severe or debilitating problem in argumentation when it is so strongly fixed that there is no real exercise of critical doubt in the argumentation. But one cannot judge exercise of critical doubt in argumentation simply by an arguer's point of view, commitment, or position. One must study the whole sequence of argumentation in a context of dialogue to see how an arguer deals with his own position and also the opposed position.

According to our new theory, a biased argument is a one-sided argument, consisting of pure pro-argumentation for one side of an issue in a dialogue, while failing to genuinely interact with the other side in a balanced way. A balanced argument, in contrast, considers all the relevant arguments on both sides and exhibits the characteristics of flexible commitment, empathy, open-mindedness, critical doubt, and evidence sensitivity.

On the new theory, bias in an argument is not necessarily harmful or negative, nor does it necessarily detract from the value of the argument as a contribution to a dialogue exchange. However, in cases where the argument is supposed to be balanced (for example, in a persuasion dialogue), if the argument is found to be biased, then that finding is a good ground for decreasing the plausibility given to that argument.

So far, we have been concerned only with the bias in arguments. But there are cases where the bias in an argument leads to a conclusion that the person advocating that argument is biased. In these cases, there is a kind of transfer effect from the finding of bias in the argument to the finding of bias in the person and then back to a reduction of plausibility assigned to the argument.

In *ad hominem* arguments, the allegation of bias is frequently used to attack an arguer's credibility. In *ad hominem* criticisms of this sort, there is a function from the person to the argument that works as follows. If the person is perceived as a bad person by the given audience, then the person's argument is reduced in credibility by that audience. But the reverse can also happen. If the person's argument is perceived as being quarrelsome or fallacious, then there will be a lowering of credibility for that person as a serious and sincere arguer.

An example here would be the backfire effect of using an *ad hominem* argument to attack one's opponent in argument. One possibility is that the argument might work and might refute or undermine the opponent's argument. But the other possibility is that by persisting in using a strong *ad hominem* attack against the opponent's argument, it may make one look overly aggressive, badgering one's opponent, while she is doing her best to be reasonable as an arguer. In such a case, one's bad argument—or, if it is perceived by the audience as bad, anyway—will make one look like a bad person.

In this kind of backfire-effect case, the credibility function goes from the argument used to the person who used it in a dialogue exchange. The lowering of credibility for the argument transfers to a lowering of credibility for the person who used that argument.

It is interesting, that if the argument continues, the function will work the opposite way. When the attacker puts forward his next argument in the exchange, the audience is likely to give less credibility to this argument, now that it has just judged its proponent to have less credibility as a person in the dialogue exchange.

In a case like this, there will be back-and-forth credibility functions working at succeeding moves of the dialogue. What happens at one move will tend to affect how the audience evaluates the arguments used at subsequent moves in the dialogue by the same person.

So when it comes to studying bias, although we are primarily interested in the bias in arguments, as opposed to the bias of persons, the two things cannot entirely be separated. The linkage arises essentially through the *ad hominem* type of argument, which connects the person with the argument. If an argument is perceived as biased, then that may affect how we perceive the person who put forward the argument. And this in turn may affect how we judge subsequent arguments put forward by that person.

The judgments will depend on the context in which an argument is used, however. If the argument is supposed to be a contribution to a critical discussion, and we see the argument as being biased—that is, as being a narrowly advocacy point of view as opposed to an appropriately balanced argument of the kind required in a critical discussion—then we will downgrade the argument in credibility in the context of it being a purported contribution to a critical discussion. But if the argument was supposed to be an advocacy argument in the first place, then revealing it to be biased or one-sided will not deduct from its credibility as an argument. And by the credibility function, nor will the credibility of the person who put forward that argument be impugned. Then in short, the working of the credibility function will depend very much on the original context of dialogue in which the argument was used.

This judgment needs to be made by looking at the sequence of argumentation leading up to the given point of dialogue in a case. What is important as evidence is how an arguer defends his position and reacts to criticisms of it. Here the maieutic function of dialogue is also an important factor. Does the argumentation move toward a refining and enriching of the arguer's position, giving it a greater subtlety and sensitivity to important qualification, as the argument moves along? Or has the argumentation only moved toward a hardening and fixing of that position into a rigid fortification? This is, over all, the evidence of the bad kind of bias.

Now the general theory of bias has been presented, the problems of identifying bias and of evaluating it, in particular cases, remains to be taken up. This problem is a practical one of devising criteria for detecting bias in a given text of discourse in an actual case.

The second of these practical problems is the problem of evaluating bias as being negative or not in a given case. This is the problem of determining, once bias (advocacy) has been found in a particular case of argumentation, whether it should be judged as just the normal or harmless kind of bias that is appropriate for this case or whether it is a bad or harmful bias, of the kind that ought to be criticized. This problem of bias evaluation will be taken up in the rest of the book, starting with chapter 5. It is not an easy problem to solve, and we will not solve it completely. But we will give a good basis for further inquiry that will go a good way toward solving it and point the way for further research.

The other practical problem is that of identifying bias in a particular case. This is the problem we now turn to in chapter 4.

Notes

1. See below in this chapter.

2. As defined in chapter 2.

3. Newman (1986).

4. Thouless (1936, 221). The term *my-side bias* was used by David Perkins in a talk at Schloss Dagstuhl, Germany, in August 1993. See the abstract (Perkins, 1993).

5. Sean Fine, "More Judges Dare to Break Silence Away from Bench," *The Globe and Mail,* Nov. 13, 1993, A1–A2.

6. See below.

7. Walton (1990c; 1992b).

8. See Walton (1991 Bias, Critical Doubt, 16–19).

9. See chapter 4.

10. On negotiation dialogue, see Donohue (1981).

INDICATORS OF BIAS IN ARGUMENTATION

In this chapter, ten indicators that can be used to detect bias in a given argument are presented: (1) something to gain, (2) selection of arguments, (3) lip-service selection, (4) commitment to an identifiable position, (5) closure to opposed argumentation, (6) rigidity of stereotyping, (7) treating comparable cases differently, (8) biased language, (9) emphasis and hyperbole, and (10) implicature and innuendo. In every instance except indicator (8), biased language—which has to do with the use of slanted definitions and persuasive definitions in argumentation and will be dealt with at length in chapter 5—a clear test that can be used to apply the indicator to specific cases of argumentative discourse is given, and/or enough examples of recognizable characteristics are given to make clear what is to be determined.

None of the indicators is, by itself, meant to be conclusive to determine that a particular given case of an argument is biased or slanted. The indicators are meant to be treated as "red flags" or defeasible warning indicators of bias in argumentation, subject to rebuttal and evaluation in light of the further particulars of a given case (as these come to be known).

In some cases of argumentation, only one indicator may be present, while in other cases, several indicators may be detected. Generally, in longer cases of extended argumentation where the given text of discourse is quite extensive, one might expect that several different indicators (possibly even all of them) could be present. However, in short examples of arguments, of the kind so often treated by the traditional and current logic textbooks, only one indicator may be present.

As the cases will show, it is often fairly evident that these indicators are in fact the criteria that people do actually use in everyday argumentation to detect bias and to weigh the credibility and bias of an argument. However, we are not attempting to carry out an empirical study here. Our claim is a pragmatic and normative one, that these indicators are the ones that ought to be used as a bias for judging evaluations of bias in argumentation and are the ones that are practically most useful for this purpose.

1. Something to Gain

One of the most important indicators of bias that people tend to use in weighing argumentation is whether the speaker has something to gain by advocating a particular view. Usually, the gain is financial, but other kinds of self-interest could be involved as well, where money is only involved indirectly. For example, it could be an interest in promoting one's career, which might involve prestige or other factors, in addition to possible financial gains.

The classic case is given in Walton (1989a, p. 149). In this case, two people, Wilma and Bob, are taking part in a panel discussion on the issue of acid rain as a matter of public policy.[1] The question to be discussed is whether acid rain is a serious harm to the environment.

> *Case* 4.1: Bob and Wilma are discussing the problem of acid rain. Wilma argues that reports on the extent of the problem are greatly exaggerated and that the costs of action are prohibitive. Bob points out that Wilma is on the board of directors of a U.S. coal company and that therefore her argument should not be taken at face value.

Bob argues that Wilma is biased because of her connection with a coal company, a group that has a clear financial interest in public policies on controlling pollution of the environment.

This type of allegation of bias, even if it is based on good evidence of a financial interest, is not necessarily a refutation of the speaker's argument. For in some cases, a person who has something at stake financially can still make the effort to weigh both sides of an issue, without being unduly influenced by this interest on the one side. Concealment is often a big factor in how we judge such a bias.

If Wilma had concealed her connection with the coal company, we would judge Bob's allegation of bias quite differently than if she had announced it to the audience at the beginning of the discussion. Apparent concealment, or having something to hide, makes us much more likely to think that a bias is affecting a person's argumentation in a negative way.

Bob's criticism of Wilma in case 4.1 is usually identified in the logic textbooks with the *ad hominem* argument of the circumstantial type.[2] Bob is citing Wilma's personal circumstances—her position on the board of directors of the coal company—as the basis of an argument against the person. Bob's *ad hominem* argument is that Wilma's argument on the acid rain issue is not credible, when we consider who is making it, because of the conflict of interest involved in her situation. The *ad hominem* argument traditionally has been classified as a fallacy by the logic textbooks, but it also has often been recognized that it can be a reasonable type of argumentation in some cases.[3]

In this case, Bob's *ad hominem* argument against Wilma could be seen as a questioning of her integrity or balance in taking part in a critical discussion that is supposed to be giving proper attention to the considerations on both sides of the issue of the harmfulness of acid rain. If Wilma is covertly engaging in an advocacy type of argumentation for one side, to protect the interests of her company, she could be simply using the public platform to support her own special interests. Any evidence of this factor will influence how the audience evaluates Wilma's argumentation for her point of view on the issue. Once the audience members learn of Wilma's affiliation with the coal company, they give less credibility to her as a balanced participant who is sincerely engaged in a persuasion dialogue, and they discount her arguments accordingly.

The basic test here is posed by the following question. Could the speaker lose anything by changing his or her opinion? Or to put it another way, What is the cost to the speaker of maintaining the opposed point of view?

It is worthwhile stressing that you cannot automatically or conclusively reject a speaker's argument because he has something to gain by advocating it, without considering other factors. For as Thouless (1936, p. 220) noted, such connections are commonplace in political argumentation.

> Practically all men desire money and comfort, and fear ruin and death, so they will tend to accept propositions whose truth would secure their wealth, comfort, and security of living, and reject those whose truth would threaten them. We can see how general this law is when we notice how nearly universal is the rule that those who have possessions (even a few) are politically on the side of preserva-

tion of the existing order, while revolutionaries are, on the whole, recruited from the non-possessors.

Thouless (pp. 221–222) gives the example of two men arguing about a proposed new tax—case 4.7, below. They might both give very general and logical arguments without going into the matter of how the tax would affect each personally. As onlookers, we should not make the mistake of dismissing their arguments simply because we find that the man arguing for the tax has no personal capital and that the man arguing against it is living on the interest of his investments (Thouless 1936, p. 222). But if we do find out such personal facts in a particular case, they are not irrelevant in considering how we judge the arguments of the two men as "onlookers," as Thouless (p. 222) puts it.

Having a financial interest is an important indicator of bias that plays a very important role in how we judge bias and use such a judgment to evaluate argumentation in a given case. But the weight and import of such a finding varies from case to case, and in many cases, the showing of a financial interest is not, by itself, evidence of a bad bias of the type that is a serious failure of critical argumentation or is sufficient to refute the argument as worthless.

Indeed, *ad hominem* arguments are very often fallacious precisely because the allegation of bias, even although it is based on a true premise and is a reasonable charge of bias *per se,* is taken as the final word needed to refute the speaker's argument as totally worthless. A good case is the following one, cited by Hurley (1991, p. 116) as an example of the circumstantial *ad hominem* fallacy.

> *Case* 4.2: Lee Iacocca has argued that cars manufactured by Chrysler are of higher quality than equally priced Japanese cars. But given that Iacocca is chairman of the Chrysler Corporation, he would naturally be expected to argue this way. Therefore, Iacocca's argument should be ignored.

It was true that Iacocca was chairman of Chrysler at this time, and pointing this out as an indication of a bias in his argumentation is not, in itself, unreasonable. The grounds Hurley offers (p. 116) for calling this case an instance of the *ad hominem* fallacy is that the speaker "ignores the substance of Iacocca's argument and attempts instead to discredit it by calling attention" to his circumstances as chairman of Chrysler. This is only a fallacy because the broader picture of evidence is ignored, and the charge of bias is blown out of proportion, as though it totally refuted Iacocca's argument.

These questions of how to evaluate charges of bias will be taken up in chapter 7. In chapter 6, we will clarify the apparent paradox of how a good argument (in the sense of presenting good evidence) can at the same time be a biased argument.

2. Selection of Arguments

Selection of arguments for and against different aspects of an issue can be an important indicator of bias in some cases. What to look for here is argumentation that selects arguments on one side of an issue and ignores arguments on the other side that should be considered. In cases of news reporting and television interviews, for example, editing is very important in making a point of view look good or look bad, depending on how it is presented.

Little, Groarke, and Tindale (1989, p. 61) identify a type of slanting of argumentation they call "selection," as follows:

> Selection is a "sin of omission," reporting those facts that favor the impression the reporter wants to create while deftly avoiding any mention of unfavorable ones. The reporter writes "nothing but the truth" but fails to give "the whole truth." By reporting only selected facts and by omitting crucial ones that offset those reported, reporters can create just the slanted impression they want.

Selection bias is not obvious to determine, in a given case, because one has to look for what has been left out. Thus one cannot just look over the given text of discourse in the case and try to identify some indicator of what is there, like key words or specific types of arguments.

The test for selection bias in argumentation is to determine what important relevant arguments have been left out. But in applying this test to make an evaluation of bias in a given case, the context of dialogue is very important. A critical discussion, for example, requires a consideration of the strongest relevant arguments on both sides of an issue. A balance is important here, and selection toward one side is an important indicator of a bad kind of bias that could prevent the discussion from throwing any real light on the issue or coming to a resolution of it. However, in a dialogue like sales or advertising promotion of a product, selection of arguments supporting the product, and ignoring arguments against the product, is a normal and expected part of the advocacy type of discourse in the case in point. Here we have bias, indicated by selection of arguments on one side, but it is not necessarily a bad bias, or an obstructive one like the case of a critical discussion.

Selection was identified by Beardsley (1950, p. 79) as a technique of slanting of discourse—see chapter 1. Beardsley very clearly saw that whether selection is a harmful type of slanting depends very much on the purpose of the type of discourse in which a speaker is supposedly engaged. And he showed (1950, pp. 79) how selection slanting, when it is deceptive and of a misleading kind, is accompanied by a pretense of being engaged in some kind of balanced dialogue, like a critical discussion.

> *Selection.* Giving only the facts favorable to one's conclusion, and leaving out the unfavorable ones, is a time-honored technique for loading the dice. Whether it is done intentionally or unintentionally, it doesn't work well unless there is some pretense that one is being fair, objective, unbiased. There are various ways of suggesting fairness, of course. Some people say, "Now, let's be honest about this . . ." or, "Now, let's look at the facts . . . ," and go on to give you a half-truth masquerading as the whole truth. They give you "nothing but the truth," but only after careful screening.

Beardsley (p. 80) gives the following more specific example.

> *Case* 4.3: A speaker may say, "We have received ten favorable letters. . . " and go on talking fast, or tell a funny story, to keep his audience from thinking that there may be fifty *un*favorable letters.

As Beardsley points out, key words or verbal indicators can be very important in judging whether selection bias is harmful or is a serious fault, from a point of view of critical evaluation of argumentation. Quite often, advocates presenting biased argumentation for one side of an issue will try to make their arguments seem more persuasive by striking a posture that they are engaging in a critical discussion or other type of dialogue that has considered the arguments on both sides of an issue or are giving balanced, judicious advice based on having considered a broad body of evidence, both *pro* and *con*. Quite often, this is a deception or trick, and a skeptical respondent or observer can easily find grounds for suspicions or reservations when judging a speaker's argumentation.

Quite often, logic textbooks treat selection bias under the heading of the "fallacy of special pleading." Carney and Scheer (1974, p. 43), for example, define this fallacy as follows: "Often we find that there are reasons for and reasons against certain statements. When someone argues for such a statement and gives only the reasons—or only some of the reasons—which support the statement, ignoring the reasons against, he is committing the *fallacy of special pleading*." They give the following example (p. 43):

> *Case* 4.4: We should legalize gambling in the state of Nebraska because, first, it would provide a rich new source of revenue; second, it would encourage tourists to come spend their money here; and third, it would cost us nothing to get these new moneys, just the passing of a law.

According to Carney and Scheer (p. 43), this argument is an instance of the fallacy of special pleading because it fails to take into account all the reasons for not legalizing gambling in Nebraska, for example, encouragement of vice, the necessity of supplementing law enforcement, and so forth.

In other logic textbooks, such as Hurley (1991, pp. 148–149), selection bias is dealt with under the heading of the "fallacy of suppressed evidence," where the premises in an argument "ignore some important piece of evidence that outweighs the presented evidence" and requires "a different conclusion than the one drawn" (p. 148). Still other textbooks do not define suppressed evidence as a distinct fallacy in its own right but treat it as a deficiency that lies at the basis of other fallacies. In fact, it is surprising how often the factor of suppressed or ignored evidence is cited as the basis for classifying many arguments as instances of this or that fallacy by the logic textbooks.

Underlying these classifications in the textbooks is the general issue of how bias is related to fallacies. In particular, it is necessary to define the conditions under which selection bias is so bad in a given case that it makes sense to classify it as some kind of fallacy or at any rate to evaluate it as an instance of a bad or critically harmful type of bias that should be subject to critical questioning or condemnation in argumentation. These issues have heretofore remained open because nobody has ever defined bias in a clear enough way to be useful for purposes of informal logic and argumentation theory.[4]

3. Lip-Service Selection

In some cases, selection bias may be harder to detect because the speaker will not entirely ignore the arguments of the other side. Instead, to give a pretense of fairness, he will put in a few contrary arguments, picking ones that are formulated in order to be weak or easy to refute. This technique could be called "lip-service selection," because the selected arguments are not ones that represent the strongest objections of the other side but are just ones that are easy to dismiss. Lip-service selection is closely related to, and often combined with, the straw man fallacy, where an opponent's position is distorted or misrepresented, in order to make it easy to refute.

Beardsley (1950, p. 80) clearly recognized this tactic as a species of selection bias: "One of the ways of covering up omissions is to put in a *few* mildly unfavorable facts and then pooh-pooh them." Beardsley gave the following example, an extension of his example of selection bias (case 4.3):

> *Case* 4.3a: Of course, there were unfavorable letters, too. We checked a couple of these, just to be sure, and it turned out that one writer was an ex-Socialist and another was in jail for bigamy. But—as I say—the ten favorable letters . . .

The technique used here is a way of covering up the bias in one's argumentation by pretending to consider the arguments both for and against, on an issue. The tactic is to put in place a means of countering the potential criticism that one's argumentation is one-sided or biased. Lip service is given to the assumption that the dialogue is one, like a critical discussion, where the arguments on both sides are being considered and weighed. However, in many cases, this is a calculated deception, an illusion designed to enhance the credibility of one's advocacy argumentation.

Lip-service selection is more noticeable where a discourse is predominantly advocacy argumentation, but where an occasional attempt is made to consider the arguments of the other side, to make the discourse appear balanced.

4. Commitment to an Identifiable Position

Any indication of a speaker's specific affiliation, position, or point of view, whether announced by the speaker or attributed by someone else, tends to function at least as a potential indicator of bias. Such positions are often summarized or typified by a key word. For example, if a political speaker is identified as a "Communist" then that label will serve as an indicator of a certain sort of bias in the speaker's argumentation.[5] Of course, such attributions can be false or made in a misleading way or even used as a fallacious *ad hominem* attack on the speaker's argumentation.[6] And any such charge is subject to rebuttal. But, generally, if such a position label is accepted by a speaker, it functions to the speaker's audience as an indicator of bias or slant in the speaker's argumentation.

When a speaker's own point of view is advocated as his prepossession or personal inclination of an issue, then this commitment to a specific view, once it is known, functions as a way of attributing a particular bias to the speaker's argument on that issue. This form of bias is not necessarily a bad bias or an obstacle to critical reasoning. It may simply indicate a partisan point of view or advocacy of a specific cause, interest, or position.

This kind of bias can be based on profession, nationality, gender, ethnic group, religious affiliation, political standpoint, and many other identifiable kinds of position, background, or interest. Francis Bacon (1605; 1620) described four kinds of idols or false appearances that color the judgments of any individual from his particular point of view—see chapter 1. These idols could perhaps be called "biases" or "sources of bias" in argumentation. Bacon made the point that it is almost impossible for anyone to be free of national, political, religious, and other biases that are an inevitable and even a necessary part of all human development and thinking.

This type of bias is normal in argumentation, and it would be unrealistic to expect anyone to be free of it. In some cases, it can be quite explicit, and even well articulated by an arguer who is well aware of it. In other cases, it can be implicit and unformulated, so that it can be conjectured only by implicature and suggestion, and made more explicit by further dialogue and questioning of an arguer. However, in neither case is it necessarily bad or harmful to critical argumentation.

However, this type of bias can become a problem in argumentation when commitment is too firmly fixed to a position. A strong adherence can become egocentric thinking, dogmatic argumentation, or even, in extreme cases, fanaticism. Thus, it is one thing to have a particular bias or point of view. But it is another thing to resist modifying, revising, or developing that point of view when good arguments criticizing it are encountered in a dialogue.

The basic tools for determination and analysis of this type of bias use the concept of 'commitment' in a logical dialogue structure, as defined by Hamblin (1970; 1971). A commitment store, defined in chapter 1, is a kind of log or repository into which propositions are inserted, or from which they are removed, as the speaker makes the various conventionalized types of moves in a dialogue with a speech partner. *Retraction* occurs where a proposition is removed or deleted from a participant's commitment store.[7] The collective set of commitments arrived at in a sequence of dialogue defines an arguer's position.

As shown in chapter 3, commitment to an identifiable position is not the same thing as bias (in all cases). But it certainly is a very good indication of bias in some cases. Moreover, commitment to certain types of identifiable positions does indicate bias of a sort that is well entrenched and is likely to be of the harmful sort. For example, suppose that in a discussion involving ethics or religion, one participant is identified as being a "born-again Christian" of a fundamentalist type. Once the nature of this person's commitment has been so identified, it will be apparent to the other party in the argument that this person is (fairly predictably) going to cleave to certain views and reject other views, quite firmly, and that his or her flexibility and openness to opposing views is likely to be very limited. So once this particular position of "born-again Christian" is identified, it is a quite good indicator of bias that is likely to be of the negative kind that is going to interfere with a persuasion dialogue.

It is important not to make such judgments of bias too harshly, however. For example, if Bob is identified as a Catholic, it does not necessarily mean that it is impossible to have a balanced persuasion dialogue with him on the issue of abortion. It would be premature— perhaps even an instance of the fallacy of poisoning the well—to say in advance that Bob's bias is of the harmful sort, so that there is no possibility at all of having a persuasion dialogue with him on the issue of abortion.

Still, once Bob's position is labeled "Catholic," it is a good indication that his bias against the prochoice thesis will be fairly strong and well established.

5. Closure to Opposed Argumentation

One very important indicator of bias is fixed commitment to a position, as shown by refusal to consider arguments or evidence from any opposed point of view. The test for this type of bias is how an arguer responds in a sequence of dialogue when her cherished beliefs are criticized. Huppé and Kaminsky (1957, p. 10) have formulated this type of test, in general terms, very well: "One test of prejudice is to see how an individual responds to criticism of beliefs which are very important to him. He may claim to be unprejudiced yet react emotionally, perhaps even violently, if certain personal views are criticized." They use the negative term *prejudice* to describe this type of bias because it is a kind of bias that is generally harmful to argumentation in a critical discussion. Too strong a commitment to a viewpoint, where the possibility of retraction will not even be considered or entertained hypothetically, prevents an arguer from really entering into a critical discussion. The failure here is one of fairmindedness in critical thinking, as defined in chapter 3, and it involves all five requirements for a balanced argument set out in chapter three.

Purtill (1972, p. 49) also uses the word *prejudice* to describe this type of bias, indicating that *bias* is a weaker term. Bias is not, in itself, contrary to logical argumentation, but according to Purtill (p. 49), "prejudices are by definition illogical." Purtill's definition of prejudice, in this sense of bias that is illogical (p. 49), is quite similar, in general outline, to the test of it given by Huppé and Kaminsky (1957, p. 10): "We will define a prejudice as an assumption or presupposition that we are extremely reluctant to change or reject, even in the face of considerable evidence." Scriven (1976, p. 235) proposes a similar test for bias or prejudice of this sort by citing an arguer's reaction to new evidence as the criterion: "If they are immune to new evidence, if they dismiss the arguments of their opposition with trivial counter-arguments or misrepresent these arguments, if they draw their own conclusions in a way which suggests that they are only providing rationalizations rather than good reasons for their opposition, then they are biased or prejudiced." Then the test here is not simply in the speaker's argument, or in how strongly she has presented or advocated it, but in how she reacts to criticisms of it, after it has been presented. Thus the criterion of bias here is dialectical in nature. It is a matter of how the speaker performs interactively in dialogue with another arguer. The evidence of bias is found in the sequence of dialogue after the argument has been presented.

This indicator is best determined by examining how an arguer actually responds to opposed argumentation. But there are a number of indicator words and phrases, noted by Fearnside and Holther (1959, p. 101), that are typically used to forestall disagreement.

> Many expressions such as "it is obvious," "everybody knows," "clearly," "of course," "as any one can see," serve the double purpose of assuring the audience that it is not necessary to think about the

problem and cowing those with the temerity not to go along. One who protests, "It isn't obvious to me!" runs the danger of appearing ignorant or boorish. Other means for forestalling disagreement are flattery of the audience ("I don't need to tell an intelligent group like this . . ."), appeals to the desire to be agreeable ("I believe everyone will agree that . . . "), appeals to the desire to be respectable ("Every decent American wants . . ."), and so on. Forestalling disagreement ranges from mild devices calculated to make agreement easy ("Of course we all believe . . .") to highly prejudicial assertions to intimidate opposition ("Only a muddled headed person would suggest . . .").

Fearnside and Holther describe such use of words to forestall disagreement as a fallacy, but this appears to be somewhat extreme. Only when such a use of words is so excessive or persistent that it obstructs a dialogue should it be called "fallacious." More generally, this type of loaded use of words is an indicator of bias, showing that an argument is being put forward in a biased way that is shielding it off in advance from potential criticism or opposed argumentation.

Of course, in extreme cases, this type of indicator of bias can be identified with certain traditional fallacies. One of these is the *argumentum ad hominem,* particularly the *poisoning-the-well* variety, where the opponent is characterized as a person who is incapable of entering into cooperative dialogue because of his bias to one side or lack of scruples in supporting his own interests or those of that one side.[8] Indicators here are personal epithets connoting blame for bad character and dishonesty, such as *liar, devil, terrorist,* and so forth.[9] The technique used is to demonize the other side so that any arguments they put forward will be discredited as worthless in advance. For example, in a negotiation, one side might say, "Whatever we offer, it's never enough for them," suggesting that the other side is inherently unreasonable and that no argumentation with them could ever be successful in coming to a conclusion.[10]

In extreme cases where this kind of indicator of bias is present, the argumentation hardens into a fanatical type of discourse characterized by slogans, preaching, propaganda, and an "evangelical" style.[11] The function of the discourse is to whip up enthusiasm for a cause, and rhetoric is used to arouse emotions to action. Loyalty to the group is the theme, and the world is divided into the insiders in the group and everyone else, defined as outsiders, that is, potential opponents to the interests of the group.

If discourse of this type is transparently factional and does not pretend to be anything but one-sided, the bias in its argumentation may not be a problem. The problem occurs where the argument began as a persuasion dialogue, supposedly considering both sides of an issue, but then covertly shifted to this evangelical type of rhetoric, masking the bias in a way that can be highly deceptive.

6. Rigidity of Stereotyping

Many generalizations on which inferences are based in everyday argumentation are *defeasible* or subject to exceptions. These kinds of generalizations are often called "stereotypes," in that they are generally true of typical persons or situations but are not absolutely true for every person or every situation. It is an indicator of bias where argumentation treats such stereotypical generalizations as absolute, giving the argumentation an absolutistic or rigid quality. This aspect of bias is very similar to the kind of prejudice Kant identified as occurring where provisional judgments become absolutized—see chapter 1.

Stereotyping as a part of reasoning is not in itself logically bad or fallacious. Indeed, it is a part of ordinary thinking that is necessary for good judgment in practical reasoning on variable matters that cannot realistically be pinned down or quantified in any absolute way. However, because defeasible reasoning is always subject to possible exceptions that may arise in variable circumstances, an arguer using it must be flexible, ready to revise an opinion or qualify a presumption.

Scriven (1976, p. 233) equated bias with the absolutizing of stereotyping in reasoning, even calling this a type of fallacy.

> The procedure of *stereotyping* is a very natural and useful type of human thinking. It amounts to representing groups of things or people by a single, allegedly typical, example. But the *fallacy of stereotyping* consists in treating this stereotype as if it represents all the individuals in the group of which it may be a fairly typical example. So the stereotype of the campus radical, or the stereotype of the hippie, or the stereotype of the businessman, or the stereotype of the surgeon or lawyer or Mexican or professor, are all useful devices in a rough-and-ready kind of way, for certain types of thinking. They may well represent the general characteristics of a population quite well, and may be useful for contrasting one population with another. (Think of the "typical" Republican vs. the "typical"

Democrat, for example.) But when it comes down to cases, you have to be willing to face the fact that an individual may, as we say, shatter the stereotype. The extent to which a human being is capable of reacting flexibly, openly, and rationally to a person who is very unlike the stereotype of the population from which he or she comes is a measure of their reasonableness, and of their capacity for justice.

What Scriven calls the "fallacy of stereotyping" traditionally has been known as the *secundum quid* (*para to pe* or in a certain respect) fallacy, or neglect of qualifications.[12] Unfortunately, however, the terminology for this fallacy has been very confusing and inconsistent, in the traditional and contemporary logic textbooks (Walton 1990b). It has often been categorized under the misleading term *accident.* Probably the best name for it is *secundum quid* or neglect of qualifications. But it is also very often treated under the heading of *hasty generalization* by the logic textbooks.[13]

This particular fallacy (whatever we call it) or the kind of reasoning associated with it is an indicator of biased argumentation, when it can be identified in a particular case. What indicates the bias in the case is not just the use of stereotypes or defeasible generalizations but the kind of rigidity of thinking that treats the generalization as being absolutely true in all cases. It is a kind of unwillingness to concede that one's position could be subject to any exceptions or qualifications.

Logic textbooks have long been aware of an association between bias and the tendency to over generalize, indicated for example in the treatment of the fallacy of hasty generalization by Hibben (1906, p. 371).

> Under the fallacies of hasty generalization naturally fall all provincialisms which arise from a narrow nature and habit of mind. The local traditions and superstitions, the prevailing winds, the social customs and manners, are taken as types of a universal experience. The inferential widening of the circle of a limited experience is always provocative of false inference and misleading results.

In this type of case, the bias appears to be a kind of stereotyping based on habits of thinking.

More recently, many logic textbooks have dealt with hasty generalization as an inductive fallacy, having to do with inductive generalizations and statistical sampling inferences. For example, Salmon (1963, p. 56) defines the *fallacy of insufficient statistics* as "the making of an inductive generalization before enough data have been accumulated to warrant the generalization. By contrast, the *fallacy of biased statistics* (Salmon 1963, p. 57), is the "basing of an inductive generalization upon a sample" known or reasonably believed to be unrepresentative of the generalized population.

Thus, there can be different types of generalizations, inductive ones based on counting of instances as well as stereotypical ones based more loosely on one's experience of typicality or normal expectations. Too strong a commitment to either type of generalization could and often is (rightly) called a "bias."

Rescher (1964, p. 322) uses the expression *fallacy of biased generalization* for the error of basing a generalization on an unrepresentative sample. He distinguishes between two forms of this fallacy, giving the following examples (p. 322):

Case 4.5: [The fallacy of biased generalization] can occur in very crude forms, as when, for example, a man believes that a great majority of his countrymen hold a certain view because he finds that a great majority of his close friends hold that opinion.

Case 4.6: But the fallacy can appear in much more subtle forms; a man who has found in a national election year that the majority of people whom he has asked have indicated that they support one particular candidate for office might conclude that most people (in general) support him, but he would be overlooking the fact that his sample is almost certainly biased because the people with whom his mode of life brings him into contact tend to be limited selectively by geographic and perhaps also by social, economic, or cultural factors.

In whichever form it occurs, this type of "hasty" or "biased" use of a generalization is certainly a key indicator of the type of bias in argumentation we are seeking to identify.

However, a clearer and more definitive indicator of bias is not just over-generalization (on the basis of too small a sample or too little evidence) or biased generalization (on the basis of an unrepresentative sample) but also clinging to or trying too hard to save the generalization, even in the face of contrary evidence.

7. Treating Comparable Cases Differently

One very clear indicator of bias occurs where a given argument treats two comparable cases that should be very similar in how a range of arguments apply to them, except that the given argument cites all the arguments on one side in the one case and all the opposed arguments on the other side in the other case. This test is particularly acute where the case on the one side is the arguer's own personal situation, or represents his personal position, interests, or affiliations, while the case on the other side is remote from his own personal situation.

Thouless (1936, p. 337) gives an excellent typical illustration of this type of biased argumentation.

> *Case* 4.7: No one who has examined the repertory of arguments of the average man can fail to notice how persistently some are applied in one context and some in another. It is a good thing that he, himself, should have a large income because (a) the amount he saves increases the capital of the country, (b) the part he spends, even on luxuries, is good for trade and increases employment. It is good that his gardener's wages should be low because (c) the country cannot afford the burden of high wages, (d) poverty and hardship produce sturdy, manly characters, and (e) if the gardener were paid more, he would only spend it on useless luxuries like going to the pictures.

The failure here is a kind of failure of consistency. The "average man" in the illustration sees all the arguments for a high income in his own case, while he puts forward all the arguments against it in the case of his gardener. But both individuals are wage earners whose circumstances may in most relevant instances be expected to be quite similar or comparable. And, in fact, all five circumstances (a) through (e) presumably apply, more or less equally well, to the situation of both the speaker and the gardener. However, the speaker selects the high wage arguments for himself, and the low wage arguments are applied to the case of his gardener.

In this case, both indicators of selection and something to gain are involved, but these factors are not distinctive of what is characteristic as an indicator of bias here. It is not just a selection of the arguments that favor the speaker and those that go against the opposed point of view that is the marker of bias. It is the doing of this in an instance where the two comparable cases are split, in this way, into two different sides yet where, all else being equal, both *pro* and *contra* considerations should be taken into account on both sides.

The indicator of bias here is a failure of balance in case-based reasoning. In general, two cases that are comparable ought to be treated equally, unless it is known or established that specific differences between them exist. This kind of bias in treating similar cases differently is also related to charges of hypocrisy frequently associated with some versions of the *tu quoque* type of *ad hominem* argument. However, although the *tu quoque* is based on an allegation that an arguer treats his own case differently and inconsistently from his treatment of a remote case, the upshot of the charge is different from a charge of bias (although bias is involved implicitly).

A typical case of the *tu quoque* argument from Damer (1980, p. 83) will clarify this difference.

> *Case* 4.8: **Father:** Owen, I really don't think that you should be drinking. Alcohol tends to dull your senses, reduces your physical control, and may even become psychologically addicting.
>
> **Son:** That's not a very convincing argument, Dad, when you're standing there with that martini in your hand.

In this case, the son accuses the father of case-by-case inconsistency—the father advocates a policy of nondrinking generally, but in his own case, he acts differently by standing with a martini in his hand. This is a kind of inconsistency between general advocacy and personal action. But the alleged inconsistency is not the whole upshot of the *ad hominem* attack. The son's reply suggests that the personal action indicates the father's real commitment, and that therefore his advice or exhortation not to drink is not credible or sincere.

It is interesting, however, that Damer (1980, p. 83) does describe this case as an allegation of "special pleading," the very same term Thouless (1936, p. 227) used to describe the fault in case 4.7 above. This same term is also widely used to describe selection bias in the logic textbooks, as noted above. This raises the question of how the term *special pleading* should be used properly in argumentation theory. Is it a species of bias or a fallacy?

The provisional answer is that 'special pleading' is best used as a name for the indicator of bias currently under consideration, that of treating comparable cases differently, as illustrated by case 4.7. Although it is not altogether inappropriate to use 'special pleading' for selection bias, or perhaps for other indicators or types of bias, the phrase is most appropriate and useful to describe treatment of 'comparable cases' bias. And we do need a shorter phrase for this.

Special pleading should not be described as a distinctive fallacy or fallacious type of argumentation. The point here is that advocacy, or pleading one's case, is not, in itself, fallacious. Nor is bias, in itself, fallacious, even though it can be at the basis of many of the traditional fallacies, and it can be a normative problem in argumentation in some cases.

8. Emphasis and Hyperbole

Hyperbole is often an indicator of bias, when one's claim is exaggerated, and dramatic appeals to emotion are used to create an atmosphere of crisis. Media reports often "hype" a story, perhaps to increase an audience or readership by making an event seem more important and newsworthy. Beardsley's account (1950, p. 81) of this factor is very indicative of how it works.

> Hence the deep and pervasive tendency toward *hyperbole* in newspapers: the use of superlatives, shocking and exaggerated words. A disagreement between Senators becomes a "clash" in which they "assail" one another, "scoff at" or "hit" or "lash out at" or "blast" one another's ideas and personalities. A fairly widespread movement of popular support for a party candidate becomes (when the news is lean) an "avalanche" of "snowballing" votes, a "deluge" or "tide" or "surge" of support, in which letters "pour in," a "rain" or "crescendo" of enthusiasm from an "army" or "hordes" of people.

As indicated, the language in which an event is described is an important factor in hyperbole. But the layout and choice of pictures also can be factors. For example, big headlines can be used for dramatic effect.

Bias indicated by emphasis on particular words, facts, or even whole arguments in a discourse often has come to be treated in modern logic textbooks under the heading of the "fallacy of accent." This broadening of the fallacy of accent came about even though the fallacy originally referred to misleading ambiguity in argumentation due to differences of verbal stress (accentuation) on words or phrases.

For example, Creighton (1909, p. 168) began by defining the fallacy of accent in the usual way, as "misconception due to accent or emphasis being placed upon the wrong words in a sentence." But then he went on to expand the definition to include bias generally, which he calls "special pleading" (p. 169):

> But these misinterpretations of single propositions are comparatively trivial instances of this fallacy. In a broader sense, the fallacy appears in connected arguments of any kind in which, while the facts are not actually misstated, certain aspects of them are so disproportionately dwelt upon and emphasized, at the expense of the rest, that a false idea of the subject in its entirety is the result. In this wider form, this fallacy is one that may be described as the particular vice of *special pleading;* and the caution that may be suggested against it is, in the language of the astronomer, to make allowances for the "personal equation" both in one's own thinking and in that of others.

This is a very broad construal of the fallacy of accent, making it indistinguishable from bias generally. Hamblin (1970, p. 25) comments that "we have come a long way from Aristotle" and are on a kind of "slippery slide"—"once verbal emphasis has been allowed as relevant, *any* kind of emphasis may be called in" (p. 25).

Blyth (1957, p. 31) also defines the fallacy of accent in such a broad way that it has come to include bias and selectivity, broadly speaking.

> *Case* 4.9: For example, it is frequently possible to achieve the effect of a lie by telling only the truth—though not the whole truth. The schoolboy explaining to his father how he happened to get into a fight may truthfully say that the other fellow hit him first but neglect to mention the fact that he had provoked the attack by making insulting remarks. Another form of the same fallacy is found in the use of a quotation out of its context. Even though the quotation is exact, an erroneous impression may be created through neglecting to mention various qualifications made in the context from which the quotation was extracted. This fallacy has sometimes been called the *fallacy of accent.*

Other textbooks adopting this very broad view of the fallacy of accent are Ruby (1950, p. 57) and Mourant (1963, p. 184). Once "emphasis" was construed very broadly by the logic textbooks, the fallacy of amphiboly was stretched to include wrenching discourse from context and other kinds of distortion that are really types of bias. This stretching of the fallacy of accent has been an unfortunate development, for accent should be seen more properly as a fallacy arising from ambiguity, comparable to equivocation and amphiboly.

Emphasis and hyperbole are important indicators of bias in their own right. Unfortunately, the standard treatment in the logic textbooks has disguised their importance in this respect, by misleadingly squeezing them into the categories of traditional fallacies.

9. Implicature and Innuendo

A more subtle sign of bias is the use of suggestion and innuendo in presumptions that are not explicitly stated. A particular statement in a text of discourse may be simply reporting a fact, if taken at a surface or literal level of interpretation. But the same statement, in context, also may suggest a conclusion or point of view that is highly argumentative and takes one side of a controversial issue. This gives the discourse a bias or slant toward a particular viewpoint.

Covering this aspect under the heading "Suggestion and Slanting," Beardsley (1966, pp. 197–218) defined this type of slanted discourse as follows: "When a discourse is true on one level, but false on a higher level, and it carries the suggestion that because it is true on one level, it is also true on the higher level, then we shall say that that discourse is slanted." Beardsley (1966, p. 202) gave the following example, analyzing it on the basis of the definition above.

> *Case* 4.10: A certain college newspaper, announcing a forthcoming talk on hallucinogenic drugs by Richard Alpert, former professor of psychology and education at Harvard, filled in some background this way: "Dr. Alpert was dismissed from Harvard for expanding the consciousness of an undergraduate." The knowledgeable reader understood several things from this. On level 1, it states that the cause of Mr. Alpert's dismissal was an event having the characteristics *designated* by "expanding the consciousness of an undergraduate"—namely, that he allegedly gave illegal hallucinogenic drugs to an undergraduate. On level 2, it states that this event had some

> characteristics *connoted* by "expanding the consciousness of an undergraduate"—namely, that the drugs opened up new areas of experience, which were beneficial and knowledge-giving, and so forth. On level 3, it suggests that Harvard University is opposed to allowing undergraduates to have beneficial and cognitively rich experiences.

In this case, the slant is indicated by the third level, where a point of view is implied by suggestion or implicature.

To detect innuendo, one has to "read between the lines" of the written or spoken discourse in a given case and draw out by implicature conclusions that are meant to be inferred by a reader or audience. This is done by reconstructing the argument as a contribution to a conversation, a conventionalized type of dialogue, in which the speaker and hearer (or reader) are supposedly engaged. In such a context, speaker and hearer may be presumed to share common knowledge and expectations and cooperatively to take part in the conversation at its different stages, by taking turns making kinds of moves called "speech acts," for example, questioning and replying, asking for clarification or justification of an assertion.

The kind of framework needed for the extraction of implicatures in innuendo is given in the structure of conversational implicature of Grice (1975), as indicated in chapter 1. One should judge implicature on the basis of Grice's conversational postulate (CP), as applied to the context of dialogue or conversation appropriate for an argument in a given case: "Make your conversational contribution such as is required, at the stage at which it occurs, by the accepted purpose or direction of the talk exchange in which you are engaged." In chapter 2, we identified the main types of goal-directed conversations of this kind.

A common example of slanting of this kind would be a case where a student, Smith, who has taken a course from Professor *X* asks him to give him a letter of recommendation to support his application for graduate school. Professor *X* writes only the following brief letter.

> *Case* 4.11: Smith's attendance at lectures was excellent, and Smith is also very friendly and congenial.

Given the normal expectations of the kind of talk exchange this process of giving references occurs within, this letter of reference would be taken as strongly negative by the person or committee who received it. The reason is that what was *not* said strongly suggests by implicature that, in Professor *X*'s opinion, Smith is an undistinguished or not very able student, to whom he is giving a very poor recommendation. For normally, in this type of conversational exchange, the referee would say lots of good things about the abilities of a student being even mildly recommended.

The trick here is that an advocate often will conceal the most controversial or extreme conclusions being put forward in an argument, which really do indicate a definite bias, by putting them in the form of suggestions and nonexplicit implicatures. This has the decisive tactical advantage of plausible deniability: burden of proof is not (explicitly) incurred, and commitment can even be retracted later, if the need arises.

Also included under this heading as a key indicator of bias is the use of presumptions and presuppositions in the asking of questions in argumentation. These include what the logic textbooks often call "loaded" or "leading" questions, and also the kinds of questions associated with the fallacy of many questions, or fallacy of complex questions, as it is sometimes called.[14] An example from Walton (1989b, p. xiii) will indicate the type of case we have in mind. During the 1988 U.S. federal election coverage, Ted Koppel asked Michael Dukakis during a television interview:

> *Case* 4.12: What is it about the Bush campaign that has absolutely nailed you to the wall?

The asking of this question (in context) clearly indicates biased argumentation. Although no explicit argument, with premises and conclusions, is directed against Mr. Dukakis' side, clearly the presumptions or presuppositions contained in the question are prejudicial to his side. Not only is it implied that he is "nailed to the wall," but any direct answer he gives to the question concedes implications that go very much against his side.

The general issue of when a question may be said to be biased, in a scientific poll, for example, will be taken up in chapter 8.

10. Using the Indicators

In order to use these ten indicators effectively, one needs to start with a target concept of bias (slant) that one is supposed to be identifying in a given case of argumentation. This target concept is the dialectical concept of bias in argumentation defined in chapter 3, meaning that bias is a matter of how an argument is being put forward in a manner to reflect the balance appropriate for the use of that argument at a particular stage of a type of conversation (dialogue) in which the arguer is supposedly engaged. Bias is determined, in an argument in a given case, by the discourse containing the argument and the manner of presentation of the argument, in a verbal or written form, in that case. This judgment should be seen as relative to what is actually known and can be documented as given, in a specific case.

It should be emphasized that bias, as identified by these criteria, is not necessarily a bad thing, a failure of reasoning, or a fallacy. It is only "bad" as a deficiency or failure of reasonable argumentation under certain conditions and where it is of a more extreme sort posing an interference with the dialogue, or a deceptive shift that is misleading and confusing. These questions of evaluation of bias will be taken up in chapters 6 and 7.

It is very easy to blow allegations of bias out of proportion, treating the charge as a devastating refutation, rather than just as a defeasible indicator of potential bias, which should only have a small weight of presumption. Indeed, as noted in cases 4.1 and 4.2, this blowing out of proportion of a charge of bias is the basis of many a fallacious *ad hominem* argument. In chapter 7, charges of bias will be evaluated.

Context of existing or known evidence in a given case is very important generally in judging whether an argument is biased. This is made quite clear, for example, in the test for selection bias, which asks, What important, relevant arguments have been left out? This kind of finding is relative to a determination of which arguments are known to have been actually presented (in context) in a given case.

Judging lip service selection is also highly contextual, because one has to look at the totality of arguments presented on both sides, *pro* and *contra*. Then one has to judge, in context, both how important these arguments are to resolving the issue and how they have been presented, as reflecting the real positions on both sides.

Commitment to an identifiable position, as an indicator of bias, also has to be judged by the dialectical context of an argument in a given case. This is done by looking over the known sequence of dialogue exchanges between the two parties, so the evolving position of each party, as reflected in his or her commitment store (and its modifications) in the dialogue, after the fashion outlined in chapters two and three.

Being closed to opposed argumentation is also clearly a dialectical criterion that needs to be determined by how an arguer reacts to criticisms or arguments during the course of a conversational exchange.

Indeed, it is not too difficult to see how all ten of the indicators presented above are inherently dialectical in nature. This means that one cannot simply look to the propositions that make up a short sequence of argument (premises and conclusion) in abstractions from the dialectical context of the larger segment of discourse in which it occurs, when using these indicators of bias.

Applying these indicators to a given case of argumentation is therefore very much a holistic judgment of weighing the significance of the indicator, when found in a case, in light of what is known about the purpose of the discourse and the use of the argument being evaluated in light of its being a contribution to the discourse at some stage of a conversational exchange. Just because an indicator of bias is present, one should not leap to the conclusion that the argument is totally discredited or refuted or that some sort of fallacy has been committed.

However, the indicators are *cumulative* in the sense that the more and more indicators are found to be present in a given case, as more of the discourse is analyzed, the more weight there is to support the charge that there is a bias in the argumentation in that case.

Notes

1. Note the previous discussion of this case in chapter 3.
2. See Walton (1989a, 141–149) and case 2 below.
3. See van Eemeren and Grootendorst (1993).
4. But see the discussion in Walton (1992b, chapter 8).
5. See Walton and Krabbe (1995).
6. See Krabbe and Walton (1993).
7. Ibid.
8. Ibid. (1993).
9. For a good illustrative case of this, see Walton (1989, 153).

10. Use of this phrase was heard by the author in December 1993, on a televised report of negotiations during a strike of construction workers in Quebec, concerning trade barriers in the construction industry.

11. For a good case, see Walton (1992c, 148–150).
12. See Walton (1990b).
13. Ibid.

14. Loaded and fallacious questions have already been analyzed extensively in Walton (1989b), and the reader is referred to that work for many case studies illustrating problems of bias in questioning.

Chapter Five
BIASED LANGUAGE

We are all familiar with the use of loaded, slanted, or biased terms in argumentation—words or phrases that have a positive slant toward one side of a disputed issue and/or a negative slant toward the other side.[1] We have all noticed, for example, that the soldiers on our side in a military confrontation are called the "freedom fighters" or described by some comparable positive terms, while the soldiers on the other side may be called "terrorists" or described by some other comparable negative terms. Here, the language used is an important indicator of bias. Biased use of language raises two normative questions we will explore in this chapter. Is it a bad thing, from a point of view of the critical use of argumentation? And if it is, or when it is, what can be done about it?

The recent influential postmodernist view is that all language is inevitably biased anyway, so it is quite all right to invent new terms that have a politically correct bias supporting one's own point of view. For, after all, the traditional language that has been in use inevitably contains a bias that supports the established institutions. The argument seems to be that since all words have political and ethical implications and biases contained in them anyway, those advocating political and social reforms (presumably, for the better) should feel free to adopt and advocate terminology that supports one's own biases.

In other words, the postmodernist climate of opinion is that there is nothing wrong with bias and that the practice of describing one's own side in positive terms and the opposed side in negative terms is quite acceptable.

The traditional informal logic textbooks, in contrast, as we will see below, generally have been pretty hard on this practice, frequently criticizing it as fallacious, under the heading of "the fallacy of loaded terms,"

115

"the fallacy of question-begging epithets," and so forth. But, as we will see below, some textbooks have been somewhat biased by their zeal to pursue their purpose of classifying and identifying errors, faults, or criticizable aspects of argumentation as fallacies.

How should we react when someone charged with one of these fallacies backs up her use of such a term with reasoned justifications in support of her usage, even offering a definition of the term in question? For example, suppose she gives extensive arguments to support the view that the cause supported by her side is a just cause and that a freedom fighter is defined, on her view, as a person who fights by fair means to defend this just cause. This type of definition has been called a "persuasive definition" by many of the current leading logic textbooks. Should we condemn such a persuasive definition as logically nonallowable or fallacious because it does show a bias in favor of one side and against the other? The textbooks seem uncertain and divided on this question. They are suspicious about persuasive definitions. Although some describe them as fallacious, others stop short of this but are generally inclined to be critical of them.

This chapter will open up the exploration of these difficult questions. We begin by considering some realistic but very controversial cases, giving the reader an indication of the seriousness of what is at stake.

1. Language Used in the Abortion Issue

Recently familiarized by the rhetoric used on both sides of the abortion issue, it is not too difficult for most of us to appreciate how each side creatively uses language to support its position. If you look at such a practice from the point of view of advocating one side of this issue, there seems to be nothing wrong with it as an obstacle to or critical defect in that advocacy. But if you take the broader perspective of viewing the argumentation in a context of the two opposed positions engaging in a critical discussion, some problems of a logical kind can become evident.

One standard example given under the heading "persuasive definitions" in logic textbooks is in fact a good illustration of how conflicts of opinion can turn on conflicting views of the meaning of a key term. According to Carney and Sheer (1974, p. 138), the following story ("Thanks and Much Love," *The Honolulu Advertiser*, February 14, 1970) appeared during hearings of the Hawaiian State Legislature on abortion law, under the headline, "Defining Abortion a Tricky Business."

Case 5.1:   Amidst the emotional debate on the abortion issue at the State Legislature, humor still lives.

Anonymous legislative staffers this week drafted and circulated to legislators a proposed "general response to constituent letters on abortion." It goes like this:

"Dear Sir:

You ask me how I stand on abortion. Let me answer forthrightly and without equivocation.

If by abortion you mean the murdering of defenseless human beings; the denial of rights to the youngest of our citizens; the promotion of promiscuity among our shiftless and valueless youth and the rejection of Life, Liberty and the Pursuit of Happiness—then, Sir, be assured that I shall never waver in my opposition, so help me God.

But, Sir, if by abortion you mean the granting of equal rights to all our citizens regardless of race, color or sex; the elimination of evil and vile institutions preying upon desperate and hopeless women; a chance to all our youth to be wanted and loved; and, above all, that God-given right for all citizens to act in accordance with the dictates of their own conscience—then, Sir, let me promise you as a patriot and a humanist that I shall never be persuaded to forego my pursuit of these most basic human rights.

Thank you for asking my position on this most crucial issue and let me again assure you of the steadfastness of my stand.

Mahalo and Aloha Nui."[2]

The writers of this letter are pointing out, in a colorful way, that the two opposed positions on the abortion issue are very much dependent on premises or assumptions about how key words in the dispute, such as *abortion,* are defined. Each side has its own persuasive or slanted definition. The writers of the letter are not accusing either side of committing any fallacies but some fallacies, or problems or obstacles to critical reasoning could possibly result from the use of such slanted definitions.

One potential problem is that of confusing a real dispute about facts or values with a merely verbal dispute—a kind of failure of communication that could result in failure to resolve the conflict of opinions by reasoned argumentation. Another is the fallacy of begging the question

(Walton 1991). For example, given that the one side defines 'abortion' as "the murdering of defenseless human beings," is that so strong that it implies the falsehood of the thesis of the other side, presumably that abortion is an acceptable practice? We return to these questions below, but first we should also note another kind of problem with the use of slanted words that is not a fallacy but is nevertheless well worth noticing.

One interesting phenomenon is that in controversies regularly debated on public issues, each side changes the key words used to describe or sum up their basic contention, in order to make their position sound more positive. The abortion issue is presumably about abortion—whether or not it should be allowed and/or supported. So, to describe the basic thesis of each side, one would think the two positions should be called "pro-abortion" and "anti-abortion."

However, being anti-abortion sounds (to many) very negative and restrictive, so this side has relabeled itself "prolife." As for the other side, being pro-abortion does not sound too good either—it sounds (to many) as if one is for something that is somehow unfortunate, regrettable, or anyhow negative. So this side calls itself "prochoice." This sounds much more positive and attractive.

It seems now that there is even a movement by the prochoice side to carry this verbal gamesmanship a step further and to call the opposite side "antichoice," according to an account given in Leo (1992, p. 18).

> "Choice" was a brilliant bit of verbal gamesmanship too, avoiding the troubling word "abortion" altogether, and completely erasing the other side's once potent term "abortion on demand." Now, there may be an effort to convert "anti-choice" into an allegedly neutral term for those who are anti-abortion. The word is being pushed hard in Op-Ed articles. The editor of a major journalism review used the term as a neutral one in a recent awards presentation. Sidney Blumenthal, the political writer, referred to "anti-choice candidates" a month ago in *The New Republic,* supplying a handy pejorative label that these candidates would never use themselves. And *USA Today* talked about a possible "anti-choice abortion ruling from the Supreme Court." Journalism marches on.

Trying to get the media to adopt one's own term, used to sum up the thesis of one's opposition in language that is less positive than the term they choose, is a tactic that seems to go too far.

In 1993, the author received a letter requesting a donation to be used for "political and advocacy work" for a prochoice group. The letter began as follows.

Case 5.2:   Dear Friend,

I have a direct *warning* for you. A warning that anti-choice groups in Canada are quickly organizing an all-out attempt to curtail reproductive freedom.

Increasingly aggressive anti-choice groups are accusing you of being a threat to the future of our nation.

Your belief in a woman's right to reproductive choice is enough for the anti-choice camp to defame your character.

Quite simply, they're out to have their beliefs supersede the right of each woman to control her own body and destiny.

That's why I'm writing to ask you to lend your financial help to the organization best prepared to protect each woman's right to reproductive freedom—the Canadian Abortion Rights Action League, or CARAL.

As a journalist, I've always prided myself on observing and commenting on events and people as accurately as possible.

The letter went on to describe the tactics used by "anti-choice" groups to "dominate the abortion issue," including "publishing lurid newsletters," sending "inflamed anti-choice videos," "stacking riding association meetings," and "targeting for defeat" politicians who put forth views they do not like. The letter concludes with a plea to "help stop the anti-choice threat to equal access to abortion" by making a donation to CARAL.

Since CARAL is an advocacy group trying to raise funds to help a cause, and in this letter explicitly describes its purpose this way, the writer of the letter is, of course, free to use advocacy language such as "anti-choice" to support its cause. There is nothing wrong with such a one-sided argument *per se*, provided it is clear to everyone that the argument is for one side. However, if one were to put the argument in a wider and different context of a critical discussion between the two opposed points of view on abortion, surely the so-called prolife side has a right to object to being labeled "antichoice" (even though that label may reflect accurately how the "prochoice" side sees them). In the context of a persuasion dialogue on the abortion issue, an argument should meet the requirements for a balanced argument.

Thus, when the letter writer adds, "As a journalist, I've always prided myself as observing and commenting on events and people as accurately as possible," a standard of impartiality or nonadvocacy is implied that is misleading and should be judged as a shift in the discourse making the statement questionable. This move is deceptive and is a bad sort of bias because it trades on the expectation that the author is engaging in a balanced, two-sided dialogue with the reader.

2. Influencing the Media through Language

Using language in a partisan fashion to support a cause or point of view is logically unobjectionable, as long as it is clear what is being done and anyone who has a different point of view is free to advocate or use different language. But such partisan practices are more worrisome when the words and phrases get into the public domain.

Journalists tend to use certain words and phrases that seem to be sanctioned by their sources as having a conventionalized sort of meaning, often of a positive or negative slant. Several of these familiar "buzz words" are cited in a recent compendium (MAL and NS, 1990, p. 21),

> *Case* 5.3: *Clean up*—a scenario for setting right oil spills, nuclear pollution, chemical releases, and the like. The phrase sounds comforting—it implies a magical vacuum cleaner at work—except that most ecological disasters can't be undone.

> *Case* 5.4: *Deterrent*—nuclear weapons pointed at the Soviet Union. (Nuclear weapons pointed at the United States never get the U.S. media's "deterrent" tag.)

> *Case* 5.5: *Military strongman*—a foreign military dictator out of favor with the White House. (In 1989, Military Strongman seemed to be the first names of Panamanian General Manuel Noriega. A few years earlier, when he was on the CIA's payroll, he was "Military Leader.")

These words are acceptable in media practices, even though they clearly contain a definite positive or negative slant, because they reflect attitudes and values of the country at the time and particularly the point of view promoted by the government as politically acceptable at the time. The problem is that the media and their readers may come to accept the usage of these words without realizing they contain a slant or "spin."

In other cases, it can be government agencies or political groups that try to get the media to use words that have a spin supporting their own advocacy point of view. The National Council of Teachers of English, meeting in Seattle on November 22, 1991, gave their annual Double-speak Award to the U.S. Defense Department. According to Macdonald (1991, p. 42), the award, for "language meant to bamboozle, befuddle and obfuscate" was given for the language used to describe the "armed situation" (war) in the Persian Gulf.

> *Case* 5.6: Bombing attacks against Iraq were "efforts" and war-planes were "weapons systems" or "force packages." When pilots went out on bombing missions they were "visiting a site." Buildings were "hard targets," people were "soft" ones.
>
> The bombs didn't kill. They "degraded, neutralized, attrited, suppressed, eliminated, cleansed, sanitized, im-pacted, decapitated or took out" targets. Killing the en-emy was "servicing the target." (p. 42)

The second prize went to a group in the Republican party who published a booklet, *Language: A Key Mechanism of Control,* telling Republicans to use positive terms such as *environment, peace,* and *freedom,* when describing their own party activities and to use words such as *sick, pathetic,* and *liberal* when describing the opposition (MacDonald 1991, p. 42).

In some cases, however, a word commonly accepted and used by the media is challenged by critics because of its positive or negative implica-tions. After the siege of the Branch Davidian compound in Waco, Texas, got so much media coverage in 1993, some commentators objected to the use of the word *cult* to apply to the many small religious communities in the United States that withdraw from society and form around a re-ligious leader (Goldman, 1993, p. L11):

> *Case* 5.7a: James Richardson, a sociologist of religion at the University of Nevada at Reno, does not like the term cult. He prefers to call them "new," "minority" or "exo-tic" religions.
>
> "We forget that 99 percent of minority religious groups are benign and peaceful and just want to be left alone," said Dr. Richardson, the author of several books on American religion. "When they abide by the law, they have this right, and the focus of the Waco tragedy should not lead to more harassment of the 99 percent. Regrettably, however, Waco may be just the excuse some

> are looking for to exercise more control over minority religious groups."
>
> Dr. Richardson, who is also a lawyer, said the Waco tragedy would only be compounded if it led to "severe limitations of religious freedom and practice."

The problem is that the word *cult* is highly negative. A highly publicized incident like the Waco siege emphasizes all the potential bad consequences and negative aspects of anything associated with the word *cult*. As the word is widely used in the media, it tends to become applied to any religious group living in a confined area under a religious leader, especially those that withdraw from society and relinquish private property. But the negative word *cult* may then apply to many religious groups that are not dangerous or do not have characteristics that should be considered bad.

Another expert cited in Goldman (1993, p. L11) cites this problem.

> *Case* 5.7b: Robert C. Fuller, an expert in new religions at Bradley University in Peoria, Ill., called the use of the word cult "an artifact of the media."
>
> "We should be careful not to become overly suspicious of all small and dissenting religious groups," said Dr. Fuller, the author of numerous books on American religious life. Many of these groups, he said, have "thoughtful and reasoned philosophies and admirable moral structures."

The problem here does not seem to be a fallacy, but it is a danger to reasoned argumentation. Once the standard meaning adopted by the media (or any other influential group in public discourse) becomes widely accepted, it may cause readers to adopt a stance to condemn certain groups by labeling them with the negative word *cult*. Given the public sanction of such usage, they may not feel free to challenge the negative judgment or be aware that there is room for disagreement or questioning.

3. Defining 'Poverty'

Many words relating to law and public policy have both political and financial implications, and alternative definitions of these terms can be subject to considerable argumentation by opposed political or advocacy groups. The definition of the word *poverty* has long been the subject of such verbal battles.

One series of engagements in this battle was related in a story "Who's Poor?" on the news program "W5" (November 25, 1993), summarized below.

Case 5.8:   Figures released by anti-poverty activists estimating three million people below the poverty line in Canada caused a "poverty panic." It appeared that Canada was going the way of Brazil or Bangladesh, and the U.N. blasted "Canada's shame." Social activists arrived at this figure using LICO, the Low-Income Poverty Cutoff ($15,509 for a single person; $33,615 for a family of five), derived from Statistics Canada figures. However a Statistics Canada representative warned that using the LICO line to define poverty is contrary to their explicit advice in their publications: "We advise people it (LICO) is not a measure of poverty." LICO doesn't take rent costs, for example, into account. Forty percent of those defined as poor by the LICO line own their own houses, and half of these are mortgage free. Also, student loans do not count as income, with the result that most students are defined as "poor," even though, if you ask them, many of them deny being poor.

Using a different definition, economist Christopher Sarlo judged only one million people in Canada to be poor. Sarlo outraged anti-poverty advocates when he said, "Those in the anti-poverty industry have a vested interest in keeping the numbers high. In order to keep your jobs, you need to keep the figures high." The response of the advocates to this charge was that this "male person, playing with his calculator," would cause payments to the poor to be cut back!

Politicians on one side of the dispute accused Sarlo's approach of "defining poverty out of existence by playing with the numbers." Politicians on the other side say that they want to make government accountable for doing something for the poor—"If you define poverty badly, you solve the problem badly." Sarlo supported this view, arguing that the advocacy definition trivializes the needs of poor people by failing to distinguish between those lacking basic needs and those lacking social comforts.

The problem here was that the two quite different definitions of 'poverty' had become part of a political battle, with exponents on both sides. The one side was explicitly an advocacy group with the goal of getting funds for "the poor," as they define this term. But they also had their political allies, who supported their views on the matter and who were in a position to make these views part of government policy.

The opposed point of view, represented by Sarlo and the political sympathizers of this viewpoint, criticized their opponents by saying they are biased, that those in the "poverty industry have a vested interest in keeping the numbers high." This criticism is that their definition of 'poverty' is a biased or slanted definition.

However, the antipoverty activists clearly see and present themselves as an advocacy group whose purpose is to help the poor. Perhaps, then, they would not see their bias or interests as a bad thing or something about which they should be defensive. In reply to Sarlo's charge of bias, the antipoverty advocate interviewed on the program used argumentation from consequences, to accuse his critic of causing bad things to happen—he would cause payments to the poor to be cut back. This suggests he is a bad person—a person who is causing harm to the poor! From their advocacy point of view, this is how they see his criticism of bias.

In this case, the antipoverty advocates are not offering an explicit redefinition of the word *poverty*. Instead, they are using a criterion that, in effect, gives a much more inclusive meaning to it than the one in normal lexical usage. It redefines people as "poor" who do not consider themselves poor, and who we would not normally use the word *poor* to designate.

Next, it is interesting to consider a case where an explicit redefinition of a term currently in use is offered, making it an instance of what the logic textbooks call a "persuasive definition."

4. Defining 'Pornography'

Among controversial revisionist definitions, it is interesting to reflect on the definition of the term *pornography* put forward by feminists. According to Smith (1993, pp. 71–72) the following definition of 'pornography' was published in a 'Policy Statement by the Campaign against Pornography and Censorship' (CPC) in 1990.

Case 5.9:   ... the graphic, sexually explicit subordination of women through pictures and/or words, that also includes one or more of the following: women portrayed as sexual objects, things or commodities, enjoying pain or humiliation or rape, being tied up, cut up, mutilated, bruised or physically hurt, in postures of sexual submission or servility or display, reduced to body parts, penetrated by objects or animals, or presented in scenarios of degradation, injury, torture, shown as inferior, bleeding, bruised or hurt in a context which is sexual.

Pornography does not include erotica (defined as sexually explicit materials premised on equality) and it does not include *bona fide* sex education materials, or medical or forensic literature.

In short, we define pornography as depicting a combination of the sexual objectification and subordination of women, often including violation and violence.

This definition is a departure from the customary lexical meaning of the word *pornography*. And it has a number of specific implications. First, pornography is defined as something bad or immoral, so that it is no longer possible to discuss the issue of whether pornography is good or bad, should be acceptable or not, and so on.

Second, it does not make it possible for men, or anyone other than women, to be portrayed in pornography. For example, sexually degrading depictions of men, made for the consumption of women viewers or readers, is not pornography, according to this definition. Nor could the portrayal of homosexual activities between men be classed as pornography.

It also suggests that this "objectification" and "subordination" of women in pornography is committed by men. It suggests strongly that women are the victims and men the culprits in all pornography.

This seems like a highly one-sided definition, and feminist writings using or advocating it often make these implications quite explicit, writing that 'pornography' contains elements of "male fascism," "phallocentrism," and other aspects indicating male aggressiveness or dominance (see Kostash 1992, p. 381).

What kind of critical commentary is appropriate for this way of defining 'pornography'? First, it should be noted that if the proponents of this definition are an advocacy or "action group" whose purpose is to support the interests of women, then it is hard to criticize the definition as part of the argumentation designed to provide that support. True, it is a one-sided definition, but evidently that is how it is supposed to be, in order to advocate the interests of women. In a purely advocacy or "interest-group" context, the definition does not seem to be objectionable on grounds that it is open to criticism or refutation as a bad argument.

Of course, if such a definition were to purport to be a lexical definition that is faithful to usage, it would be open to criticism that would decisively refute it. Or if the definition were put forward in a critical discussion on the ethics of pornography, supposedly discussing the issue of whether or not pornography is immoral, it would beg the question by opting in a foreclosing way for one side over the other. An example will help to clarify this.

> *Case* 5.10: In a philosophy seminar, the designated topic for a class discussion is: Is pornography something that should be allowed, or not? A participant in the discussion puts forward and advocates the definition of 'pornography' stated in case 5.9. Another participant replies: "That definition begs the question, because according to the definition given, pornography is very bad, and even illegal, implying that pornography definitely should not be allowed. The definition, once accepted, closes off the discussion in favor of one side. If we accept it, we can no longer have any discussion of the proposed seminar topic."

What are we to say about this type of criticism of the use of a persuasive definition of this kind in a critical discussion? Perhaps the advocate of the definition might reply, "Yes, this definition closes off the argument in favor of one side. But that just shows this one side is right. And anyway, I'm free to offer any definition I like, and this one truly reflects my point of view on the issue." This reply seems to have some elements of legitimacy in it. The discussion, after all, is about values and morals, so it should not be regarded that a definition put forward in the discussion is "persuasive" or reflects the values or viewpoint of the one side. And, of course, the other side is free to argue against the proposed definition.

As a preliminary to addressing this tricky question, some further matters need to be taken into account—especially the standard textbook accounts of persuasive definitions and the fallacy of question-begging epithets.

5. Biased Terminology in Scientific Research

One might presume that bias related to the definition of a term could occur only in a type of dialogue where there is an explicit conflict of opinions or values involved and would not occur in scientific research. For surely scientific research is meant to be a collaborative type of investigation based only on verified facts and knowledge, and as such, it would be designed to exclude bias. Even though this may be true, as an ideal of scientific research, it seems that, in practice, bias related to the definition of terms can come into the argumentation.

In an article published in a medical journal, Morabia and Flandre (1992) showed how bias due to the definition of the term *menopause* led to inconsistent findings (spurious differences) in breast cancer studies. The abstract of the article (Morabia and Flandre, 1992, p. 222) outlines the problem posed by this alleged misclassification bias, due to the definition of a term.

> *Case* 5.11: It is often assumed but has not been consistently observed, that some characteristics of reproductive history are specifically related to breast cancer of pre- or postmenopausal onset. To determine whether inconsistent reports may be due to differences in definition of menopause, we computed the relative odds (RO) of breast cancer for nulliparity, age at first live birth, family history of breast cancer and prior history of benign breast disease, separately in pre- and postmenopausal women, using seven different definitions of menopause. Results show that (i) relative odds of breast cancer and their confidence intervals may vary according to definitions of menopause; (ii) age-based definitions of menopause are associated with moderate differential misclassification bias between cases and controls; (iii) nulliparity, late age at first birth and family history of breast cancer seem to be specific risk factors for pre- but not postmenopausal breast cancer when cutoff for menopausal status is 10 years or more after last menses; and (iv) when information on menstrual history is not available, 50 years of age may be the best proxy for all menses-based definitions of menopause. We conclude that inconsistent findings on the effect of menopausal status in the association of breast cancer with some re-

> productive factors are partly due to statistical imprecision and differential misclassification bias associated with different age-based or menses-based definitions of menopause. Researchers should either test whether their conclusions hold using several definitions of menopause or give a biological rationale for the choice of a given definition of menopause.

The problem here is partly one of ambiguity—Morabia and Flandre (p. 226) show that there are three age-based definitions of menopause in use by medical researchers and four menses-based definitions in use. However, it does not seem, according to their account, that the ambiguity can be eliminated simply by picking one definition as the "correct" one. They write that the age-based definitions lead to some degree of misclassification bias, compared to menses-based definitions (p. 226). But age-based definitions can be appropriate where information on menstrual history is lacking (p. 222). Hence the conclusion Morabia and Flandre reach (p. 227, and see the abstract, above) is to warn researchers to test whether their findings hold for several definitions or give a "biological rationale" for the definition used.

As this case indicates, definitions in science also are open to challenge and revision and can be quite legitimately subject to argumentation. In this case, the problem is that some researchers may be unaware that there is more than one correct definition in current patterns of scientific usage. Once an awareness of this exists, then the danger of a research outcome's being biased is overcome.

6. Origins of Concern about Slanted Terms

Logic textbooks and critical-thinking guides, as well as manuals on rhetoric and language, have generally recognized (and even emphasized) that the use of slanted language can be a serious obstacle to reasoning in some instances. But they have not always been consistent or unified in directing their readers on how to deal with the problem. Some textbooks have treated "loaded terms" as a fallacy. Others have dealt with the problem under the heading of "persuasive definitions." Still others have dealt with it under the heading of the "fallacy of question-begging epithets" (or "question-begging appellatives"). This last category was introduced into the logic curriculum by Bentham (1824), and many textbooks have been strongly influenced by his treatment of the subject—see below.

However, if we go as far back as Aristotle, it can be seen that he was well aware of the problem. A good deal of his concern in the *Topics* and *Rhetoric* has to do with argumentation relating to or based on definitions and word usage.

Aristotle did not treat the use of slanted terms as a fallacy in his *Sophistical Refutations*. It does not fall under the heading of any of the five fallacies "dependent on language" that Aristotle distinguished: equivocation, amphiboly, combination and division of words, accent, and form of expression. Although some modern logic textbooks have included bias and slanting of various kinds under the category of "accent," this is an unjustifiable broadening of the fallacy of accent, beyond what Aristotle would have intended or what we should properly allow.

However, in book 3 of the *Rhetoric*, Aristotle did clearly recognize and identify the eulogistic and vituperative use of epithets as a distinctive tactic of argumentation. This is made clear by two examples Aristotle gives (1405b14).

> *Case* 5.12: As for epithets, they may be applied from what is vile or disgraceful, for instance, "the matricide," or from what is more honorable, for instance, "the avenger of his father."

> *Case* 5.13: When the winner in a mule-race offered Simonides a small sum, he refused to write an ode, as if he thought it beneath him to write on half-asses; but when he gave him a sufficient amount, he wrote,
>
> > Hail, daughters of storm-footed steeds!
>
> and yet they were also the daughters of asses.

In case 5.12, Aristotle alludes to the *Orestes of Euripides*—when Meneleaus accuses Orestes of matricide, Orestes replies that Meneleaus should rather call him the avenger of his father, Agamemnon, who had been murdered by his wife—Orestes' mother, Clymaenestra. This shows that the act carried out by Orestes could be described in a positive way, by the epithet *avenger of my father,* or in a negative way, by the epithet *matricide* ("killer of my mother"). Either way clearly has (opposed) persuasive or rhetorical effects.

Case 5.13 shows that an epithet can be biased to one side or the other, in a positive or negative way, depending on which aspect of something the speaker chooses to emphasize. A "half-ass" or donkey is half horse and half ass. To call such a beast "the daughter of an ass" makes it sound not very impressive. However, Simonides made the same beasts sound glorious by calling them "daughters of storm-footed steeds." Here Aristotle is recognizing the rhetorical tactic—nowadays it would be called "puffery" in public relations—of using a dramatic and glamorous phrase to give added rhetorical glamour or positive "oomph" to something, making it sound very positive and attractive. By its usual name, the same thing might seem everyday, ordinary, and unexciting, perhaps even negative.

7. *The Fallacy of Loaded Term*

Johnson and Blair (1983, p. 127) define the *fallacy of loaded term* as the use of evaluative or non-neutral terms, where there is not adequate evidence given to support the evaluative component. Their analysis of the fallacy falls into two parts, indicated by their figure (p. 129) below.

---

1. *M* labels something, *X* (a person, act, event, situation, etc.), in a way that is either debatable or else false.

2. *M* uses that classification of *X* without defense as support for some conclusion, *Q*.

Figure 5.1. Loaded Term

They give the following example (p. 128) from an advertising circular by the Imperial Oil Company, arguing for higher prices for petroleum products.

> *Case* 5.14: Over the past quarter century, because world prices for crude oil have been *depressed,* and because of intense competition, petroleum energy has been available in Canada at *bargain* prices. The price of energy generally in Canada has been so low that, in the words of the Ontario Government Advisory Committee on Energy, it has been taken for granted and regarded almost as a free commodity. (Emphasis ours.)

As Johnson and Blair point out (p. 128), *depressed* is a loaded term in this case because it implies that prices are lower than they should be, but this claim is not supported. Similarly, *bargain prices* is a loaded term, as used here, because it implies that we have been getting petroleum more cheaply than we would normally expect, but this is not supported adequately by the argument given.

This case illustrates very well what is wrong with using loaded terms, from a critical perspective of normative evaluation of argumentation. But does it justify calling the use of loaded terms in this case, and ones like it, a "fallacy"? Not if a fallacy has to be more than just an inadequately supported or "weak" argument, where a premise is not backed up by sufficient evidence to prove it. Such a failure to meet burden of proof should not be equated, at least necessarily, with the committing of a fallacy.

However, in Johnson and Blair's view (1983, p. 129), the fallacy of loaded term is a special case of a more general type of fault or error they call "problematic premise."

> We must emphasize that *loaded term* is a special case of *problematic* premise. Essentially what you are doing in locating a term which has questionable application is pointing to a premise which requires defense; that is, the arguer needs to provide some reason for thinking that the term does indeed apply. Therefore, a charge of *loaded term* must not be pictured as a devastating rebuttal of an argument. It's more appropriately seen as exposing the argument's weak or tender spots. There is no presumption that the arguer cannot produce the needed defense of the classification that is questioned. For instance, Imperial Oil may well be able to demonstrate that, despite the questions we have raised, all the evidence taken together does justify their describing world crude oil prices as "depressed" and Canadian petroleum prices as "bargain."

Problematic premise, as a species of fallacy, according to the account of Johnson and Blair, then, is a failure to meet a burden of proof in an argument by failing to adequately justify one or more of the premises, where that premise (or premises) should have been supported adequately.

There is room for argument on this classification of loaded term as a species of fallacy, however, depending on what is meant by 'fallacy.' Is a fallacy a failure to support a premise adequately, or in many instances, could this be merely a blunder, error, shortcoming, or fault other than a fallacy? It depends on what you mean by 'fallacy'. According to one theory (Walton 1994), a fallacy has to be more than simply a blunder, error, or inadequately supported argument. It has to be an underlying, systematic error of the use of reasoning meeting certain requirements—generally it is a type of sophistical tactic of argumentation or a systematic, structural type of error that fools someone and he or she unwittingly falls into committing in an argument.

On this account, a problematic premise, or a failure to meet burden of proof in an argument, is not, in itself, or by itself, a fallacy. It is a weak or inadequately supported argument, and that is a critical type of failure in argumentation. But it could be simply a blunder, or generally a failure to meet burden of proof, that is not necessarily a fallacy—a fallacy being a more serious, systematic type of logical failure than just failure to prove something.

This is a general question of what 'fallacy' means that has not yet been resolved in the field of argumentation. However, unfortunately, the failure to resolve it has proved to be a continuing problem affecting the treatment of fallacies in the logic textbooks. As shown in Walton (1991, pp. 273–276), there has been an unfortunate tendency in many textbook treatments, to treat the fallacy of begging the question as being simply failure to meet a burden of proof. The origin of this tendency would appear to have been Bentham's treatment of question-begging appellatives.

8. Question-Begging Appellatives

Bentham (1824) in *The Book of Fallacies* appeared to have been the first to draw attention to the use of loaded terms in argumentation as a logical or critical defect appropriate for treatment in a logic textbook format. Bentham noted (p. 337) that begging the question was one of the fallacies listed by Aristotle but that Aristotle did not point out "the mode of using the fallacy with the greatest effect, and the least risk of detection—namely, by the employment of a single appellative." To fill the gap, Bentham introduced "the fallacy of question-begging appellative."

To see how Bentham defined his new fallacy, we have to begin by examining his doctrine that appellatives (epithets, words, and phrases) as used in language can be divided into three categories (p. 377): neutral, eulogistic, and dyslogistic, depending on commonly accepted attitudes of approval or disapproval ("general approbation or disapprobation").

Among the appellatives employed for the designation of objects belonging to the field of moral science, there are some by which the object is presented singly, unaccompanied by any sentiment of approbation or disapprobation attached to—as, *desire, labour, disposition, character, habit,* &c. With reference to the two sorts of appellatives which will come immediately to be mentioned, appellatives of this sort may be termed *neutral.*

There are others, by means of which, in addition to the principal object, the idea of general approbation as habitually attached to that object is presented—as, *industry, honour, piety, generosity, gratitude,* &c. These are terms *eulogistic* or laudatory.

Others there are, again, by means of which, in addition to the principal object, the idea of general disapprobation, as habitually attached to that object, is presented—as, *lust, avarice, luxury, covetousness, prodigality,* &c. These may be termed *dyslogistic* or vituperative.

The common tendency in argumentation, according to Bentham (p. 338) is to use dyslogistic terms to describe something if one is arguing against it and to use eulogistic terms if one is arguing for it.

But why is the use of such a practice an instance of the fallacy of begging the question? Bentham argued that it can be so classified on the grounds that the proposition in which such a eulogistic or dyslogistic term is used is really an implicit argument, with a nonexplicit premise "secretly" smuggled into it. Bentham's point of view has turned out to be influential, and the analysis upon which he based it (p. 338) is worth careful examination.

To the proposition of which it is the leading term, every such eulogistic or dyslogistic appellative, secretly, as it were, and in general insensibly, slips in another proposition of which that same leading term is the subject, and an assertion of approbation or disapprobation the predicate. The person, act, or thing in question, is *or* deserves to be, or is *and* deserves to be, an object of general approbation; or the person, act, or thing in question, is or deserves to be, or is and deserves to be, an object of general disapprobation.

The proposition thus asserted is commonly a proposition that requires to be proved. But in the case where the use of the term thus employed is fallacious, the proposition is one that is not true, and cannot be proved: and where the person by whom the fallacy is employed is conscious of its deceptive tendency, the object in the employment thus given to the appellative is, by means of the artifice, to cause that to be taken for true, which is not so.

Although Bentham gives many examples of eulogistic and dyslogistic terms, he does not work out an actual example of his analysis in detail. However, it will clarify how his analysis works to apply it to an example.

Suppose Bob and Helen are discussing a particular doctrine, and Bob uses a proposition in his discussion of the term *this heretical doctrine*. Here Bob has used a dyslogistic term, as applied to the doctrine in question. According to Bentham's analysis, Bob's statement has "secretly" slipped in another statement, namely, *This doctrine is, or deserves to be an object of general disapprobation*. In other words, Bob's asserting the first proposition tacitly commits him to asserting (or presuming) a second approval (disapproval) statement. But this approval statement "needs to be proved," according to Bentham's analysis. But if this approval statement is not true, and can't be proved, and Bob knows it, then Bob has committed a fallacy of question-begging epithet. In other words, Bob has inappropriately, and even deceptively, assumed something he was supposed to prove but did not. This sounds very much like Aristotle's fallacy of begging the question (*petitio principii*), and that is how Bentham classifies it.

Schopenhauer (1851) adopted a position very similar to Bentham's, in his *Art of Controversy*. Schopenhauer (p. 22) suggested that a widely used and effective tactic of argumentation is to choose words to describe one's position that are favorable to it, or alternatively to choose words to describe one's opponent's position that are unfavorable to it. Schopenhauer classified this tactic as a "stratagem" of argument, characterizing it as follows (pp. 22–23): "Of all the tricks of controversy, this is the most frequent, and it is used instinctively. You hear of 'religious zeal,' or 'fanaticism'; a *'faux pas,'* a 'piece of gallantry,' or 'adultery'; an 'equivocal,' or a 'bawdy' story; 'embarrassment,' or 'bankruptcy'; 'through influence and connection,' or by 'bribery and nepotism'; 'sincere gratitude,' or 'good pay.'" Another example Schopenhauer gives is this case (p. 22):

> *Case* 5.15: What an impartial man with no further purpose to serve would call "public worship" or a "system of religion," is described by an adherent, as "piety," "godliness": and by an opponent as "bigotry," "superstition."

It is easy to appreciate that this kind of tactic is indeed a common "stratagem" in everyday argumentation. But what, exactly, is wrong with it, from a logical point of view? Schopenhauer's answer (p. 22) is very similar to Bentham's.

> This is, at bottom, a subtle *petitio principii*. What is sought to be proved is, first of all, inserted in the definition, whence it is then taken by mere analysis. What one man calls "placing in safe custody," another calls "throwing into prison." A speaker often betrays his purpose beforehand by the names which he gives to things. One man talks of "the clergy"; another, of "the priests."

This answer is less explicit than Bentham's analysis, but it seems to amount to pretty much the same account. An approval or disapproval proposition (one which is "sought to be proved") is "inserted in the definition," instead of being made explicit and proved.

9. *Question-Begging Epithets*

Michalos (1970, p. 27) defines the fallacy of question-begging epithet as the use of epithets that not only describe but also evaluate an issue: "The fallacy of *question-begging epithets* is committed when, describing an issue, epithets are applied to it which not only describe it but evaluate it. Instead of introducing the issue in neutral or nonbiased terms, one introduces it using laudatory or vituperative epithets." To illustrate the fallacy, Michalos (p. 27) asks us to compare the following claims.

> *Case* 5.16: Johnson introduced a new tax bill.
>
> Johnson introduced a long-awaited and extremely needed tax bill.
>
> Johnson introduced another tax gimmick to fill the government's pockets.
>
> Quick-draw Johnson unloaded another get-rich-quick tax bill.

According to Michalos (p. 27), the last three claims not only describe an event but also evaluate it, "and the evaluation is presented as if it were a simple statement of fact." The fallacy then is a deception or pretense that a fact is only being described, when actually it is being evaluated.

There are a number of problems with this account of the fallacy of question-begging epithets. One is that the four sentences in case 5.16 do not seem to be arguments. They are in fact single propositions, with no indication of premises or a conclusion being stated or put forward.

Michalos calls them "claims," suggesting perhaps that they are conclusions. But a claim could also simply be an assertion (as opposed to an argument).

Another problem is that while the last three propositions are "evaluations," in a sense in which the first is not, there remains the question of what is wrong with making such an evaluation. Surely using such evaluative language is not, in itself, fallacious. It could be justified, in the appropriate context. In other words, it is simply not evident, in the absence of any given context for these three propositions, that the evaluation is deceptively or inappropriately presented "as if it were a simple statement of fact."

The third problem is that the fallacy of question-begging epithet is supposedly a species of question begging. Yet it is not clear why any of these three evaluative propositions begs a question, or commits the fallacy of begging the question, in the context of some argument. Begging the question, as a fallacy, implies a circular argument, where the conclusion depends on, or is equivalent to, some premise in the argument.[3] This is simply not evident in this case, for there is not enough context of conversation given to tell us what these premises and conclusions are, or might be, and how they are related in some way that clearly indicates a circle in the reasoning.

Instead of cases of the fallacy of question-begging epithet, what we have here is a set of three cases of uses of evaluative language. But there is nothing wrong or fallacious in the use of evaluative language *per se*. What is lacking is enough context for the case to show that the fallacy of begging the question has occurred. The definition of the fallacy of question-begging expression given by Damer (1980, p. 27) is very similar to the account of question-begging epithet of Michalos.

> **Definition:** This fallacy consists in discussing an issue by means of terms that imply a position on the very question at issue. Typically, certain evaluative terms or phrases are used as if they were purely descriptive terms, in such a way as to direct the listener to a particular conclusion about a situation or issue. In other words, a value judgment is presented as if it were factual.

As with Michalos, the fallacy is defined in relation to a shift from a purely descriptive type of discourse to an evaluative type of discourse.

However, the examples given by Damer, (1980, p. 28) unlike the case given by Michalos, do offer enough context to indicate why such a shift is problematic.

> *Case* 5.17: A U.S. Congressman recently sent a questionnaire to his constituents that included the question "Do you favor the give-away of the Panama Canal?" To include the expression *give-away* in such a question was very clearly an attempt to lead constituents to a particular conclusion on the issue of the Panama treaties (Damer, 1980, p. 28).

In this case, the term *give-away* does indicate a bias or slant, favoring one side of the issue. And such a bias is generally regarded as an error or fallacy in polls, statistical surveys, and referendums where a yes-no question is asked. In such cases, the context of the poll is that it is an attempt to get a true indication of support for opinions on either side of an issue. In this context, to stack the question to one side by using evaluative or loaded terms is to bias the poll. Whether such a bias is question begging is another question. At any rate, we can see why such a bias due to word selection is a kind of error or failing in a poll of this sort.

Another example given by Damer (1980, p. 27) does seem to be an instance of question begging judging by our discussion of this fallacy in connection with case 5.1.

> *Case* 5.18: Suppose that you are engaged in a discussion of the moral permissibility of abortion. One of the more important issues related to abortion is whether the fetus is to be considered a human being. If one of the discussants constantly refers to the fetus as *the baby*, he or she has begged the question on the very point at issue.

If an issue to be disputed is whether the fetus is to be considered a human being, then one side's using the term *baby* to describe the fetus is circular and question begging. For the conclusion to be proved by one side is that the fetus is human. And if that side refers to the fetus as a baby, in premises of her arguments, then she is already presuming the conclusion (which she is supposed to prove) that the fetus is human. This type of question begging is clearly a fallacy, and the context given in case 5.18 is sufficient to yield the evidence needed to show why.

However in cases 5.16 and 5.17, there is no circular reasoning in the argumentation or the kind that would properly justify our classifying either case as an instance of the fallacy of begging the question. These are just cases of slanted (loaded, biased) use of terms. We seem to have a serious confusion here between "loaded terms" and "question-begging epithet" as categories of logical fault, defect, or error. This confusion has become entrenched in the modern textbooks, as shown by Engel's treatment, compared with that of Johnson and Blair.

What Johnson and Blair call the "fallacy of loaded term" is identical to the error Engel (1982, p. 119) calls the "fallacy of question-begging epithets": "the error lies in the use of slanted language that reaffirms what we wish to prove but have not proved." Engel (p. 120) gives the following examples.

> *Case* 5.19: When one reflects on how this country's unemployment insurance program has encouraged the indolence of skid-row bums and Cadillac-driving welfare cheats, it becomes obvious that this legalized highway robbery must be revoked.

> *Case* 5.20: The councilman's shocking proposal is calculated to subvert the just aspirations of hard-working men and women.

> *Case* 5.21: No right-thinking American could support this measure, a cunning plot hatched in the smoke-filled rooms where bossism rules.

One can certainly appreciate what is objectionable or questionable in these cases. They all use terms that are slanted in an argumentative way. But why is this a fallacy? Engel's answer (p. 121) is very much like that of Johnson and Blair:

> The question-begging epithets used in these arguments are logically objectionable because they assume attitudes of approval or disapproval without providing evidence that such attitudes are justified. To call someone a "welfare cheat" or a "hard-working citizen" is not to establish that the name fits him or her; nor does calling a certain measure a "cunning plot" or "shocking" make it so.

And the same question needs to be asked: Why is "assuming attitudes of approval or disapproval without providing evidence that such attitudes are justified" a fallacy? Perhaps these attitudes are, or could be justified. And even if they have not been justified, or are not justified from the opposed point of view, why is that a fallacy?

Of course, the arguments in these three cases could be question begging in certain contexts. For example, if the issue being disputed in case 5.19 is whether this country's unemployment insurance policies are good or bad, then describing these policies as "legalized highway robbery," as in case 5.19, would beg the question (assume the truth of the thesis to be proven by the party speaking). But this is not necessarily the real (or the only legitimate) context of dialogue for case 5.19, as far as can be determined by the evidence given by Engel in his description of this case. The case, as presented, is open to other interpretations as well, as far as we know. Much the same remarks apply to the other two cases.

10. Question-Begging Definitions

Michalos (1970, p. 28) defines the *fallacy of question-begging definitions* as "committed when some essential words of a presumably factual but questionable assertion are defined in such a way that the assertion must be certain, but cannot be factual." He gives the following example (p. 28).

> *Case* 5.22: Suppose, for example, it is claimed that all farmers are slow learners. Then a man who has been farming for *ten* years comes along who, according to all tests, would be considered a fast learner. Rather than admit a *counter* or *negative instance* to the generalization, we might define "farmers" as those who have been farming for *twenty* years. When a man who has been *dairy* farming for twenty years appears to be a fast learner, we claim that dairy farming is not "really" farming at all. Similarly, the fast-learning *mink* farmer is not a "real" farmer. Little by little it becomes clear that the generalization cannot possibly have a counterinstance because the key word "farmers" is being defined and redefined to meet all challenges. That is, all farmers are slow learners because anyone who learns fast is immediately excluded from the class of farmers. The truth of the questionable empirical assertion is guaranteed by the persistent *question-begging definition* of "farmers." Therefore, while the assertion must not be questionable, it cannot be empirical either.

The fallacy in this case is a genuine fallacy of some sort, but it is a very complex kind of failure, and it is not really a species of question-begging fallacy.

In a case such as 5.22, giving a more precise definition of a term in a generalization that excludes a counterexample to the generalization is, in principle, a legitimate move in argumentation. This practice relates to the *secundum quid* fallacy, to making exceptions to a generalization, and to nonmonotonic reasoning generally.[4] In scientific argumentation, for example, it may be legitimate to define a key term in a hypothesis more precisely, in response to a falsifying or negative instance to that hypothesis, where the precising definition saves the hypothesis. However, if carried out again and again, this way of saving a hypothesis can become highly questionable. In fact, in some cases, it may be evidence that the hypothesis is not really falsifiable—and hence is not really an empirical hypothesis at all. This is the traditional problem of verifiability, or an important aspect of it. If the process of qualification by definition is too persistent, it may indicate that the hypothesis is not empirically verifiable (or falsifiable) and is, in a sense "meaningless" or a "pseudo-hypothesis."

The problem here is not one of begging the question but of a one-sided refusal to countenance legitimate counterevidence to one's claim. The problem is one of a close-minded attitude, which is inappropriate in a critical discussion, where a conflict of opinions is supposed to be resolved by balanced argumentation. The problem is that each side must take into account the reasonable arguments of the other side, by making retractions in their positions where appropriate. The necessity for these requirements of a balanced argument in a persuasion dialogue was established in chapter 2.

11. Persuasive Definitions

Many logic textbooks have a section on definitions, separate from their section on fallacies, and among the various kinds of definitions treated are persuasive definitions. A *persuasive definition,* as generally conceived in these texts, is a definition that is slanted to one side of an issue; that is, it is directed toward persuading a respondent to accept or be favorable to one point of view, as opposed to another, on some issue of contention.

Hurley (1991, p. 89) gives the following example as an exercise in his textbook (exercise 2.3, question 2).

> *Case* 5.23: "Football" means a sport in which modern-day gladiators brutalize one another while trying to move a ridiculously shaped "ball" from one end of the playing field to the other.

From this kind of example, it is easy to recognize the familiar tactic of everyday argumentation to which Hurley is drawing our attention.

But is this type of definition a fallacy? As stated above, definitions are generally treated separately from fallacies, in those texts having a section on both. And persuasive definitions are not usually categorized as fallacies.

Even so, the textbooks are generally negative in their judgments on persuasive definitions, seeing them as somehow deceptive, misleading, or dishonest. Hurley's characterization of persuasive definitions (1991, p. 88) makes this attitude evident.

> The purpose of a *persuasive definition* is to engender a favorable or unfavorable attitude toward what is denoted by the definiendum. This purpose is accomplished by assigning an emotionally charged or value-laden meaning to a word while making it appear that the word really has (or ought to have) that meaning in the language in which it is used. . . . [A] persuasive definition masquerades as an honest assignment of meaning to a term while condemning or blessing with approval the subject matter of the definiendum.

Hurley does not go into the question of why persuasive definitions are "dishonest" or "masquerading," simply commenting (p. 89) that they are "effective" as "instruments of persuasion." But this leaves us with a number of unanswered questions. If persuasive definitions are wrong or deceptive, what exactly is it that is wrong about them? Or maybe they are not wrong, if they are simply part of advocating a point of view. Or if they are only sometimes wrong, dishonest, or deceptive, how can we identify these wrong cases and separate them from cases where persuasive definitions are not wrong?

What could be wrong with using a persuasive definition, from a logical point of view, is that it may conceal deceptive shift in the meaning of a term used in an argument. An existing term already has an accepted lexical meaning in a language, and when re-defined, through a persuasive definition, that existing lexical meaning has a tendency to stay in place. Hence, there is usually an ambiguity involved when one party in dialogue uses a persuasive definition. On the one hand, the persuasive definition presents a new meaning for the term in question. But on the other hand, the old meaning may not be entirely eradicated. It may linger on. What is especially significant is that the old emotive connotations of the term may linger on. Such emotive connotations are hard to eradicate, because the term may have old associations, positive or negative, that stay in the mind of an audience. Theoretically, the term has been re-defined. But in practice, the term may still have favorable or unfavorable connotations that stay in place, at the emotional level. Such a shift can be deceptive. Although the term seems to have been given a new meaning, elements of the old meaning linger on.

Because of this deceptive shift, it may even be tempting to hypothesize that every use of a persuasive definition gives rise to a fallacy of ambiguity. The fallacy, according to this hypothesis, is that there is an equivocation between the accepted (lexical) meaning of a word, and the proposed new (persuasive) meaning. Certainly such an equivocation is possible when a persuasive definition is used. But does it have to happen in all cases? Or can persuasive definitions sometimes be reasonable? It is possible to argue that every use of a persuasive definition commits a fallacy of equivocation, by arguing that every such use takes the following general form as an argument.

> Premise 1: You (the respondent) approve (disapprove) of all things denoted by term T.

> Premise 2: Term T is redefined so that it now denotes object O.

> Conclusion: You should approve (disapprove) of object O.

This argument can be said to be an instance of the fallacy of equivocation. The reason is that the class of things denoted by term T has shifted. In premise 1, the expression 'all things denoted by term T' referred to things denoted under the given lexical meaning. But then in premise 2, there is a shift. Object O is some new thing, not covered under 'all things denoted by term T' in premise 1. This shift in meaning from premise 1 to premise 2 can be described as a fallacy of equivocation.

To see how this diagnosis of the fallacy works, consider an illustration.

> *Case* 5.24: Suppose that a speaker is giving a talk to an audience of teachers who, it is reasonable to assume, generally approves of things that would be described under the term 'education'. The speaker, however, proposes the following persuasive definition; "The true meaning of 'education' to provoke a student through discussing a con-

troversial issue so that her critical thinking abilities are brought out, and she is led to make up her own mind about the issue." It becomes evident as the speech proceeds that the purpose of this redefinition is to persuade the audience to come to accept the new teaching methods proposed by the speaker.

According to the hypothesis on persuasive definitions outlined above, the speaker is committing a fallacy of equivocation. The reason is that even though the speaker has re-defined 'education,' the old positive connotations of the term for the audience will tend to linger on. Even though they may not approve of the speaker's thesis that the process of education should be one of the teacher's provoking of critical thinking in the student, they persist, at the emotional level, in seeing anything called 'education' as being a good thing. Therefore, when the speaker redefines 'education' as process of provoking critical thinking, they are impelled towards seeing his thesis in a positive light. According to the hypothesis above then, the shift in the meaning of the term 'education' is an ambiguity. Not only that, it is a deceptive ambiguity, a shift in the meaning of the term within the speaker's argument. Therefore, the evaluation of case 5.24 should be that the speaker has committed the fallacy of equivocation, according to the hypothesis outlined above.

But there is another hypothesis that could also be used to evaluate the speaker's argumentation in case 5.24. According to this hypothesis, the speaker's legitimate aim is to persuade the audience to come to accept his thesis that education is provoking the student to critical thinking. The speaker is advocating what might be called the Socratic view of education. The purpose of his speech is to persuade the audience to accept this Socratic view. Therefore if the speaker wants to redefine 'education' as a process of provoking a student to critical thinking, he has a right to do that. After all, from his point of view "real education," the kind that is most important, is precisely this process of discussing a controversial issue to provoke the student into thinking out the issue for himself. It may be true that the term 'education' already has an accepted meaning that is different from the new Socratic meaning proposed by the speaker. But so what! If the speaker wants to redefine the term to fit the view he is advocating, he should not be accused of having committed a fallacy simply for that reason. He should have every right to argue for his own viewpoint, just as the audience has every right to argue against it, or to agree with it, however they see the issue.

What needs to be seen is that although the logic textbooks tend to be against persuasive definitions, there are fundamental questions about even the simplest cases of the use of such definitions that have not been answered. One hypothesis is that using a persuasive definition involves a shift in the meaning of a term resulting in the committing of the fallacy of equivocation. According to this hypothesis, any use of a persuasive definition is inherently ambiguous, deceptive, and fallacious. According to this hypothesis, it is best, from a logical point of view, to avoid persuasive definitions altogether in rational argumentation. According to the opposed hypothesis, an arguer should have a right to use a persuasive definition. According to this hypothesis, there is nothing inherently wrong with the use of a persuasive definition. There may be the possibility of confusion or deception, but it is up to the audience, or respondent of the argument, to make up his or her own mind on the issue. According to this hypothesis, banning persuasive definitions altogether is too strong a restriction. Which hypothesis is right? To get to the bottom of this issue, a careful analysis of how persuasive definitions work in argumentation is needed.

12. Stevenson's and Robinson's Analyses

Stevenson (1944, pp. 210–226) has given a very useful analysis of persuasive definition that explains very insightfully how this type of definition works to redirect emotions as a tactic in argumentation.[5] According to Stevenson (p. 210), the purpose of a persuasive definition is to redirect the descriptive meaning of a term without making any substantial change in its emotive meaning. By exploiting this interplay between the emotive and the descriptive meanings of a term, the definition is used to redirect people's attitudes. Stevenson gives an example (p. 211), where two parties, *A* and *B,* are discussing a mutual friend.

> *Case* 5.25: *A:* He has had but little formal education, as is plainly evident from his conversation. His sentences are often roughly cast, his historical and literary references rather obvious, and his thinking is wanting in that subtlety and sophistication which mark a trained intellect. He is definitely lacking in culture.
>
> *B:* Much of what you say is true, but I should call him a man of culture notwithstanding.

> *A:* Aren't the characteristics I mention the antithesis of culture, contrary to the very meaning of the term?
>
> *B:* By no means. You are stressing the outward forms, simply the empty shell of culture. In the true and full sense of the term, "culture" means *imaginative sensitivity* and *originality.* These qualities he has; and so I say, and indeed with no little humility, that he is a man of far deeper culture than many of us who have had superior advantages in education.

Stevenson comments (p. 211) that, in this case, *B*'s purpose was to redirect *A*'s attitudes, urging *A* to stop using 'culture' to refer to "grammatical niceties, literary allusions, and the rest" and to "use it, instead, to refer to imaginative sensitivity and originality." His purpose, on this analysis, was to redirect *A*'s attitudes, so that *A* would have a greater appreciation of the merits of the friend *A* and *B* were discussing.

Stevenson notes that persuasive definition often can be recognized by their use of words such as *true* or *real.* In case 5.25, *B* was telling us what "true" culture is, as opposed to the more superficial meaning or "shell" of culture (p. 213).

Stevenson also brings out how clever the use of persuasive definitions is, as a subtle tactic of shifting attitudes in argumentation. The shift to a new descriptive meaning leaves the emotive meaning of the word unchanged, and hence the hearer is not "sharply reminded that he was being influenced." The same word, with its same connotations, continues to be used. So the shift in the descriptive meaning, of what the word refers to, is beneath the surface. Another advantage of persuasive definition (p. 212) is that, if successful, it makes "its results permanent by embedding them in the hearer's linguistic habits." Stevenson's analysis is quite clever because it shows how persuasive definitions can tend to be misleading and deceptive, by their very nature, without condemning them as always being fallacious.

Persuasive definitions certainly can be deceptive and misleading, and although most of the logic textbooks stop short of calling them "fallacious," they are generally portrayed in a negative light. Some textbooks see them as bad or critically defective, while others hover between condemnation and acceptance. Stevenson's analysis helps to explain this suspicious and at the same time ambivalent attitude toward persuasive definitions.

Robinson (1950, pp. 169–170) sums up this ambivalence very well.

What is hard to decide is whether persuasive definition is a desirable way of trying to change people's opinions. The argument against it is that it involves error and perhaps also deceit. The only persons who are influenced by a persuasive definition, it may be said, are those who do not realize its true nature, but take it to be what every real definition professes to be, a description of the objective nature of things. A persuasive definition, it may be urged, is at best a mistake and at worst a lie, because it consists in getting someone to alter his valuations under the false impression that he is not altering his valuations but correcting his knowledge of the facts.

However, it is unwise to be too negative in condemning persuasive definitions because, as Robinson (pp. 167–168) shows, they are frequently used in famous literary and philosophical writings. When Plato asks "What is justice?" and gave his account of "the true meaning of justice" in the *Republic,* he is giving a persuasive definition (Robinson, 1950, p. 166). When Marx (p. 167) defines the "value" of a commodity as "constituted solely by the human labor contained" in it, this is a persuasive definition that contains a moral demand to redistribute goods, and it "arouses some responses in every heart." When Tolstoy (p. 168) asks "What is art?" he redefines 'art' away from the objects of art he disapproved of, in an attempt to "transvaluate" or reorient our aesthetic values. In all of these cases, we may disagree with these attempts at redefinitions of terms currently in use, but given that they are based on careful argumentation, we are reluctant to condemn them as fallacious or erroneous arguments, just because they advance persuasive definitions.

Both Stevenson and Robinson see persuasive definitions as making a normative claim, about how people ought to behave, or see things, ideally. Accordingly, Robinson proposed that persuasive definitions ought to be seen as "stipulative" rather than "real." This would rob them of their power to deceive the hearer who does not realize how his emotions are being redirected implicitly by a persuasive definition. It would make it clear to a hearer that she is free to challenge the proposed definition or to disagree with it. It would also leave the proposers of persuasive definitions free to make them, without necessarily having committed a fallacy or having made an erroneous move in argumentation. But, at the same time, it would rob persuasive definitions of their appeal, as tactics of argumentation, and of their power to persuade the unconvinced in an argument. This proposal is an insightful one that has some virtues. But in the end we will reject it.

13. Context of Use of Arguments

Using slanted language or persuasive definitions is not an obstacle to balanced reasoning in argumentation, provided it is clear to everyone that the purpose of the argument is persuasion or advocacy for one side of a particular interest or point of view. The realization of this point should be the starting point of our analysis.

In all argumentation in everyday conversation, there is a normal tendency to use language in such a way that the words and phrases are slanted toward supporting one's own point of view. It is natural to describe one's own position in terms that imply that it is right and to describe opposed positions in terms that imply that they are wrong or imperfect. Although this practice has often been condemned by textbooks on critical thinking, it is a perfectly natural and normal part of much everyday conversation. It is not, in itself, fallacious or erroneous, as a part of argumentation of the most familiar sort. Yet we can get into trouble with it sometimes, and it can lead to certain logical problems and fallacies.

This practice could be described as verbal bias, in the sense that the bias is built into the terms used. In this way, the bias is concealed in the meaning or use of words, rather than being made explicit, as a statement that something is being asserted outright to be good or bad. Even so, however, verbal bias is not inherently bad, an obstacle to resolving a conflict of opinions in a critical discussion, for example. Here we might distinguish once again between bad bias, of the kind that is obstructive to argumentation in a dialogue, and the kind of benign bias that is not, in itself, a critical defect in an argument.

A good deal of everyday argumentation is advocacy or partisan discourse, in the sense that it promotes one side only of a one- or many-sided issue. But that, in itself, as we have maintained, is not necessarily a fallacy or a critical defect in the argument. Only in some cases have we judged advocacy dialectically inappropriate in the sense that it blocks a dialogue or becomes a critical problem so that some normative standard of goodness of the argument is not met. And so with these one-sided uses of words and phrases in verbal bias. They are slanted or biased with respect to the conversation of which they are a part. But this slant or bias is normal, expected, and unproblematic, or so we should often judge, by the standards of chapters 3 and 4.

We rightly expect a critical discussion to examine the arguments on both sides of an issue. But a critical discussion has advocacy of opposed arguments on both sides. We expect a participant in a critical discussion to put up the strongest advocacy arguments she can, those that support her own point of view, and those that criticize or go against the opposed point of view. So how we judge argumentation as biased or not should depend on the dialectical framework in which the argument is supposed to be placed (see figure 5.2), according to the new theory of bias.

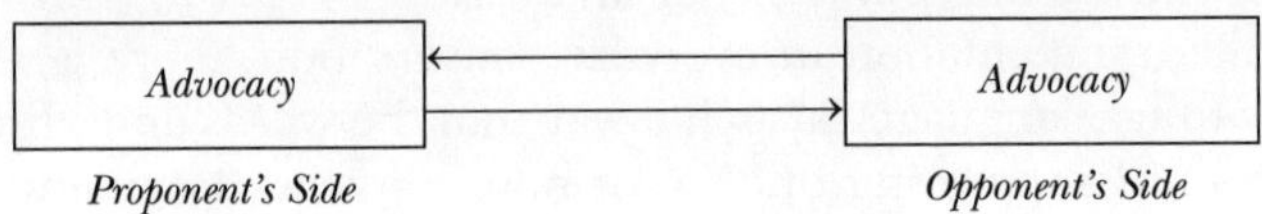

Figure 5.2.

If a salesman in a car showroom is showing you a new car you are thinking of buying, you expect him to present an advocacy argument designed to get you to buy the car. If you read *Consumers Reports,* your expectations are (and should be) quite different. The report on this model of car should give you negative as well as positive information on the qualities, features, and judgments on whether or not the car is a "best buy."

Negotiation is an interest-based type of dialogue, where one expects an arguer to try to define the terms and framework of an argument in language that is favorable to her own side. By contrast, in a scientific research investigation that is supposed to take the form of an inquiry, it could be a serious bias, subject to criticism, to define a term in a way that is "friendly" to getting favorable results, especially if other researchers have or might use or define the term another way, getting (not surprisingly) different results. This defeats the goal of reproducibility of experimental results.

The upshot is that when we turn to an evaluation of loaded terms or persuasive definitions, we should judge them as having a harmful kind of bias or not, in relation to how the language is used in a context of conversation or dialogue in which two parties are involved.

14. Uses of Slanted Terms

Our recommendation on *loaded term* (or *slanted term* or *biased term*) is that it be defined exactly as Johnson and Blair define it but that it not generally be considered a fallacy. It should only be considered an obstacle or problem in argumentation, and subject to critical questioning or correction, if the context of dialogue is one where such a slanted use of language is inappropriate. Generally, this problem is deceptive or is dialectically harmful because there has been a shift from one type of dialogue to another. In such a case, the appropriate question that needs to be asked is: In what type of dialogue was this argument supposed to have been put forward (according to what is known of its context of use in the given case)?

Once we start paying serious attention to such dialectical contexts of use, it can be seen that careful attention needs to be paid to questions such as the following. If the argument was put forward in a critical discussion, then what conflict of opinions was supposed to be resolved by the discussion? Once this has been clarified, in a given case, we can distinguish between arguments containing question-begging epithets and those using terms that are loaded or slanted to one side, but not in a way that is question begging.

The use of the term *anti-choice* in the letter in case 5.2 is not fallacious (as things stand). From the tone of the letter, which could be described as defensive to the point of quarrelsomeness, it sounds like 'antichoice' reflects the point of view expressed in the letter. The so-called antichoice groups are described as "aggressive" and "out to have their beliefs supersede the right of each woman to control her own body and destiny." Certainly, from the point of view being expressed by the letter writer, these antichoice groups are made up of very bad people.

However, this letter is not meant to be, nor should it be supposed to be, an unbiased critical discussion of the abortion issue, representing the views of both sides fairly. It is in fact an action letter, a plea for funds to support the interests of one side, despite the letter writer's pose in one sentence as a "journalist" who is "commenting" on the issue "as accurately as possible." If the letter is supposed to be a journalistic presenting of "news" or information in a nonadvocacy sort of article or a critical discussion of the issue representing both sides accurately and fairly, then we could be justified in judging that the use of the term *antichoice* to refute the view of the opposition by making the position of its members appear extreme and negative (in a way to which they themselves would clearly object) is an instance of the straw man fallacy.

So it depends on what the purpose of the letter is, or can rightly be supposed to be. If it is a plea for funds to support the interests of a group, then the slanted language used is not fallacious or critically biased in a bad sense that interferes with the argumentation in the letter.

However, the "prolife" side would clearly object to its argument being described, or even defined characteristically as "antichoice," and it has a right to object to this label. So in any critical discussion between the two opposed points of view, it would be quite appropriate for this side to object to the other side's use of the phrase *antichoice* as biased language, an unduly negative way of defining or describing its viewpoint.

However, the basic problem with the notion of vituperative and laudatory epithets introduced by Bentham and Schopenhauer is the tendency to define all uses of such slanted terms as fallacious. Although the use of such terms reflects a slant or bias, in many cases this bias may be appropriate to reflect a point of view being advocated in an admittedly partisan way. Moreover, even where such bias is inappropriate and subject to questioning or criticism, it is not necessarily the case that the bias is so bad or is a systematic error or specific tactic of deception of the kind of which it is correct to say it is fallacious or a fallacy (like begging the question, for example).

Where Michalos' description is right, that "an evaluation is presented as if it were a simple statement of fact,"[6] there has been a shift from one type of discourse to another and it is appropriate to say that there is a bias or slant of the kind that is a critical failure in the argument. If the shift is concealed or deceptive, it could even be right to conclude that the bias is of the bad or negative kind that interferes with the type of dialogue in which the speaker was supposed to be engaged.

The problem in the textbook treatments generally in this area is one of fallacy inflation. In cases 5.19, 5.20, and 5.21, for example, there is very definitely slanted use of language, indicating a bias on the part of the speaker. But is this bias a bad bias that interferes with the correctness of the speaker's argumentation on an issue? We simply are not given enough context, in any of these three cases, to make a reasoned judgment, one way or the other. In the absence of evidence then, we must not presume to conclude that the speaker has given evidence of a bad bias or has committed some sort of fallacy. Of course, given the use of such biased language, it could be that the speaker is putting forward an argument that commits the fallacy of begging the question. But we do not have sufficient evidence to reach that conclusion in these cases.

15. Handling Persuasive Definitions

Our recommendation on how to handle persuasive definitions in argumentation is quite different from that of either Robinson or that of Copi and Cohen. The best way to handle persuasive definitions is to view them as a distinct, and in principle legitimate type of definition in their own right. This means that they should not be treated as if they were stipulative definitions, as Robinson recommends, and they should not be treated as inherently fallacious, as Copi and Cohen recommend. Instead, we propose that they should be treated as a legitimate type of definition in their own right, but a contestable type, that is, open to criticism, questioning, counterargumentation, and even, in some cases, refutation. Indeed, we even go so far as to say that, in some cases, they can be judged reasonably to be fallacious.

Advocacy is a distinct context of argumentation in its own right. Advocacy, *per se*, is not inherently bad or fallacious, although, to be sure, it can be excessive in context. Advocacy in a critical discussion, for example, has to be restrained by the rules and requirements or the various stages of the discussion.

A persuasive definition should be seen as a definition that advocates a particular viewpoint in argument, and as such, it should be appropriate for someone who does not share that viewpoint to question the definition and to demand that it be supported by argument or given up. Moreover, a critic should have the right not to accept the definition, or even to propose an alternative definition that conflicts with it. This way of seeing persuasive definitions is a new viewpoint on them that stresses that they have a legitimate function in argumentation, at least when properly and appropriately used. Of course, it should be clear, in a given case, how the definition is being used to support an argument, in a context of dialogue. And this factor seems to be the source of the problem.

Perhaps the reaction against persuasive definitions as inherently illegitimate stems from a positivistic attitude that any attempt at persuasion, or advocating a point of view by using language with argumentative connotations, is inherently partisan and therefore subjective and unscientific. However, it is our contention here that advocacy is not inherently bad or fallacious in itself in persuasion dialogue.

Persuasive definitions should not be seen as something bad, fallacious, or inherently suspicious, but as a normal part of persuasion dialogue. The kind of case where a persuasive definition should be treated as fallacious or dubious is one where there has been a dialectical shift so the definition is not what it really appears to be in context. Thus Robinson's solution of treating persuasive definitions as though they were stipulative can be seen as too limiting and drastic a way of treating them generally. For a persuasive definition should be looked at as a distinctive type of definition in its own right that has its proper place, when overtly used as such in a persuasion dialogue. It is only when it purports to be a lexical definition, or some other kind of definition that is not subject to reply to by an opposing persuasive definition representing the point of view of the other side that it is fallacious or subject to suspicion because it is deceptive and illegitimate.

The postmodernist argument on behalf of persuasive definitions is that lexical definitions, which report customary usage of words in natural language, already have connotations built into them. So they are argumentative in nature, at least implicitly, and are not value-free. So why, goes this argument, should we not have the right to replace the lexical meaning of such a word with a new persuasive definition? This argument has a point, but it also conceals a problem. For lexical definitions do report or reflect usage and so can be verified by empirical data measuring the intuitions of native speakers. So with a lexical definition, there is an objective basis for telling us what the correct lexical meaning should be or should not be. A persuasive definition is different, because it is inherently subject to argument. A respondent in a dialogue can accept or reject a persuasive definition, but an empirical, linguistic survey, an appeal to common usage or to the native speaker's intuition, will not resolve the question of whether the persuasive definitions are more like stipulative definitions. They are put up for acceptance, and if the respondent accepts them, then they are acceptable in the dialogue, and that is, at least for the moment, the end of the matter.

Still, the point is rightly made that lexical definitions themselves are not value-free, and therefore they do have a persuasive aspect, so to speak. They do direct people to specific courses of action as approved or disapproved. Because they have this directive function, they do have a persuasive aspect built into them, certainly in many cases.

So the postmodernist is right in thinking that we do have a right to question traditional terms and to put up new terms or new persuasive definitions in their place. Where the postmodernist approach goes wrong is by implying that there is no basis for questioning or rejecting the new persuasive definitions advocated "for a good cause," on the grounds that one definition is as good as another because all are equally biased. A persuasive definition is really advocacy of a particular position, and as such, it should be open to critical doubt and challenge.

A persuasive definition is a tool of advocacy, and as such, it has the legitimate function of defining terms in order to support one's point of view in an argument. If the context is that of the eristic dialogue, or its subspecies, the quarrel, there is very little in the way of restraint on advocating one's own point of view. However, if the context is that of a critical discussion, one must always put forward one's argumentation in a way that leaves it open to critical questioning or even defeat (refutation), if evidence strong enough to refute it is brought forward by the opposing side.

For example, in case 5.1, when the prolife side brings forward the definition of 'abortion' as "murdering of defenseless human beings," that move in the argument is not illegitimate or fallacious *per se*, provided the other side in the critical discussion or debate has a right to put forward arguments giving objections to it or even proposing an alternative (and opposed) definition. Then both sides can argue out which definition is better, agree on some other definition, or simply concede that they are using the same word to mean different things. Hence, according to this analysis of the argumentation in case 5.1, there is no fallacy in it, nor is the suppositional entertaining of the two opposed persuasive definitions of 'abortion' by the letter writer an objectionable argument or a failure of logic or critical reasoning.

A similar analysis applies to case 5.9. The redefinition of 'pornography' is a persuasive definition put forward to support the interests and point of view of a particular advocacy group (women).

It would seem that by the Copi and Cohen test, for example, this definition would come out as fallacious on the grounds that it commits a fallacy of ambiguity by shifting from the lexical definition of pornography to a quite different definition. And according to Robinson's analysis, it should be seen as a stipulative definition. So any attempt to portray it as otherwise by its defenders would be illicit or fallacious.

But what if we see this case as an instance of a persuasive definition that is, in principle, acceptable as a kind of legitimate definition, even though it is argumentative, being used as part of an advocacy type of discourse? It is no longer a fallacy, nor is it objectionable on purely logical grounds, as long as it does not pretend to be something it is not. Since there is no contextual evidence of misuse in case 5.9, we conclude that the persuasive definition used in this case is nonfallacious.

Then on this analysis a persuasive definition like the one given in case 5.9 should be judged fallacious or an obstruction to a dialogue only if it is presented in certain ways, as shown by the evidence from the discourse. Suppose, for example, Bob and Helen are having a critical discussion on the issue of pornography, and Bob replies to Helen's presentation of the definition given in case 5.9 as follows.

> *Case* 5.26: **Bob:** Well, I object to this definition as unfairly biased toward one side only. Don't women now have magazines that portray men as sex ob-

> jects? This is surely pornography in my sense of the word, and in the conventional, lexical sense. I think we need a definition that can accommodate these facts.
>
> **Helen:** Don't you realize that women are dying now because of your way of defining 'pornography'? Anyone who does not accept my definition hates women and is a bigot, sexist and insensitive!

In this case, it is not the original definition that is critically problematic or that blocks the progress of a critical discussion on the issue. It is the closure of the definition to a hardened advocacy, a dogmatic kind of move that refuses to allow critical questioning or to concede the possibility of an opposed or alternate point of view, even for the sake of argument. Here then is a critically problematic use of a persuasive definition, as indicated by the discourse in Helen's speech when she replies to Bob's objection.

If the context of dialogue in this case was that of eristic dialogue or quarreling, or if the conversation were purely a vehicle for Helen's advocacy point of view, then there would be no fallacy or critical failure of her argument to promote her definition of 'pornography'. However, presuming that the dialogue is supposed to be a critical discussion, open to viewpoints on both sides, the evaluation of the use of biased language is quite different.

This aspect of the use of definitions in a context of continuing dialogue was nicely brought out by case 5.22, Michalos's case of the arguer who keeps redefining 'farmer' creatively so that it meets all challenges. The problem in this case is that the arguer keeps redefining 'farmer' to defeat all counterexamples and objections to his claim that all farmers are slow learners.

The problem here is not that the definition is question begging. It is that the man's argument, which is supposed to be an empirical argument, we are told, is made immune to criticism or questioning through a sequence of redefinitions that takes it farther and farther away from the conventional, lexical definition of 'farmer'. The problem is that the man's sequence of argument, as revealed in the context of the dialogue in this case, is closed to arguments representing any skeptical or opposed point of view. It is one-sided argument used in a context where balanced argumentation is to be expected and would be appropriate.

Notes

1. See Walton (1989a, pp. 243–250).

2. This same case is cited in Copi and Cohen (1990, p. 138), under the heading "Persuasive Definitions."

3. Walton (1991).

4. Walton (1992b, pp. 75–80 and 282–284).

5. According to Robinson (1950, p. 168), it was Stevenson who introduced the idea of persuasive definition. Robinson, quite rightly, comments that Stevenson's analysis of it was "brilliantly set out" in Stevenson's book, *Ethics and Language.*

6. See the discussion of case 5.16, above.

CHAPTER SIX

ARGUMENTS IN SALES AND ADVERTISING

This chapter poses a theoretical question for the study of bias that turns out to be quite difficult to answer. Yet the question will not go away, because it is ubiquitous in studying cases where bias is alleged and has very wide and significant implications. The question is whether the kind of argumentation commonly encountered in sales and advertising dialogue—typified by a conversation between a salesman and a potential buyer in a new car showroom or by the kind of discourse used to promote a product in a television commercial—is of a type that should properly fit contextually into one of the known normative models of dialogue outlined in chapter 2.

This question was prompted by the presentation of some new research work in the field of artificial intelligence that has the goal of modeling dialogue between a computer and a user. The example of a dialogue chosen for modeling was that of a car salesman who is attempting to persuade a potential customer to buy a car.[1] It will be the conclusion of this chapter that the argumentation in this type of encounter, despite its down-to-earth ordinariness in some respects, is extremely complex, when one tries to pin down what sort of general normative structure it exhibits as a goal-directed type of conversational exchange. It will be argued here that it is a composite mosaic, rather than a single type of dialogue.

One problem posed specifically by this kind of dialogue concerns the status of the argumentation put forward by the salesman or the advertiser. It can be described as advocacy, and therefore, according to the analysis given in chapter 3, one would be correct to describe it as argumentation containing a bias—a bias to promote or sell the product. But is this a bad or harmful bias, in the sense that the argument is open to

157

criticism? Or is it an acceptable kind of bias that is normal and appropriate in the kind of dialogue or conversational exchange of which it is a part?

This turns out to be a surprisingly difficult theoretical question to answer decisively. But our attempt to answer it will throw interesting light on the concepts of advocacy and bias in commercial speech.

This theoretical question also has some very practical implications for informal logic. For in the sections on fallacies in the logic textbooks, many of the examples of arguments cited as fallacies are in fact cases of dialogue from sales and advertising. This treatment seems to imply that arguments used in sales and advertising can be criticized routinely as logically faulty, presumably on grounds that they are biased and that the bias they exhibit is of the harmful sort that violates normative standards of a successful conversational exchange of some kind. The logic texts, as we will see illustrated below, tend to condemn such commercial arguments as fallacious on the grounds that they "fail to present relevant evidence," and so forth, implying a failure to meet high standards of burden of proof and presentation of information and evidence appropriate for, say, a critical discussion or an information-seeking, or advice-giving type of dialogue. In this chapter it will be questioned whether such a standard is an appropriate one for television commercials and sales exchanges.

So here we have some very practical, down-to-earth questions for informal logic. Are these examples of admittedly biased arguments rightly condemned by the textbook treatments as logically deficient on the grounds that they fail to meet a normative standard of dialogue, like that of persuasion dialogue, for such a case? And, if not, what is the normative framework appropriate to judge the argumentation in such a case as fallacious or not?

1. The Standard Treatment

As Hamblin (1970, chapter 1) pointed out, the textbook treatment of fallacies has tended to be superficial, because serious scholarly investigation of this branch of logic has been systematically neglected. Although it is good that the study of fallacies has retained some place in the logic curriculum in the textbooks, the basis of evaluation of many of the examples treated tends to be questionable. Instead of giving an analysis of why a particular example falls short of some clear standard of correctness, too often the textbooks condemn arguments as fallacious without much analysis or explanation, just presuming that the reader will agree that the example appears offensive, objectionable, or dubious.[2]

But not all arguments that appear offensive or objectionable commit logical fallacies. Generally, according to the account in Walton (1995), to be evaluated as fallacious, a text of discourse in a given case must (a) contain an argument and (b) it must be an argument that falls short of some normative standard of correctness, and (c) the normative standard in question must be appropriate for that argument, as it occurred in the given case.[3]

Arguments can be objectionable for all kinds of reasons. They can be in bad taste, they can be illegal, they can violate ethical standards, they can be offensive to specific groups or individuals; they can be annoying, repetitive, impolite, and so forth. None of these deficiencies is exactly the same as the fault of being fallacious, however.[4] Hence when the textbooks make the leap of condemning an argument as fallacious simply because it (quite rightly) is objectionable or bad, for some unspecified reason, it is a questionable inference.

Looking through the textbook sections on fallacies, one sees that a good number of the examples classified as fallacies of one type or another are commercial advertisements and sales pitches. Some books stress this type of case quite heavily.

Kahane (1992) has a whole chapter on advertising, indicting many commercial advertisements of products of committing various logical fallacies. Celebrity endorsements of products in commercials are said to be instances of the fallacy of *appeal to authority,* for example, Ray Charles and Joe Montana choosing Diet Pepsi over Coke (p. 195). Kahane goes on (p. 198) to accuse commercial advertisements of committing a wide range of fallacies.

> Ads also frequently are guilty of *suppressing evidence.* They tell us the good features of products and almost always hide their warts. (Why should they do otherwise?) *Example:* Ads for the Tylenol brand of acetaminophen, for Bayer aspirin, and for other brand-name painkillers don't mention that drugstore and supermarket brands sell for much less and are pharmaceutically identical.
>
> Advertising audiences also are invited to make *faulty comparisons.* *Example:* Ads for Kraft Cheese Slices that compare this second-rate product to third- and even fourth-rate processed cheeses (but never with any of the many truly excellent cheeses).
>
> Of course, advertisements run the range of fallacies, challenging theorists to invent pigeonholes into which to put them all. How, for

instance should we categorize the fallacious reasoning that leads people to be swayed by endlessly repeated, mostly empty, slogans? *Examples:* "Magnavox. Smart. Very smart." "Nike: Just do it." "Nobody beats Midas. Nobody." "The World's Greatest Newspaper" (that's the *Chicago Tribune,* by the way). "I love what you do for me, Toyota." And so on, *ad* infinitum.

One certainly can be sympathetic to these criticisms. We are inundated with these ads in our daily lives, and some of them are loud, offensive, and annoying. But does not Kahane seem to be going a little too far in condemning them as arguments that fail to live up to some pretty lofty standards?

As Kahane himself admits, why should the Tylenol ads not "present the good features of their products" and "hide their warts"? Would we reasonably expect a commercial to stress all the bad features of a product, and not mention any of the good features? Wouldn't this defeat the whole purpose of the commercial? Should we expect or require that Tylenol ads should function like *Consumer Reports,* telling the viewer objectively which painkiller is a *best buy,* according to their comparative tests of all the products available? Or does this standard seem somehow unreasonable and inappropriate for a commercial advertisement?

And why should we fault Kraft for failing to compare its product with that of some other cheese that might be much better? It would seem pretty silly of them to do this or of us to expect them to do it, would it not? After all, Kraft is trying to promote its own product, not that of its competitors.

It is certainly true that these ads exhibit a bias in their blatant advocacy of one side of a case. But is that bias not exactly what one would expect in a commercial?

With the remaining examples that Kahane mentions—the various slogans—it is not even clear that these are arguments—or, if they are arguments of some sort, what their premises and conclusions are. But if they are not clearly identified as arguments, then it is premature to declare that they are fallacious arguments, or biased arguments, meaning bias in the harmful sense. Although they may be "empty slogans" and perhaps not very informative, is it right to categorize them as fallacies, as Kahane does, claiming that they exhibit "fallacious reasoning"? Instead, this approach seems to be a blanket condemnation of advertising as fallacious, by a general presumption of guilt, even before examining particular cases.

Let us go on to examine a few cases where ads or sales pitches are criticized in the textbooks for committing specific fallacies, without by any means trying to cover all the fallacies at issue or all the textbooks that use this type of case.

2. Appeal to Pity

Several logic textbooks offer examples of the *argumentum ad misericordiam,* the fallacy of appeal to pity[5] that are cases of sales dialogue. Rescher (1964, p. 79) defines the *ad misericordiam* as the type of argument where the premises make an "appeal to pity" to "secure acceptance" of the conclusion and gives the following example (p. 79):

> *Case* 6.1:   These brooms are of fine quality and you'll be very satisfied with the one you buy, Lady. I've got a sick wife at home, and four kids, and I've got to sell at least ten each day to make ends meet.

The fallacy in such a case, according to Rescher, is that the proponent tries to move the respondent to sympathy, "rather than showing actual evidence" (Rescher 1964, p. 79) for the conclusion claimed.

Frye and Levi (1969, p. 221) describe the *argumentum ad misericordiam* as a fallacy that works by addressing pity or sympathy as an irrelevant basis for a conclusion. They give the following case (p. 221).

> *Case* 6.2:   The man who comes to the door with a product to sell may avoid discussing the merits of his article or the housewife's need for it, and instead tell a story designed to arouse pity for himself.

The use of this case, similar to the one given by Rescher, implies that the salesman has a claim or conclusion to be argued for, that the brooms are of "fine quality," or that the article for sale, whatever it is, has "merits." The presumption is then that in a sales dialogue of this type, the seller has a burden of proof. He has a claim or conclusion he is supposed to prove by means of an argument, and his argument is good or reasonable to the extent he can successfully prove this proposition by presenting actual, relevant evidence that backs it up.

To the extent he uses appeal to pity or other emotions or considerations not relevant or sufficient, as good evidence to prove his conclusion, the salesman may be judged to be engaging in inappropriate, irrelevant, and fallacious argumentation. At least this is the presumption behind the use of these examples of the fallacious appeal to pity.

But is this not demanding quite a high standard of correct argument that the salesman's presentation should have to meet in order to be charged with committing a fallacy? Could not an appeal to pity, or at least to sympathy or compassion, be somewhat relevant to the salesman's argument—perhaps a minor but not altogether irrelevant consideration—if the woman is deciding whether to buy the product from him or the same product at the same price from a store? It is not relevant to the merits of the product, but is that the only or complete and sufficient reason in every case for deciding whether or not to buy something?

Of course, an overly dramatic, false, or deceptive appeal to pity could be irrelevant or faulted on other logical grounds as a bad argument. But is any use of appeal to compassion or sympathy wholly out of place or inherently fallacious as an argument?

And what about the criticism that the salesman's argument is a fallacious appeal to pity because it fails to show "actual evidence" for the conclusion that the product has merits or is of good quality? If the woman does not ask for such evidence, is the salesman's argument fallacious if he fails to include it? This ruling seems a little harsh. Perhaps she is already familiar with the product and requires no convincing of its merit or would not believe the salesman if he tried to argue for it anyway. However, there is a difference between case 6.1 and case 6.2 on this point. In case 6.2, the salesman "may avoid discussing the merits of his article," while in case 6.1, the subject is not "avoided," at least as far as we are told.

It is argued in Walton (1992c) that appeals to emotion, such as sympathy and compassion, should not be judged inherently fallacious, in every case where they occur. Hamblin (1970, p. 43) concurs that where "a proposition is presented primarily as a guide to action, . . . it is not so clear that pity and other emotions are irrelevant." None of this is to deny that some appeals are outrageously fallacious, however. But the question is whether sales presentations fall into this category, and if so, why.

Soccio and Barry (1992, p. 135) give some specific reasons.

> Salespeople are fond of appeals to pity, particularly in selling life and health insurance. It's not surprising. After all, if a pitiful picture is painted of a provider's children scratching around for food and clothes in the absence of the provider, the person is likely to take out some life or health insurance. The beauty of such an appeal is that it makes a person live with guilt *before the fact*. The pitches for

purchasing a "preneed" burial plot work the same angle. It's tough for people to live with the guilt of making their loved ones scurry around making funeral arrangements for them, so why not arrange for all that "before the time comes"? In that way people can presumably just sit back and enjoy your funeral.

Here we are talking about psychological tactics used in sales presentations to exploit emotions such as fear, pity, or guilt. These tactics are what Johnson and Blair (1983, p. 247) call "creative strategies" or *gimmicks,* attention-getting devices with a "persuasive hook," designed to create a climate or ambiance that is favorable for a product.

But, as Johnson and Blair point out, criticizing sales presentations that use such gimmicks just on the grounds that they make an emotional appeal or use psychological strategies is somewhat naive.[6] For that is exactly what the advertising firms are trying to do, and everybody knows it (or at least, reasonably well-informed viewers are normally quite well aware of this). We ought to have reservations about condemning sales presentations as logically fallacious in a blanket way, simply because they use psychology to sell a product. Yes they have a bias, but we should not leap to a blanket condemnation of all such arguments purely on this basis.

3. Appeal to Popularity

Some reservations about the citing of certain types of television commercials as fallacious already have been indicated in Walton (1989a, pp. 84–85). A particular type of example often cited as an instance of the *ad populum* fallacy in logic textbooks is illustrated by the following case (Walton 1989a, p. 84).

> *Case* 6.3:　A television commercial for life insurance portrays a scene of a happy, handsome family having a picnic on a river bank. They are fishing in the river and generally having a good time together. The commercial message is a series of slogans about happy family life, including phrases like "peace of mind today" and "security for the future." The insurance company is described as a place where the family and the insurance agent can "work things out together." No mention is made of the types of policies available, the interest rates paid on these pol-

> icies, or other specifics for anyone interested in shop-
> ping for the best insurance coverage at reasonable rates.

This case would be cited routinely as an instance of the *ad populum* fallacy by the standard treatment of the textbooks (Hamblin, 1970, chapter 1) on the grounds that the message has failed to present any useful information about the specific clauses, benefits, costs, and other particulars of the policies advertised. The criticism of the ad, which is at the basis of calling it a fallacy, is that it substitutes a folksy, emotional, popular appeal for relevant information useful to the consumer.

But, as noted in Walton (1989a, p. 85), the insurance company that ran the ad, if confronted with this criticism, would probably reply that the purpose of the ad is not to present factual information about costs, interest rates, and specific coverage of the policies. The time to go into these questions is during a conversation with the company's representative. The purpose of the ad is only to draw attention to the company's product and present it in a positive light, so that a consumer will want to inquire further into it.[7] Thus the emotional appeal to popular sentiments or values, perceived as positive in the consumer's eyes, is not a fallacious cover-up or deception. It is what the message is, quite properly, all about.

One of the most widely used logic textbooks for many years contains an outstanding passage that is vitriolic in its condemnation of advertisers as fallacy committers.

Copi (1986, p. 96) defines the *argumentum ad populum* as the fallacy committed by "the attempt to win popular assent to a conclusion by arousing the emotions and enthusiasms of the multitude rather than by appeal to the relevant facts." Describing this fallacy as a "favorite device with the propagandist, the demagogue, and the advertiser" (p. 96), Copi is particularly severe in his condemnation of the latter for committing it.

> It is to the huckster, the ballyhoo artist, the twentieth-century adver
> tiser that we may look to see the *argumentum ad populum* elevated
> almost to the status of a fine art. Here every attempt is made to set
> up associations between the product being advertised and objects
> of which we can be expected to approve strongly. To eat a certain
> brand of processed cereal is proclaimed a patriotic duty. To bathe
> with a certain brand of soap is described as a thrilling experience.
> Strains of symphonic music precede and follow the mention of a
> certain toothpaste on the radio and television programs sponsored
> by its manufacturer. In pictorial advertisements, the people using

the products advertised are always pictured as wearing the kind of clothing and living in the kind of houses calculated to arouse the approval and admiration of the average consumer. The young men pictured as delightedly using the products are clear-eyed and broad-shouldered, the older men are invariably "of distinction." The women are all slim and lovely, either very well dressed or hardly dressed at all. Whether you are interested in economical transportation or in quiet comfort on the road, you will be assured by each automobile manufacturer that his product is "best," and he will "prove" his assertion by displaying his car surrounded by pretty girls. Advertisers "glamorize" their products and sell us daydreams and delusions of grandeur with every package of pink pills or garbage disposal unit.[8]

To do justice to Copi's textbook, it should be said that it is generally one of the best and gives a much better balanced and careful treatment of the fallacies than many of the other texts. But one can see how difficult it is to resist the tendency to take advantage of the students' tendency to chortle at all the heavy-handed attempts of commercials to exploit "role models" and "peer pressure" to promote their products. We are all so familiar with these commercials in our daily life and so cynical about them that any condemnation of them in front of a student audience is assured to meet with sympathy and enthusiastic approval.

And, of course, appealing to popular acceptance or approval is generally a defeasible type of argumentation that often turns out to be erroneous as an argument and is subject to exploitation as a sophistical tactic.[9] But can we say that advertisements commit the *ad populum* fallacy on a blanket basis, simply because they try to show attractive people using their product or because they associate the product with people or things that are generally approved? Is using "clear-eyed and broad-shouldered men" in a commercial fallacious, because it "glamorizes" the product?

Once again, it comes back to the issue of what type of communicative exchange the advertisement is supposed to be about. Is it supposed to give us information about the cereal or toothpaste advertised? Is it supposed to convince us by rational argumentation, on the merits, that this is the best product, the best buy, or the most nutritious or healthy product for a specific purpose? Is it supposed to be a balanced critical discussion of the evidence both for and against the values of this product as opposed to its competitors?

Or are these goals too lofty and unrealistic? Is not the real purpose simply to sell the product, to try to get the consumer to buy it? After all, the advertising firms go by the "bottom line" and for practical purposes use or drop commercials on the basis of whether or not they appear to increase sales of the product. And, certainly, advertisements have to meet ethical standards of decency, standards that are in fact enforced, if not always in ways that we like. But should they also have to meet logical standards of freedom from bias and selectivity of evidence, so that any commercial that fails to convince the viewer that the product advertised the best buy, based on relevant, actual evidence that proves this claim, can be condemned as a fallacious argument?

4. Suppressed Evidence

Hurley (1991, p. 149) defines *the fallacy of suppressed evidence* as committed where an argument that presents evidence for a conclusion ignores stronger evidence that supports a different conclusion.[10] Hurley (p. 148) gives the following example, quoted as case 6.4 below.

Case 6.4:   Example:

> *Used car salesman to buyer:* Mrs. Webb, I have just the car you need. This 1978 Chevrolet was recently traded in by a little old lady who kept it in the garage most of the time. The odometer reads low mileage, and the engine was recently tuned up. If you buy this car, it will give you trouble-free service for years.
>
> Mrs. Webb accepts the salesman's argument and buys the car, only to have it fall apart two months later. Unfortunately, the salesman had failed to tell her that whenever the car was not in the garage the little old lady was driving it cross-country, that the odometer had rolled around twice, and that even though the engine was recently tuned up, it had two cracked pistons and a burned valve. By suppressing this evidence, the salesman made it appear that Mrs. Webb was getting a good deal, whereas in fact she was getting a pile of junk for her money.

Here, one can debate the ethics of the case. The salesman has (presumably) acted unethically by failing to inform Mrs. Webb about the cracked pistons and burned valve. In some jurisdictions, he has also probably

166

broken the law. He has lied about the mileage, and by giving wrong information about the odometer, he has probably committed a crime.

However, these ethical defects and lies are not necessarily fallacies or logical faults of biased argumentation. Ethical and legal guidelines on commercial speech are at issue. Some would argue that everyone knows it is "Buyer beware!" when buying a used car and that it should be up to Mrs. Webb to have the car inspected by an independent mechanic (preferably one she knows and trusts) before buying the car. One could even argue that she was imprudent and careless in not doing so and that this, itself, is a sort of ethical or prudential deficiency.

Whatever is the right ethical point of view on this issue, it seems that the trend in law is increasingly toward making the vendor responsible for informing the buyer of all aspects (including known defects) of the item sold. This trend is a development that the textbooks appear to be supporting, and that, presumably, their readers can be counted on to approve.

But is it good grounds for making the salesman guilty of having committed a logical fallacy in his argument in this case by "ignoring evidence," or for making him guilty of a harmful bias in his argument?

To impose such a criticism puts quite a strong requirement of adequacy on the salesman's argument. It must "tell the whole truth," so to speak.[11] It must present enough of the relevant evidence in its premises for its conclusion so that no stronger evidence supporting any other conclusion is omitted. It must be balanced, in the sense of presenting all the relevant evidence on both sides of the issue. This is quite a strong requirement of balance for an argument to meet. Should the salesman's argument have to meet this standard in order to qualify as nonfallacious?

Of course, leaving out relevant evidence would be an indicator of selection bias, of the kind identified in chapter 4. Using this indicator, we could say that the salesman's argument exhibited an indicator of bias, because it failed to mention facts that were relevant to the case. Thus the salesman's argumentation was biased.

But is this bias a bad bias, in the sense that it is a defect in his argumentation, as a contribution to the talk exchange in which he was engaged? Even if you look at his argument from the point of view of a persuasion dialogue, it may be hard to see this bias as a critical defect, error or fallacy in his argument. For, after all, he is supposed to be engaged in advocacy or pro-argumentation for his point of view. He is not obliged to point out arguments for the other side.

If Mrs. Webb were to consider buying the car and then go to an independent mechanic, consumer's bureau, or car inspection depot, for expert advice on the car's roadworthiness and value, then certainly, in this advice-giving dialogue, the expert would have an obligation to meet a two-sided standard of balance and relevance of evidence. But is it appropriate to impose this same standard of balanced argument on the salesman?

Some would argue that such an imposition would be inappropriate and unduly harsh and restrictive because the salesman is not supposed to be a consumer advocate, who presents all the evidence on both sides in a balanced and objective way. This portrayal is an overly idealistic and unrealistic distortion of his role in this type of exchange. Everyone knows that the salesman, and the dealership, and the manufacturer he represents are basically in business to sell their product and make their income from doing so. They are an "interest group," so to speak, with a bias.[12] And to portray them otherwise or to try to make them have to function otherwise to be "reasonable" is a kind of distortion, or twisting of their function, that is bound to be unrealistic.

To be sure, they should be held ethically and legally accountable for selling unsafe products, deceptive advertising, and other breaches of good business practices. But to hold them as logically deficient for bias or for committing the fallacy of suppressed evidence whenever they fail to mention all evidence on both sides of an issue in their sales presentations and advertisements seems an absurdly high requirement.

5. Sales Dialogue

So to what kind of dialectical standard of adequacy and balance would it be reasonable to hold an argument, in a given case of advertising or sales presentation? The first step toward investigating this question is to consider a relatively typical case of a sales presentation and examine both the context of use and the kinds of arguments generally used in such a context. This step is a preliminary to the next step of looking at the various different normative models of dialogue that have been studied as contexts of use in which argumentation takes place. First then, consider the following case.

> *Case* 6.5: A customer walks into the showroom of a car dealership, and starts to look at one of the cars. A salesman walks up to her and asks if he can be of any assistance. They start to engage in conversation. She tells him that she is looking for a two-door six-cylinder model like the one she

has been looking at in the showroom. They begin to discuss the various aspects of this model, and he asks if she would like to take one for a test drive. She says yes, and he makes arrangements to get a car ready. After they return from the test drive, during which they talked at length about the car and her situation and needs with respect to car buying, they sit down in his office and begin to discuss prices.

The kind of situation is a familiar one to most of us. We know that it is a conventional kind of conversational exchange that passes through various stages and that each of these stages has a different and distinctive purpose within the goal-directed cultural construct of which it is a part. From a sociological perspective, the whole process as it currently exists in America could be described as a kind of ritual that has its expected conventions and standards of politeness. From this point of view, it could be defined as a speech event, a cultural construct that has rules of comportment and verbal interaction that are understood implicitly by both parties.

But from a point of view of the critical analysis and evaluation of argumentation, how could we construct a normative model of the type of dialogue in which the two speakers in such a case are engaged? This is a subtle and difficult task because normatively such a conversation is extremely complex. As it proceeds from one stage to another, there are dialectical shifts in the purpose and type of dialogues in which the speakers are engaged. And, at any given stage, there may also be shifts from one type of dialogue to another.

Are they engaged in a critical discussion of the kind defined by van Eemeren and Grootendorst (1984)? The purpose of this dialogue is to resolve a conflict of opinions. This type of dialogue is a subtype of a persuasion dialogue (see chapter two), where the purpose of the one party is to persuade the other that a certain proposition is true (or false). In general, the goal of this kind of dialogue is for the one party to convince the other party that the first party's point of view is the right one, based on concessions or commitments of the other party. This seems to be partly what is involved in the car sale conversation above. Certainly, the salesman is trying to persuade the other party to accept the proposition that the act of buying this particular car would be a good idea.

Yet, this way of construing the conversation is not quite accurate. What the salesman is trying to do (his goal) is not just to persuade the other party that buying this car would be a good idea. He is actually trying to get her to act—to actually go ahead and buy this car. His goal is more one of action than of mere persuasion or of convincing her that a certain proposition is true (or false). So one could say that the salesman is engaged in a kind of argumentation that can be described best as a species of practical reasoning. He is trying to get her to buy the car. Of course, that may not be his actual motive (in a given case). But we presume that, in general, that is a pretty good description of what his goal should be, given his acknowledged role as a salesman. We all know, for example, that he is not a disinterested party who is giving advice of the kind we might find in *Consumer Reports*. He is a salesman. That is his job. He is paid to do it, probably on a commission basis. And if asked, he will not deny it.

Another hypothesis is that the salesman and the customer are engaged in a negotiation dialogue. For neither is a disinterested party, and both have their own interests at stake in the exchange. The customer is shopping around for a good car at a good price. The salesman has the goal of making a sale, preferably one that maximizes profits for the dealership, or at any rate one that makes some income for him. This aspect of self-interested negotiation pervades the whole conversation. But it seems to become especially prevalent at some stages, for example, when they sit down to discuss prices.

You could say then that the conversation is a mixture of persuasion dialogue and negotiation dialogue. But at some stages, negotiation comes more to the fore, and at others, persuasion dominates as the type of dialogue.

At the initial stages of their encounter, both parties seem to be primarily engaged in an information-seeking dialogue. The customer wants to find out about cars available at this dealership, or perhaps she is especially interested in a car of a particular type. She may want to find out information on the features of this particular car. The salesman, in turn, probably wants to know more about the customer—her needs, what she likes, and how much she can afford to pay for a car, for example.

At the latter stages of their dialogue, if it gets to the point where an offer is made or discussed, the information-seeking part may be pretty well over, and negotiations in the form of offers and counteroffers may typify the verbal exchange.

Another characteristic feature of this type of conversational exchange generally is that it is hard to see the dialogue as having some single, well-defined goal. Indeed, the goals of the participants are quite different and asymmetrical in nature. To some extent, too, the relationship is adversarial. The customer knows very well that the salesman and his company are in business for profit and that they make this profit by selling cars with a good margin of profit for them. However, the customer wants to get a *good* car, for her purposes, and preferably at as low a cost as possible. Thus, the customer is deliberating, primarily, whereas the salesman is pressing forward with a one-sided dialogue that could be described as almost eristic in nature. Not only are the goals of the two parties at conflict financially, but their general objectives are clearly different. The customer has the practical objectives of getting a *good* car, or a car she likes, according to her own standards of goodness and her own likes and dislikes. The salesman also may be generally committed or motivated to sell a *good* car, that the customer likes—at least as customers, we hope this is true. But it is likely to be more central to the immediate job, as he perceives it on the spot, to keep his overhead moving, that is, to sell off his existing stock quickly enough to stay in business. Certainly, this aspect of it is known to the customer, and the customer should be aware of it. In other words, the salesman has the job of selling, and it should be presumed that he has a strong interest is selling something, independently of how he himself might personally feel about the merits of his product or the competitiveness of its price. In short, we can presume, and we generally know, that the salesman is an advocate whose job is to emphasize the arguments on one side and not necessarily present a balanced argument on both sides of an issue (even though he may often make a show of doing so).

In sales dialogue, there tends to be a lot of internal shifting from one type of dialogue to another. Sometimes, what is going on seems to be a persuasion dialogue, where the salesman is trying to persuade the buyer that certain propositions are true or false. At other junctures, it seems that what is going on is a type of goal-oriented, action-directed practical reasoning in deliberation, where the salesman is advising the customer on how to achieve his or her goals by taking a proposed course of action.

The problem with case 6.5 is that it does not fit any of these normative models of dialogue exactly in all its phases. As noted, what is characteristic of case 6.5, in fact, is that the sequence of argumentation seems characteristically to shift through several different types of dialogue at various stages.

Indeed, as observed in the discussion of case 6.5, the sequence of argumentation almost seems to indicate that the salesman and buyer are at dialectical cross-purposes—one is engaging in one type of (sales) dialogue, the purpose of which is to sell a car, to cause action, while the other is essentially trying to deliberate on the pros and cons of which is the best car for her to buy, a species of deliberation. This dialectical analysis suggests making a closer study of what the salesman is (presumably) trying to do.

6. Forms of Advocacy

The kind of argumentation in which the salesman could be described as being engaged could be called "advocacy," in the sense that he is arguing for one side only, on an issue in which there is more than one side. Everyone knows that a car salesman is paid to sell cars and that he has an interest in persuading potential buyers to purchase the particular cars he has for sale. Everyone, perhaps except for a few naive people, is aware that the salesman's function is different from that of *Consumers Reports* April issue on cars, as noted above. There the purpose is to give balanced information, both strong and weak points, of the various new cars for sale. Nobody expects a car salesman in a showroom to exhibit this level of balance, or lack of bias, in presenting all sides of the choice to be made. It would be unfair and unrealistic to hold the salesman to this standard of objectivity. We all know that although the salesman may be expected to be knowledgable about a lot of facts and to report them accurately and willingly, he is engaged in an advocacy type of argumentation where he can be expected to emphasize the facts that tend to be in favor of making his car seem like a good one to buy.

To make sense of advocacy argumentation of this sort, we must recall the place of pro-argumentation or advocacy in persuasion dialogue, as analyzed in chapters 2 and 3. In a critical discussion, there is a conflict of opinions, and the two participants each advocate one side. That is their goal, and the participant's burden of proof is to prove her own thesis or to refute or criticize the thesis of the other side successfully. In the eristic type of dialogue, this adversarial property is even more dominant—the goal is to refute the other side by almost any means possible, even if it means committing fallacies. The critical discussion, in contrast, has dialectical rules and procedures that both sides must observe, and these rules are the basis of normative standards that rightly lead one to condemn the committing of fallacies as inappropriate for this type of dialogue. In a critical discussion, one-sided arguments are legitimate in principle. But that is only part of the picture. One-sidedness has to be tempered by limits and normative requirements. How an argument is used to interact with the argumentation and commitment in the dialogue is normatively important.

In other types of dialogue, like the inquiry, advocacy dialogue is generally even more inappropriate, except in contexts where both sides are presented and where such an interlude might be necessary. But the inquiry generally strives to remove doubt where possible and generally to eliminate argument based on uncertain, unestablished premises or (even worse) open doubts and conflicts of opinion.[13] Thus, in scientific research, advocacy of one's personal opinions or interests would be seen as irrelevant and inappropriate.

There are other familiar social institutions that provide contexts of argumentation, however, where advocacy is generally appropriate and is an integral aspect of the structure of dialogue.

The legal trial is based on an adversary system of argumentation and jurors may find undetected fallacious arguments persuasive. This raises the question of whether it is acceptable in a trial for an attorney to knowingly use a fallacious argument to help win a case for his or her client. Can lawyers exploit ambiguities, fallaciously loaded questions, appeals to pity, fallacious appeals to expert opinion, and the like, if such arguments turn out to be effective in persuading a jury and are not exposed by the other side's counsel?

This is a hard question, because a lawyer is an advocate who is paid to argue a case, one side of a case that is, for a client. The lawyer's job is to make the best possible case on behalf of the client. Waller (1991, p. 48) argues that the knowing use of a fallacious argument in court by a lawyer is "an unmixed wrong, which subverts the truth-seeking purpose of the adversarial system of justice." Waller argues that not (knowingly) using fallacious arguments is a requirement of the "morally legitimate adversarial practice of law." But this is not a legal requirement of courtroom dialogue specifically stated in legal rules of evidence or procedure. It seems to be more a moral rule of conduct for members of the bar as ethical professionals or perhaps as persons of conscience.

Then it seems that advocacy is not itself a type of dialogue or a normative model of dialogue in its own right but an aspect of various types of dialogue. The possible exception here is the eristic type of dialogue, the most dominantly adversarial type of all, where each side is almost purely an advocate for his or her own point of view and uses personal attacks, "irrelevant" emotional appeals, and the like, without regard to rules of conduct appropriate for a critical discussion. But other types of dialogue, such as the critical discussion, can contain advocacy on both sides, even though that advocacy is moderated or balanced by normative requirements that restrain it.

Advocacy, as defined in chapter 3, is pro-argumentation of a kind that can occur in all of the types of dialogue defined in chapter 2. This is a context-free definition of advocacy. But the problem is that advocacy cannot be fully defined in a purely context-free way.

Advocacy never exists, in any real case of argumentation, apart from the context of dialogue in which it occurs. It is therefore misleading to operate on the assumption that advocacy, as a concept that occurs in argumentation, can be defined in a context-free way, at a high level of abstraction as pro-argumentation for a particular proposition or thing. But what kind of advocacy it is depends on the nature of that proposition or thing.

Advocacy exists in its purest form in the eristic type of dialogue, because this type of dialogue is least governed by Gricean maxims of politeness that constrain advocacy in certain situations. A quarrel "breaks out" precisely in the kind of situation where it is appropriate to cast aside the usual rules and constraints of polite discourse to give vent to a deeply felt grievance.

In other types of dialogue, however, advocacy is limited by the rules of politeness governing argumentation. For example, in a critical discussion, strong advocacy of one's point of view is very important and is to be generally encouraged, but it is curtailed by the need to recognize a good argument put forward by the other side. A participant in a critical discussion must not be such a strong advocate of his point of view that he relentlessly attacks the argumentation of the other side, by personal attacks or other specious tactics, even when he recognizes that the argument in question is based on good evidence. The rules for a critical discussion do not permit this sort of excessive or inappropriate advocacy of one's point of view.

The kind of advocacy found in negotiation dialogue is somewhat different in nature from that found in a critical discussion. Advocacy in a negotiation dialogue is for one's interests, and usually, at least in the simpler cases, this is some sort of financial interest. In a critical discussion, in contrast, advocacy is for one's point of view, which is essentially a proposition plus one's attitude toward that proposition. Thus these two kinds of advocacy are quite different in nature.

Then advocacy in two kinds of cases, might be quite different. In the case where the argumentation is supposed to be part of a critical discussion, an indicator would be relevant arguments, based on good evidence, that would support the arguer's point of view in the dialogue.

7. The Mosaic Theory

On the whole, we have not been able to pin down a single type of dialogue as a normative framework for the kind of argumentation put forward by the salesman in case 6.5 or by the commercial advertisement of a product. It seems to be a composite type of dialogue, a mosaic of different types of dialogue that in some cases may not even contain a clearly identifiable line of argument.

However, we can say some things about ads and sales presentations, when they do contain an argument. They do seem to use broadly, but variably, a kind of persuasion dialogue. But unlike persuasion dialogue generally, the goal of the arguer is not to persuade the respondent or audience that a particular proposition is true or false or is justified as such by evidence presented. Instead, the goal is to persuade the respondent to act in a certain way, that is, to buy something. Unlike argumentation in a critical discussion, however, there seems to be no constraint or set of rules and agreements, that require the proponent to convince the respondent by "reasonable" argumentation only, based on actual, genuine, good, and relevant evidence. On the nature of claim and evidence, the reader might read Ehninger (1974) and recall the requirement of evidence sensitivity stated as a requirement of a balanced persuasion dialogue in chapter 2.

Second, the respondents know in advance that the salesman or advertiser is being paid to sell a product. They know, or should know, that the speaker has a bias and is engaged in advocacy. It would be naive for the respondents to assume that such a speaker is engaged in a kind of advice-giving dialogue or joint deliberation with them, in such a way that he can be expected to objectively present both sides of an issue.

Thus, appeals to emotion, like the *argumentum ad misericordiam* and so forth, which could rightly be judged fallacious in a critical discussion, might not be fallacious in an advertisement or sales presentation. And it would be a mistake to presume that such emotional arguments are generally or always fallacious in these contexts, without having to argue for the special circumstances of the argument in the given case, on its merits.

Moreover, although commercials and sales presentations, at some stages and in some cases, do have a function of presenting information and facts to the respondent, it should not be presumed generally that such an argument commits the fallacy of suppressed evidence if it does not give all the relevant information. Generally, it should not be presumed that a sales pitch is a species of information-seeking, advice-giving, or two-sided persuasion dialogue.

As indicated by the samples above, too often the textbooks have classified arguments in sales and advertising as fallacious, based on this sort of presumption but without presenting a dialectical analysis of the case.

One textbook account of advertising that explicitly rejects the assumption that ads commit fallacies because they fall short of normative standards of rational persuasion and presenting information is that of Johnson and Blair (1983). Johnson and Blair think that we are often annoyed by ads that are offensive, false, deceptive, degrading, and so on, and that ads do have a function of informing us about new products, but it would be naive to conclude from these two premises that ads commit logical fallacies because their arguments fall short of standards of rational persuasion.

> It would be extremely naive to think, however, that the sole purpose of advertising is to provide information and rational persuasion. If that were the case, we could comb them for fallacies, just as we would any argument. It's true that many ads have a superficial resemblance to arguments, so they encourage us to approach them in this way. Think of ads which use the line, "Here are the reasons this product is the best." But this line is usually nothing more than a façade or window dressing, for, although advertising is an attempt to persuade, the type of persuasion generally used is not rational. Instead, advertising attempts to persuade us by appealing to our emotions (our hopes, fears, dreams), to the vulnerable spots in our egos (our desire for status and recognition), by applying pressure to the tender areas of our psyches. (Johnson and Blair 1983, pp. 246–247)

As Johnson and Blair put it, "advertising has a logic of its own" (p. 247). The standard logical point of view in the textbooks, by wrongly assuming the ads have rational persuasion by argument as their sole purpose, has fallen into a "gratuitous exercise" of condemning them as fallacious (p. 247).

What then is the dialectical framework of advertising and sales dialogue, if it is not solely that of rational persuasion? The best answer seems to be that the two parties are engaged in different types of dialogue that only partially overlap. The salesman or advertiser is (primarily) trying to get the respondent, the potential buyer, to buy his product. The respondent is (primarily) deliberating on which of several available products is the best for her to buy. If she is a new car buyer, for example, she goes around to several showrooms, test drives several cars, and then chooses from the evidence she has, including the various sales presentations, which car will be the best for her purposes, at the best price.

So there is a framework of dialogue surrounding the commercial sales argument, but it is not a single normative type of dialogue that is involved. It is a complex mosaic, composed of several different types of dialogue that are appropriate for different stages of the sequence of argumentation. The goal of dialogue of the kind in which the one party is engaged is only indirectly related to the goal of dialogue in which the other is engaged.

The goals are somewhat opposed in certain respects, and it seems that the goal of one is different in its general nature from the goal of the other. In a way, they are arguing at cross-purposes. At any rate, these are the goals of the primary participants. But the dialogue itself as a goal-directed cultural institution, as a familiar type of transaction in which there are cooperative exchanges according to standard expectations and rules of politeness, is a composite speech event. A *speech event* is an existing cultural or organizational framework that defines specific (often institutionalized) rules in which argumentation is put forth and evaluated.[14] For example, an argument in a university library committee meeting will be run by a committee chairperson in accord with specific rules of procedure (see chapter 2). Legal and scientific arguments are also part of social institutions and can be described as speech events (see chapter 8).

In a similar way, a sales presentation is a speech event of a familiar kind, with certain cultural expectations and standards. But from a normative viewpoint, it is not one distinctive type of dialogue, but a composite of several types, in which there tends to be shifting from one type to the other during the sequence of argumentation.

8. Infomercials

The somewhat negative and pluralistic thesis of the previous section may appear to be too generous to advertising and sales presentations. Surely in some cases, the arguments in these contexts do commit logical howlers and use tactics that definitely should be judged as fallacious or contrary to logic.

First, it should be noted that in some cases advertisements and sales messages do shift to a subdialogue where they clearly purport to engage in advice-giving dialogue by appealing to "scientific experts" and the like. And in such cases, the ad can be criticized for its failure to do so properly. In such cases, however, the key presumption of the evaluation is in what type of dialogue the message is supposed to be engaged, as far as we can judge from the textual and contextual evidence in the given case.

It may come as a surprise to find, in light of the foregoing remarks, that there do actually exist cases where a commercial advertisement is presented to viewers or readers in a context where the argument is supposed to be some other type of dialogue (not of such a one-sided advocacy type). A new type of television program called the "infomercial" has the initial format and appearance of a talk show or news program but is actually a half-hour commercial advertisement for a product.

> *Case* 6.6:   According to a "20/20" report (1990, p. 16), a television program "Rediscover Nature's Formula for Youth" used terms such as "investigative team" to suggest it was a news program. One presenter on the program even introduced himself as "your Inside Information investigator" (p. 15). When confronted with the charge that he was pretending it was a news program to sell a product, the producer replied (p. 16), "Come on, John, it's the real world" [to interviewer John Stossel].

Here the deception lies in the shift between one type of dialogue and another. The producers are trying to portray the program as a news investigation—a type of dialogue that is supposed to gather and present information in a way that shows all sides of an issue or at any rate does not advocate one side only in an uncritical and unbalanced way. The viewers' expectations are exploited by introducing the program in a format and style of delivery that makes it appear to be a regular news report. But then there is a shift in the discourse to a dialogue that is really a commercial advertisement to promote a product.

The key aspect of the deceptive tactic of argumentation in such a case is the dialectical shift from one type of dialogue to another. There is nothing wrong or fallacious *per se* about a sales pitch or a commercial ad for a product. But if the producers are trying to disguise the pitch by enveloping it in another format, which raises quite different expectations and standards of argumentation for a viewer, there is a pretense here that does give good grounds for calling their argument deceptive and fallacious.

Another tricky format of this type that has become a new trend is the *magalog* (Lee 1993, p. 69):

> With their flashy layouts and high-gloss paper, they look like magazines. With their slick writing and precious trendy stories, they read like magazines. And with their four-color advertising and carefully targeted circulations, they even do business like magazines. But they're something else entirely. The corporate folks who

brought you the Walkman, the PC and sweaters in every shade found in the rainbow have hit upon a new merchandising device: the magalog. Part life-style book, part catalog, there are now more than 100 of these hybrids whose strategy is to reach customers directly and treat every page as a marketing opportunity.

For example, in *Sony Style,* a magalog produced by the Sony Corporation, stories that appear to be critical discussions turn out, on closer inspection, to be sales pitches for new Sony Products (p. 69):

> *Case 6.7:* A story about "freedom of speech" turns out to be a paean to cordless telephones.

> *Case 6.8:* [A story about] the heartbreak of information overload is a pitch for a new floppy disc.

The format and style of these magazines suggests to readers that they are the regular type of magazine where the articles report on or critically discuss issues of current interest or controversy. The expectation is that the issues will be discussed in a relatively balanced way or at least that the purpose of the article will be to inform about something or discuss some issue and not to sell a product.

Another recent case of a comparable type is the following example of a dialectical shift:

> *Case 6.9:* A videotape on trees and the environment was distributed free to teachers in the public school system as an educational tool for use in classes on geography and the environment. However, the video was produced by a logging company who had a large financial stake in the geographical regions covered in the program, and it clearly expressed a point of view on environmental issues favorable to the interests of the loggers. After the video was played to one class for a while, one observant child said, "Hey, it's a commercial!"

Here the dialectical shift occurred because the video presentation posed as an educational resource to be used to educate children about the environment. Thus, it was supposed to be a factual and objective scientific resource for teachers to use in the classroom. However, it was clear to viewers that it was really an advocacy argument, designed to support one side in the issue—a side that also had a financial stake in the outcome of the debate. This could be called "corporate advocacy" in the sense of Schuetz (1990).

In these cases, there is an advocacy argument put forward. Advocacy *per se*, is not illegitimate or fallacious. But, in context, we judge that there is a bias in such cases, of a sort that is negative or open to normative/dialectical criticism, on the ground that the dialogue is of a different kind than it originally purported to be. The concealed dialectical shift is an illicit shift, from a critical perspective of judging the argumentation in it.

In these cases, we can say correctly that the argument is of a deceptive kind that is compatible with its being evaluated as fallacious or sophistical. This type of deceptive shift is a paradigm of dialectical bias of the harmful kind in argumentation.

9. Can a Good Argument Be Biased?

An argument that is biased can be quite a good argument, in the (narrower) sense that the premises do provide some evidence to support the conclusion. For example, in case 4.1, Wilma's argument that acid rain is not as harmful as people think may be based on good scientific evidence. Even so, if it is revealed that she is director of a large coal company, the audience may be justified in perceiving her argument as biased toward her point of view or the one she is defending on the issue.

But this point is often perplexing to some people. How can an argument be biased and at the same time be a good argument, based on genuine, relevant evidence? And if this is the case, of what value is it, in judging an argument, to know that it is biased? To answer these questions, we have to begin to understand certain subtleties about the dialectical concept of bias.

The first thing to understand is that dialectical bias has to do with how an argument is presented, with how it is used in a context of discourse. The bias is not internal to the argument, so to speak, but is in how the argument is used for a purpose in speech.

The second thing to understand is that dialectical bias often comes into play as an important factor in evaluating an argument when objective evidence, of a scientific kind, for example, is insufficient for us to make a decision whether or not we should accept the argument. For example, in the Wilma case, we may be uncertain what the body of scientific evidence should lead us to conclude on the issue of the harmfulness of acid rain. As nonexperts on the subject, and given the conflict of opinions on the part of the speakers in the debate, it may be hard to say for sure what conclusion the scientific evidence proves. So we are cast back upon trying to judge the credibility of the speakers, on the basis of how they have presented their arguments. Bias could play an important part in making this kind of assessment.

Similarly, in a court case, the crime may have happened a long time before, and the circumstantial evidence may not be sufficient to prove the defendant guilty or not guilty. When eyewitnesses are then brought in to testify, we may have little in the way of objective evidence to confirm or refute what they say. Hence, bias could be an important factor in judging the worth of their testimony as evidence, especially if a definite bias, one way or the other, is apparent. It is not that the bias is the whole story in deciding on the question of the guilt of the defendant. But it is one factor that can swing a weight of presumption one way or the other in deciding on the worth of an argument.

When we find bias in an argument, we give it less credibility or judge it more critically than we would if the same argument were seen as nonbiased. But this should not lead us to leap to the conclusion that because the argument was biased, it must be completely worthless, fallacious, and so on. Such judgments of evaluation should be made in relation to the type of dialogue of which the argument is supposed to be a part. If there has been a deceptive and illicit dialectical shift of the infomercial sort, then a highly negative evaluation could be appropriate. But not all sales and advertising arguments fall into this category.

10. Conclusions

The answer to the difficult question posed at the beginning of this chapter is the following. Commercial advertisements and sales presentations and arguments are both distinctive types of speech events, and as such, they share a lot in common. Both are complex interactions where a proponent is arguing to sell a product to a respondent buyer or audience and where the respondent may be presumed to be deliberating or choosing between buying this product or that. However, when we try to apply a normative model of dialogue to this familiar speech event in a given case, in order to criticize the argumentation in it as deficient in certain respects identified in the logic textbooks as fallacies, we find that no single normative model (of the existing, known types) clearly fits. Instead, we see, in such cases, that the context is a mosaic of different types of dialogue, at different stages of the sequence of argumentation, with a good deal of characteristic shifting from one type of dialogue to another.

Although this conclusion is (to a considerable and perhaps disappointing extent) a negative one, its implications for evaluating cases of sales and advertising arguments are highly significant. It means we can no longer engage in the traditional practice of the logic textbooks of gratuitously presuming that all such arguments are fallacious because they fail to present all the relevant evidence of the kind appropriate for a critical discussion (or information-seeking dialogue, and some other types of dialogue identified in chapter 2) in a balanced way.

However, it does not follow that we can never pin down advertisements and sales arguments as committing logical fallacies or as containing harmful bias. What it does mean is that in order to do an adequate job of backing up this kind of criticism, we must first of all identify the type of dialogue in which the speaker is supposed to be engaging. Definite textual and contextual evidence is, in fact, available, in some cases, that can be used for such a determination, as shown above.

In a case where dialectical evidence of this kind can be found, the argument can then be criticized as falling short of the normative standards of balance appropriate for that type of dialogue. But the negative form of this conclusion also applies. If evidence of this sort is not found in a given case, then the finding of fallaciousness or of harmful bias should not be judged as justified.

When there is a dialectical shift during a given sequence of argumentation in a case, the evaluation of the argument should proceed by "looking backwards," by determining what the original context of dialogue was supposed to be. Then the argument should be judged dialectically by the normative standards for argumentation in that type of dialogue.

When the evidence is insufficient in a given case to determine the type of dialogue in which an arguer was supposed to be engaged, often the best that can be given is a conditional evaluation of the argument: If argument *A* was originally supposed to be put forward in context of dialogue *D*, then it can be evaluated provisionally as fallacious or critically deficient for its failure to meet a normative requirement of *D*.

Thus, in the cases examined, where textbooks charge cases of arguments in sales and advertising as fallacious, the best we can do here is to agree provisionally: if these arguments were supposed to be part of a critical discussion, scientific inquiry, information-seeking dialogue, pedagogical dialogue (or some other type of dialogue requiring a balanced approach, in which straight advocacy for one side of the sales dialogue type would constitute a faulty, inadequate, or fallacious type of argumentation), then they can be evaluated as fallacious (faulty, etc.) relative to that hypothesis. However, as shown in detail in the analysis of these cases above, there has been too often, in the textbook treatments, little or no real evidence that these cases are supposed to be arguments put forward in dialogues of one of these types. And, as also shown, there is little or no reason to think that sales and advertising arguments are generally well-classified as being one of these types of dialogue (at least in any exclusive or clearly dominant way, generally), requiring balanced argumentation.

Empirical research of cases of sales and advertising dialogue in argumentation might do better to see it as a complex mosaic of other types of dialogue, characterized by dialectical shifts and by what we have called "advocacy."

In many cases, detecting dialectical bias in argumentation in a given case may be relatively easy and nonproblematic, compared to the job of properly judging or evaluating that bias as having a harmful effect on the worth of the argument. In many instances, as we will see in chapter 7, an arguer can be brought to agree that there is a bias in his argument, but he will energetically dispute any charge that this bias detracts from the worth of his argument or should have any negative impact in evaluating it.

Notes

1. Anthony Jameson, "Dialogue Partner Modeling and Argumentation," a presentation at the seminar on Argumentation and Reasoning at Schloss Dagstuhl, Germany, August 26, 1993.

2. Recently, there has been some controversy on just how bad the standard treatment really is. See Johnson (1990) and Walton (1991c).

3. See Walton (1989a; 1992b).

4. Ibid.

5. See Walton (1992c) for an extensive analysis of the *ad misericordiam* fallacy.

6. See the quotation from Johnson and Blair below.

7. Ostensibly, at any rate, this seems a reasonable presumption.

8. This same passage also occurs in Copi and Burgess-Jackson (1992, p. 133).

9. See Walton (1992b; 1992c) on default reasoning.

10. Copi (eighth edition, with Carl Cohen, 1990) and Hurley (4th ed., 1991) are probably the two most popular introductory logic textbooks in use at this time.

11. Hurley (1991, p. 149) describes the fallacy of suppressed evidence as a "device used by unscrupulous individuals to pass off half-truths as the whole

truth." However, the use of the word *unscrupulous* here suggests that what is being presumed is an ethical fault of the person, as a basis for condemning that person's argument as logically fallacious.

12. See the discussion below on forms of advocacy.

13. Walton (1998, chapter 3).

14. Defined in chapter 2.

TESTING ALLEGATIONS OF BIAS

In this chapter, a number of case studies of argumentation are examined that contain allegations of bias—all, except for the first case have "something to gain financially" as the type of indicator. What we find in all these cases is that when the charge of bias is brought forth, it is on the basis of a definite kind of evidence, which does definitely indicate a bias in the argument. The problem is how to judge correctly, or justifiably, whether or not such a finding of bias should have a negative impact on the worth of the argument.

In chapter 6, the general tendency to overreact was noted—this is the tendency (itself a sort of bias) to leap to the conclusion to reject an argument as worthless, or even fallacious, once any indicator of bias is found. In chapter 7, a more carefully laid out sequence of steps is identified, guiding a reasonable critic from a premise of an indictor of bias in a given argument, to a negative, critical judgment of the worth of that argument.

1. Evidence for a Charge of Bias

An allegation of dialectical bias is best understood as a kind of claim or argument where one party in a dialogue exchange of argumentation is putting forward a charge that the argument of the other side is biased. It is important to recognize that such a claim can be justified in some cases and unjustified in others. Evidence can be brought to bear, for or against the claim.

Typically, when the word *bias* is used in this sense, it has negative connotations. It is used to condemn, refute, or criticize an argument. But the charge of bias is often put forward in a specious or unjustified way, as a means of attacking an opponent's argument unfairly. Such misuses have frequently have been observed in the logic textbooks, under the headings of the various fallacies, such as the *ad hominem* fallacy, where the unjustified charge of bias is often classified as a species of circumstantial *ad hominem* fallacy.[1] See, for example, Hurley (1991, p. 116).

The charge of bias becomes especially significant as a negative allegation when an arguer purports to fairly considering the arguments on both sides of a contentious issue. This prior commitment to treating an argument in a balanced way, where no significant argument on one side or the other is overlooked or ignored, applies to all types of dialogue discussed in chapter 2, except the eristic type.

For example, suppose a news program such as "20/20" is criticizing some practice it finds reprehensible, such as dentists charging people large fees for unnecessary dental work. Feelings no doubt run high on both sides in this type of "story." Dentists will be very apprehensive or perhaps defensive about it, while many of us who have felt taken advantage of by unscrupulous dentists will have strong emotions on the other side. Although a news program on this topic might very definitely be an argument supporting one side, there is an expectation that a balanced treatment will consider relevant evidence on both sides.[2]

In some cases, evidence external to the argument itself can be made available to judge a charge of bias (Alter 1993, p. 65).[3]

> *Case* 7.1: "20/20" reporter John Stossel seemed to prove in a 1989 story that a Philadelphia dentist recommended an unnecessary procedure when Stossel cited only mild jaw discomfort. The dentist last year lost his defamation suit, but outtakes aired recently on Court TV suggest that he had good reason to feel wronged. This edited-out footage shows that Stossel actually complained of much more pain than the viewers heard, and the dentist at first recommended much less expensive treatment. In other words, the editing of the piece seriously distorted the truth.

This was a case in which it was alleged that the argument was biased because certain relevant facts were left out. Hence, the indicator of bias is that of selection of arguments (see chapter 4). Although the complaints of pain and the dentist's recommendation were left in, they were not fully represented in a way that was consistent with that indicated by the larger footage (according to the allegation in case 7.1 above). This, according to the charge, made the argument misleading, by distorting the evidence.

In a case like this, there is quite a large body of evidence in the original footage recorded. To arrive at a conclusion on how appropriate or justified the dentist's recommendations were, the whole body of evidence needs to be viewed in perspective. Altering or deleting some small but key parts can affect the conclusion greatly.

The allegation made by Alter in case 7.1 is that the argument as presented on "20/20" did have a bias in it that was negative, in the sense that it "seriously distorted the truth." The evidence cited to back up this charge is the series of outtakes viewed on "Court TV," indicating that certain key items in the footage were edited out.

This case suggests that a claim of bias can be supported or refuted by evidence and that therefore such a claim is testable by evidence. The problem is that the evidence is contextual in nature. It is not in the argument itself, at least explicitly, without evaluating the argument in a broader context. In this case, the evidence came in the form of the outtakes, the parts omitted in the argument, with the argument as presented to the TV viewers. What is left out (negative evidence) can be as important as what is in an argument.

The other contextual factor is the type of dialogue exchange of which the argument was part—a TV news program, which could be called a type of "information-seeking dialogue."[4] This program definitely contained an argument, but one supposedly based on facts uncovered by an investigation and presented to the viewers in a way that fairly represented the facts. In such a setting, journalists are supposed to have certain standards of presenting information, and consequently an allegation of bias, of the kind given in case 7.1, is a negative criticism.

Generally then, judgments of whether there is an identifiable bias and whether this bias is of the bad or interfering kind in argumentation depend on the kind of dialogue in which one is supposedly engaged. Standards will be quite different for information-seeking dialogue than for a critical discussion, and different again where the argument is explicitly meant to advocate one point of view.

Generally, the format and expectations of the news program "20/20" identify it as a species of information-seeking dialogue. The expectation of viewers is that this program will present information to the audience. Although the stories typically are overlaid with advocacy and treat of controversial topics where strong viewpoints on two sides of an issue will be considered and weighed, a bias that is perceived as too strong or that viewers might object to strenuously is generally avoided.

Normally, editing is done privately by the producers of this kind of program, and the audience is not privy to whatever footage may be edited out. Hence, there would be normally no visible indicators of the type of bias criticized in case 7.1.

In this case, the situation did not provoke the charge of bias until the new evidence provided by the outtakes was revealed. Generally, in a given case, whether or not a charge of bias can be supported by the evidence may change, as new information is added into our knowledge of the case. Thus, the questions of identifying and evaluating bias in a given case should be seen as rebuttable or defeasible, that is, subject to change or withdrawal as new information on the case is made available.[5]

All charges of bias in a case should be seen as weighted one way or the other, subject to the given information in the particular case. We are typically given a text of discourse in a case—in this case it was a televised presentation—and we should judge the bias in the argumentation relative to and conditional upon the information given. Should new material be added to the case, our evaluation is subject to revision and/or correction.

2. Potential for a Charge of Bias

In certain cases, there is a potential for a charge of bias to be brought forward as a particularly effective form of criticism. If one is aware of this potential in advance, it can be dealt with in a proactive way in argumentation.

In some cases, the potential for a charge of bias is significant because the dialogue is a balance-of-considerations situation, where there is a good deal of evidence on both sides, but the evidence on neither side is conclusive. It comes down to a question of whom you believe, one would say, in this type of case. If the argumentation on one side is perceived to contain a bias, it will swing the burden or weight of presumption toward the other side.[6]

Sometimes, arguers are well aware of how important perceptions of bias are in this kind of situation. So when one side attacks the argumentation for the other side as bias, he will argue, pre-emptively, that the argument on his side is not biased in the same way.

The following case was broadcast on the news program "Dateline," April 19, 1994. The story concerned billions of dollars being lost to the government by fraudulent electronic income tax returns. Thieves had learned how to submit phony income tax returns by computer and were making a fortune. It seemed that the Internal Revenue Service could do little to stop these thefts unless it wanted to slow down the speedy processing and delivery of income tax rebates to taxpayers.

Case 7.2: "Dateline" interviewed one man (*A*) who argued that the electronic processing of income tax returns was a big advance that made the tax system much more efficient and that the new system was very popular with taxpayers, because they were able to get their refunds quickly. *A* argued for the electronic system and was experienced with its use since he was employed in a company that helped to set up the system and was operating it for the government.

Then a second man (*B*) was interviewed. He had formerly worked for the government agency that was responsible for electronic processing of income tax returns. *B* argued that this system was losing billions every year and ought to be stopped because it could not deal with the problem that it was so easy for thieves to make fraudulent returns. When referring to the argument of *A*, *B* said that *A* was biased because he was making his living from this electronic system. *B* added that *A* would say that (*B*) was biased, but *B* said that he had nothing to gain. He said that his only motive was to be the spokesman for the people still working in that government office, who were very frustrated but could not speak out.

In this case, *B* realized rightly that once his charge of bias was made, the next question asked would be whether he himself did not have something to gain by speaking out. The role of such a proactive move in dialogue, as related to bias, will be taken up in chapter 10.

Having something to gain financially is one of the most powerful indicators of bias, and if people see a financial connection between an argument and the person who has supported that argument, then it will cause them to have reservations about the support given. This situation raises questions about the seriousness or honesty (credibility) of the person putting forward the argument. But not only that, it also raises questions about how much weight of presumption or credibility should be rested on the argument itself.

This raising of suspicion can even occur in the case of a scientific inquiry, as the case below illustrates. In this case, Bob Fenton, a professor of economics at the University of Winnipeg, was conducting independent research on different types of product packaging, to provide consumers with information on the most environmentally friendly packaging available to them (Research Profile, 1992, p. 2). In an interesting comment on the funding of his research, Professor Fenton commented that it was important that his research not be funded by any industry because of the suspicion of bias.

> Case 7.3: Although studies similar to Fenton's have been done in the past, he says that many are not considered entirely credible although conducted by professional firms and scientists.
>
> "People are suspicious when they see that a study is being done by someone connected to the product being researched. For example, a plastics manufacturer studies the environmental impact of cardboard versus plastic egg cartons. When the results come back showing plastic as a better choice, people are automatically doubtful. It's important that my research isn't funded by any industry," says Fenton. "People shouldn't think that I'm being influenced by any financial contributions from businesses."

In this case, the potential for a charge of bias is inherent in the given situation. Manufacturers of shopping bags and many other products had been aware for some time that a significant number of consumers had been choosing products that they thought were more environmentally friendly. Hence, the manufacturers and retailers were spending a lot of revenue in advertising trying to portray their products as being more "green" than those of their competitors. Part of this kind of advertising campaign often involves hiring scientists who conduct studies that supposedly support the environmentally friendly properties of this or that product. The public is aware that these scientists are paid to conduct research by a company that has something to gain, so there tends to be a skepticism about this kind of alleged scientific support.

With this initial skepticism already in place, a researcher in an area such as environmental economics has to be careful to deal with the potential for suspicions about bias, especially in relation to sources of funding.

3. Suspicions of Unconscious Bias

Thouless (1936, pp. 221–222) presents an interesting case that raises questions about how we judge bias.

> Case 7.4: Let us suppose that two men are arguing about the proposal of a capital levy. One of them is in favor of the

> levy. He argues the case in its favor entirely on general grounds, with logical arguments as to its general economic effects. His opponent argues hotly against it with equally general arguments. Neither of them argues the question would affect him personally, and both would indignantly repudiate the suggestion that the effect of the levy on themselves plays any part in determining their opinions about it. Yet, as onlookers, we are not surprised to learn that the man arguing for the levy has no capital, while the man arguing against it owes much of the comfort of life to the interest on a capital sum greater than £5000 either saved by himself or inherited. Nor are we likely to be wrong in guessing that these facts are much more important influences in determining the opinions of the two men than any of the logical arguments they bring forward so impressively.

Both men have something to gain or lose—a financial interest at stake—on the outcome of the disputed question of the levy. But that does not mean that either of their arguments is biased in the bad or harmful sense of being critically defective or erroneous. Surely we, as onlookers or critics, owe the two men an obligation to look at their arguments on their merits, on the basis of the evidence they put forward to support their respective conclusions.

But, as onlookers, once we know the background financial facts about these two men, it is difficult not to weigh this into the balance. We may not believe or have any evidence to support the view that either of these men is intentionally deceiving us, in the sense that they are merely promoting their own interests by putting forward arguments in which they do not really believe. But there may still be a suspicion that part of the basis behind the stand each takes is an unconscious motivation or bias to support his own interests.

As Thouless (p. 223) puts it, *rationalization* occurs when "our minds construct an apparently rational set of reasons for supposing a belief to be true" because "our desires lead us to accept." Such a belief is really held on "irrational" grounds, that is not on the basis of the evidence given in a critical discussion, but simply on our interests or desires. Rationalization can be quite unconscious, so that the arguer "honestly believes that his reasonable arguments are the real grounds for his belief" (Thouless 1936, p. 222).

The problem posed by case 7.4 is that the onlookers may not hold reservations about the arguments of either side because they think that either side is being dishonest or hypocritical, by intentionally trying to deceive, simply in order to promote their own interests. The reservations of the onlookers may be much more subtle than that. The problem posed by this case is that the onlookers are likely to suspect that the two arguers are rationalizing (in Thouless's sense) by being unconsciously influenced by their interests. In weighing up the balance of considerations on both sides, an onlooker is strongly tempted or inclined to rate the argumentation on both sides as somewhat less credible, once the facts of personal financial interests in the outcome are made known. But this is a problem from the point of view of the critical analysis and evaluation for argumentation because it is based on a suspicion. It is a question-raising suspicion, as opposed to a definite argument against the argumentation of either side, based on hard evidence.

This kind of reservation or suspicion probably would be a factor in how we judge argumentation in a case such as 7.4. But it is based on suspicion concerning something by which the participants may be influenced at an unconscious level. How should this sort of factor be dealt with from a critical point of view?

The best way to treat such a suspicion of bias is as a rebuttable presumption or as a ground for reservation that should be put in the form of an allegation. The participants should be asked whether it is true that they have such interests at stake in the case and how they can defend themselves against the suspicion of bias that could be raised against their argumentation.

The subtle thing about this sort of suspicion is that it relates to something that may be unconscious as a ground of belief. Hence, it may be very hard to get to any kind of hard evidence whether or not it really exists in a given case. Alleging bias using the indicator of having something to gain is a subtle form of criticism that may be very hard for an arguer to rebut or defend himself against.

What is indicated here is that having something to gain as a basis for a criticism of bias should be taken as a rebuttable allegation. The party accused or suspected should be given a chance to dispute such an allegation once it has been brought forward.

4. The Last Battleground Case

The following case is based on the transcript of a news program "The 5th Estate," broadcast on October 12, 1993, by the Canadian Broadcasting Corporation. The program consisted of an interview by reporter Trish

Wood of several participants in public debate on environmental issues concerning the logging of the Clayoquot Sound area in British Columbia.

For the past decade, the environmentalists had campaigned for preservation of the rain forests of Clayoquot Sound. But now the supporters of logging had begun to fight back by forming advocacy groups of their own, advocating what they saw as a more balanced viewpoint that supported both the environment and the economy. However, since these groups contained many members who made their living from the forestry industry in one way or another, the issue of bias affected their credibility. The problem for the logging corporations was that if they tried to argue against the environmentalists, the public saw them as biased because they were making their income from logging, whereas the environmentalist groups were seen as unbiased because they had nothing to gain financially.

To deal with this problem, MacMillan Bloedel, the logging corporation, was instrumental in the founding of an advocacy group, Share B.C., composed of loggers, truckers, their families, and people who made their living from the forest economy. Composed mostly of people from small towns in B.C., Share portrays itself as a "grassroots revival" or citizens group that denies it is an instrument of the logging companies or even has formal ties with the forest industry.

Share describes itself as an advocacy group, as indicated by the statement of its director, Mike Morton: "We are an advocacy group, we're concerned about environmental values, we're concerned about the economy, and our purpose is to promote community stability by supporting the principles of sustainable development."

The Share Movement does not see itself as acting for the interests of the logging companies. As the interviewer in the program, Trish Wood, states: "The Share Movement denies it has any ties with the forest industry." The movement sees itself as an activist group with a message, who gets its inspiration from the American Wise Use movement. Ron Arnold, executive director of the Centre of Free Enterprise in Bellview, Washington, is quoted as an activist who has expressed the kind of political platform advocated by Share (p. 3).

> The environmental movement really isn't what it seems. It's not saving the earth. It's killing jobs and trashing the economy. Every single law that's drafted and lobbied into existence by environmentalists and environmental leaders hurts people in some definite way. It either regulates them out of making a profit if they're a small

business, or a big business—it doesn't matter, and without profits you can't survive. It takes private property away from people and you find the most outrageously deliberate statements—we can't save nature until we eliminate private property—coming out of environmental groups. Where's your food, clothing, shelter, and fuel going to come from if you believe that everything people do harms nature? That industry, the big bad wolf, is destroying nature? Where are you going to get breakfast if you destroy industry?

Learning how to get this message across to the public from their American counterparts, a group of community leaders in Port MacNeil—a logging and mining town at the north end of Vancouver Island—created a study group with the goal of warning people about the dangers of listening to "extremist" environmentalists. Other groups like this one were formed to support the B.C. Share movement.

However, it was a problem for Share that it was supported by meetings organized by executives of MacMillan Bloedel. This link with the logging industry, particularly in the form of financial support, indicates to critics of Share that its purpose is not one of providing information or of supporting the public interest in an unbiased way. In the program, this question of bias is raised by interviewer Trish Wood when she questions Dennis Fitzgerald, a spokesman for MacMillan Bloedel (pp. 3–4).

Trish Wood

Is it ethical for the industry to fund so called citizen groups who downplay their affiliation with the industry?

Dennis Fitzgerald

Sure, I think it's ethical. I mean it's not something you can buy. You know, you can sort of facilitate it and pay a few of the bills and things like that, but it goes only if people want to make it go. So you don't, it's not something you buy. You can help them out and certainly we've done that.

Trish Wood

So what did you do?

Dennis Fitzgerald

You give them some seed money and that's pretty much been it ever since. It's been you pay some amount of money so people can pay their phone bills and run their fax machines and stuff like that, and then you've got a volunteer organization that sort of works on the enthusiasm of its own membership.

Trish Wood

How much money did they get from the industry, and MacMillan Bloedel specifically?

Dennis Fitzgerald

Right now I think it's in the neighborhood of about $100,000 a year.

Mike Morton

If they're willing to fund us, terrific. Whatever we receive, there's no strings attached, whether it's forest industry dollars or Joe's garage down the street.

Trish Wood

My question to you then is why would the forest industry fund you unless it was in their interest to do so?

Mike Morton

Well, there's obviously some commonalties of interest. We want to see a healthy sustainable forest industry, and they want to see a forest industry. They may not be funding the Western Canada Wilderness Committee because they might not want any forest industry.

The problem here is one of public perceptions. The Share movement wants to portray itself as being "at arms length" from MacMillan Bloedel and other companies that profit directly from logging. They cannot deny that they accept money from these groups. But to effectively oppose environmentalist advocacy groups, they have to present themselves as independent from the big corporations.

Later in the interview, Trish Wood asks why industry has funded the Share movement, and Mike Morton answers that the funding was simply a gift (p. 4):

Mike Morton

Again, any money that we've accepted from the forest industry, there's absolutely no strings attached as far as our association with the forest industry is concerned.

Trish Wood
  So this is a gift. This is a gift.

Mike Morton
  Well, sure it is. Of course it is.

This position is easy to criticize, however, and another speaker is interviewed, alleging that MacMillan Bloedel is "simply using these groups to bolster the company position which is that the company wants to retain control over as much of the resource as they possibly can." Trish Wood follows up this line of questioning by pointing out that another group allied with Share, the Forest Alliance of Canada, created to deal with the environmentalists in urban areas, brought in public relations "top guns," paid for by the forest industry (pp. 4–5).

Trish Wood
  The top guns were Burson-Marsteller, the largest public relations firm in the world. The company has made its name advising corporations involved in environmental disasters. When Exxon needed help to deal with an angry public after the Exxon Valdez spill, and when Union Carbide needed help after the Bhopal disaster, they called in Burson-Marsteller.
  The Forest Alliance of B.C. wasn't only the brainchild of the world's largest public relations firm; Burson-Marsteller actually created the alliance. Together with the forest industry, the PR company hand-picked the Alliance's key employees, its executive director, and its chairman. In fact, the Alliance's first executive director was a Burson employee. He still maintains an office here to keep an eye on things for the forest industry.

Although the Forest Alliance portrays itself as an independent body and even as an environmental organization, the revealing of such close financial ties to the forestry industry poses a criticism of bias.
  Jack Munro, the chairman of the Forest Alliance, is then interviewed. He portrays the group as believing in the need for a balance between the environment and a good economy. But when he is questioned in the interview, what comes across is that this claim is "tainted" by bias (p. 5).

Jack Munro
  We are being widely accepted with open arms by the public. Finally the public of British Columbia are saying, finally we've got

an independent body who is in the center trying to find once again a balance between a healthy economy and a healthy environment.

Trish Wood

You don't believe that the fact that the Alliance was set up by a public relations firm, spin doctors, in any way taints the Alliance.

Jack Munro

The firm advised the CEOs that they establish a citizens board independent, not controlled by the industry. That's what they did. Now Burson-Marsteller or Gary Lee or anybody else does not run the Alliance.

Trish Wood

So there's no conflict here even though the Alliance gets most of its funding from the forest industry.

Jack Munro

Not at all, not at all, not at all. Because we can be—I've fought with these characters, for goodness sake, for 30 years. I'm not afraid to have a scrap with them about anything.

This reply is not very convincing, especially when Trish Wood (p. 5) follows up by openly saying that the Forest Alliance is "operating in the interests of the forest industry." In support of their position, the best a representative of the Alliance can do is to insist "It operates at arm's length from its funders." But Trish Wood, commenting on the "educational" programs produced by the Forest Alliance, puts forward an even more explicit charge of bias: "These programs look like documentaries. They appear to be open, unbiased presentations of the industry and its problems. But every program contains a bottom line message from the industry to the public." At this point, one might think that the arguments of the Share movement and the Forest Alliance spokespersons have been so thoroughly discredited that there is not much point in continuing. But the program goes on to further examine the claim of these groups that they are environmentalists. The members of the groups claim that they have a right to this description of the view they represent.

5. Defending against a Criticism of Bias

The big question raised by this case concerns the first indicator of bias—having something to gain. If this indicator is present in a given case of argumentation, is it still possible for the arguer to defend himself against a criticism of bias by claiming that his argument stands on its own, independent from this financial interest? The Last Battleground case shows that there is room for such a defensive line of argumentation.

The Share movement admits its financial links to the logging industry, and indeed most of its members seem to have jobs that are in, or depend on, logging. They admit to facts that are clear indicators that their argumentation on the issue of the environment contains a bias. They even admit direct financial ties to the logging corporation, MacMillan Bloedel. This admission definitely indicates bias, yet they seem to be arguing against the criticism of bias as counting against their argumentation.

The Share movement was founded and funded by the forest industry. Thus Share has a financial link to an industry that gets its income from logging. It is interesting that although this is a clear and definite indicator of bias on the issue of, the Last Battleground, it does not, in this case, completely destroy the credibility of Share, by showing that its argumentation exhibits a bad sort of bias that would refute it. Share does appear to put up a fairly plausible and convincing defence of its argumentation against this line of criticism.

Mike Morton admits that Share is an advocacy group and that it was founded and funded by the forest industry. None of the supporters of the Share movement deny these things, although they maintain that they have their own point of view on environmental issues, which should be evaluated on its own merits as a point of view, and that they are at arm's length from the forest industry.

Dennis Fitzgerald admits that Share grew out of the Wise Use movement funded and founded by MacMillan Bloedel and was itself funded by "seed money" and continuing support from the logging industry. But he claims it is a "volunteer organization" that "works on the enthusiasm of its own membership." Dennis Fitzgerald concedes that Share gets around a hundred thousand a year from MacMillan Bloedel, but Mike Morton adds that there are "no strings attached" and that this money is "a gift." According to Trish Wood, the local members are all volunteers, who "resent any suggestion they are in the industry's pocket." Hence, the members of the Share movement admit that there is a financial link with the logging corporation MacMillan Bloedel, but they deny that this link means that they are just paid advocates of the corporation viewpoint.

This argument seems implausible on first evaluation. If there is a financial link to the corporation via the funding given to Share, surely Share is gaining from its advocacy of this particular viewpoint. So how can it be said that its argumentation is not biased, in the same way that the corporation's advocacy of their view is generally perceived as biased?

The difference here seems to be that the corporation directly profits from logging, so it very definitely and directly has something to gain from its argumentation for a particular point of view. In contrast, the Share group may be receiving financial support from the corporation, and many of its members may be employed in or receive income in their employment as side benefits of the success of the logging industry, but it need not be true (in the same way it is true for the corporation) that they have something to gain financially from their efforts of advocacy on behalf of the view that they put forward. In other words, there is still a financial connection here, but members of Share can distance themselves from the making of profits, to some extent, by maintaining an "arm's length" from the corporation.

Thus, while there are still grounds for alleging that the arguments of Share on environmental issues contain an identifiable bias, evidenced by a financial connection to those who gain directly from logging, this kind of bias seems less serious, less destructive of its credibility as an advocate of a point of view. For even though there is evidence of a bias there, the arguments put forward by Share could be based on good evidence that is worth listening to even by those of us in the cities who are not directly involved in logging or directly affected by the logging industry activities.

6. Burden of Proof in This Case

The basic parameters of burden of proof in this case are set in place by two given public perceptions or received opinions. One is that big corporations are in business to make a profit. They are perceived as primarily pursuing their own interests, even if this may conflict with the interests of the broader population. The other received opinion is that environmental groups, such as those that protest against logging, are ethically motivated—that is, they are acting not for profit or from self-interest, but from some moral motive. The perception is that such a group is acting on the basis of what it perceives, rightly or wrongly, to be in the interests of the general population.

It follows from these received opinions about these two groups that big corporations are seen generally as having a bias because they have something to gain, when they venture any opinion on public issues related to the source of their profits. By contrast, a protest or environmental group, such as Greenpeace, is not perceived generally as having this same type of bias, when it speaks out on some environmental issue.

The success of the environmental protesters had historically posed a difficult public relations problem for the logging corporations. They had been portrayed as the offenders, who were causing damage to the environment, according to the arguments of the environmentalists. But if they tried to defend themselves, by denying the charge or raising arguments against it, their arguments were not perceived as being very credible by the public—for, after all, these were the "big corporations" who are in business to make a profit for themselves. Hence any argument they might use to try to defend their position on environmental issues is automatically perceived as biased. This put them in a position that was difficult to defend with any credibility because their argumentation was perceived as biased, whereas that of the opposition was not.

How did they deal with this difficult problem? Their solution was essentially to copy the methods used so successfully by their opponents. They staged demonstrations and other political-media events put on by "protesters" and "concerned citizens." The strategy was to portray these arguments as being advanced, not by the big corporations, but by concerned citizens who were independent of or at arm's length from the corporations, even though they shared the same conclusion as that supported by the corporations. The idea was that even though they may share the same view, their argumentation for this view is based on their own ideas. Thus the protesters for this view cannot (presumably) be tarred with the brush of bias, in the same way that the corporations had been.

Ron Arnold (CBC transcript, p. 1) encapsulated this strategy graphically:

> Industry cannot save itself by itself. It needs citizen allies, for the simple reason, who's ever going to love big business? I mean that's a joke. I've said look industry, you take your money, you give it to one of these grassroots groups, and get the hell out of the way because there's no way you're ever going to convince people. Let the people who it's going to affect tell that story.

Dennis Fitzgerald also indicated in his remark that this was essentially the strategy: "So what you have to do is to find some way to identify people who would be your advocates and move to empower these people" (p. 3). Then Bob Skelly admits that this strategy was the method carried out by MacMillan Bloedel. They set up and funded Share groups among their workers in areas where job loss was threatened by environmental initiatives p. 3).

How successful has this strategy been? Evidently, it has had some success in drawing public attention to a point of view that previously could not seem to mount a credible public campaign. But the problem is that it is still open to suspicions of bias. Trish Wood keeps raising these doubts when she asks questions—for example, she asks, "Is it ethical for the industry to fund so-called citizen groups who downplay their affiliation with the industry?" Dennis Fitzgerald answers this question by saying that this is just "seed money" to help a "volunteer organization" (p. 3). But how convincing is his response? It certainly does make a good point. But given the heavy weight of presumption in favor of the perceived bias of an organization directly funded by the industry that profits from logging, one would have to think that this kind of questioning is doing some damage to the credibility of Share's argumentation for its point of view.

What impact these suspicions of bias have in the wider arena of public opinion on logging in British Columbia is hard to say. Judging from a massive protest of some 20,000 loggers and forestry workers chanting "No more lost jobs" at the British Columbia Legislature buildings in March 1994 (Cernetig 1994), it seems that opposition to the demands of the environmentalists is being vocally advocated in the arena of public opinion.

7. Harmful Bias and Duplicity

In this case, it is clear from the outset that both parties to the dispute have a bias in their argumentation. For both parties are committed to an identifiable position on the issue, and this is an indicator of bias. But this bias is not, in itself, a bad bias or a reason for impugning the credibility of the argumentation of either party.

The doubts raised by the interviewer are based on a different indicator. The interviewer presents evidence that Share is funded by the forestry industry, those who primarily stand to gain if Share's point of view is accepted by the public, and those who determine public policies. The presumption raised by this indicator of bias is that Share may be a "front" for the forest industry, and hence its advocacy for industry's point of view in the dispute with the environmentalists would be based on a kind of deception or concealment of bias of a harmful or illicit kind. These doubts, once raised, suggest that we may not be able to trust Share to give a sincere advocacy of its point of view, based on arguments it believes to be convincing as evidence that should be acceptable to the uncommitted. Instead, it is suggested what Share could be doing covertly is bargaining to promote its own financial interests and those of the forest industry. In other words, the suggestion is that Share does not really believe its own arguments but is merely "putting up a front" to win over others for financial gain.

This would be a bad or harmful kind of bias with respect to the critical discussion on the issue of logging and the environment in which Share is supposedly engaged. For it suggests that Share is not really looking at the evidence on both sides, and deciding the issue on the basis of this evidence. Instead, the allegation is that Share has made up its collective mind in advance and will always declare the strongest argument is on the one side, on the basis of its financial interest in making it seem that this side has the best arguments in its favor.

Then the allegation here is one that indicates a kind of duplicity. This aspect of the allegation of bias especially came out in the second half of the interview. It was made clear there that the B.C. Forest Alliance made a point of portraying itself as an independent body. According to Trish Wood, the Forest Alliance says it has the purpose of "informing the public on forestry issues." The Alliance presents itself as an "environmental organization" (p. 5). The stance taken by the Forest Alliance is that it is providing "information" to the public on forestry issues. It does not portray itself as an advocacy group that is pushing for one side on controversial environmental issues. However, Trish Wood's questions suggest that this stance is phony. She immediately asks whether "the fact that the Alliance was set up by a public relations firm, spin doctors, in any way taints the Alliance" (as quoted above). She then goes on to indicate in detail how the Alliance is funded by the forest industry and is operating in the interests of the forest industry.

This allegation of duplicity is most pointed when Wood cites a television series paid for by the Forest Alliance where the programs "look like documentaries" and "appear to be open, unbiased presentations," but "every program contains a bottom line message from the industry to the public" (p. 5). At the end of the interview (p. 6), Wood even gets Dennis Fitzgerald to agree to the proposition that those at MacMillan Bloedel are "the environmentalists in this debate" (p. 6). This would be an absurd proposition for most of the viewers to accept.

The case here is comparable to that of the infomercials, where the program presents itself as some sort of documentary that has the purpose of giving information to viewers but is covertly an advocacy argument to sell something (see chapter 6). At least that is an implication of the criticism posed by Trish Wood's questions in the interview, and she gives plenty of evidence that would indicate this kind of bias on the part of the Forest Alliance. This is a misleading and critically harmful or obstructive type of bias, based on a concealed dialectical shift. What appears on the surface to be a kind of information-presenting type of dialogue is revealed as advocacy, a kind of selling of a product.

8. Evaluation of the Case

In the end, the Share movement and the other advocacy groups questioned in the Last Battleground case are, by and large, unsuccessful in defending themselves against the charge of bias posed in the interview. Their attempts to portray themselves as on the same footing as environmental groups, or even as independent bodies informing the public on environmental issues, are largely a failure. The interview presents such well-documented evidence of financial and other connections with the forest industry that the burden of proof remains pretty well set in place on the side of perceiving them as having a strong bias.

Nevertheless, from a point of view of studying allegations of bias, it is very interesting to see that there is room for them to mount argumentation against this allegation of bias. Even though the argumentation is not successful in this case, it does show that a line of argumentation of this type is, in principle, possible. That is, the charge of bias is rebuttable. Even though both sides concede that the groups in question had something to gain and were even funded and founded by the forest industry, there was room for them to maintain that, despite this, they had an independent point of view and an arm's-length relationship.

The basic point is that even if a group admits it is an advocacy group and that its argumentation has a bias, it is possible for this group to defend this argumentation as being based on good evidence that should command itself to anyone's rational assent or consideration. The allegation of bias is a defeasible one, and the indicators of bias are defeasible "red flags" or warning signals that function as signs of bias, not conclusive refutations of an argument.

Then, it is interesting to see that a distancing strategy is available for anyone accused of the kind of bad or harmful bias that would detract from the credibility of her argumentation. The strategy is to portray oneself as being at arm's length, as having one's own reasons for one's point of view, even though one may admit to having something to gain by taking one side on an issue.

A bias in the sense of commitment to an identifiable position is not necessarily something that detracts from the argumentation for that position. It is only if that bias can be shown to be an obstacle to or prevention from one's genuinely and sincerely looking at the arguments on both sides, on their merits, that it becomes a so-called bias that can be used to criticize or undermine one's argumentation. Even if one has something to gain, one can still defend one's argument against the criticism that it contains the bad sort of bias.

9. Raising Critical Questions

Throughout the case, the interviewer, Trish Wood, raises questions that focus on the issue of whether or not the advocacy groups, such as Share and the Forest Alliance, that oppose the environmentalists' arguments for restricting logging, really represent an independent viewpoint of their own or are merely pawns or paid advocates of the logging corporations. This issue is really the substance of the interview. The facts arising from the interview, not contested by either side, of the various financial connections between the logging corporations and the advocacy groups, set in place a presumption of bias. The representatives of the groups interviewed use arguments that attempt to rebut this presumption. But the questions posed by Trish Wood raise the presumption and strengthen it, making it quite an uphill struggle for the groups to try to distance themselves from corporate interests. It is interesting to try to evaluate to what extent their arguments are successful in doing this.

The interview starts out with a history of the facts of how Share developed from the Wise Use movement. Most of this part of the interview seems to be concerned with sketching in the background facts. And much of it seems to be positive toward the views of Share. Ron Arnold, for example, is allowed to attack the environmental movement, portraying it as "killing jobs and trashing the economy." However, this first part of the interview also makes it quite clear how Share evolved from earlier organizations that were specifically founded and funded by those who had something to gain by supporting logging—loggers, truckers, people from logging communities, and representatives of MacMillan Bloedel. Indeed, it is indicated that it was this logging corporation that was primarily responsible for setting up Share and continuing to support it financially. Bob Skelly even admits that the first meetings were called by the chief executive officer of MacMillan Bloedel, with "booze and food spread out so you could enjoy as much as you want" (p. 3). Understandably, these admissions, by the very people who support the Share cause, set in place quite a heavy presumption of bias, indicated by such strong and definite financial links between Share and those who have much to gain or lose by the fate of the logging industry.

The first serious critical question, once the facts are set in place, to raise the issue of bias, is Wood's asking whether it is "ethical for the industry to fund so-called citizens groups who downplay their affiliation with the industry." This is a loaded question for the Share advocates. It suggests that they could be unethical and attributes deception to them, by using the phrases "so-called citizen groups" and "downplay their affiliation." This suggests, subject to rebuttal by the reply, not only that these groups have a bias but also that they are trying to conceal it by portraying themselves as something they are not. The presumption raised by the question is that these advocacy groups have a bad or harmful kind of bias, that they are trying to "downplay" their affiliation with those who gain financially from logic in order to deceive the public.

Dennis Fitzgerald, in his reply, does give a good argument in reply, supported by Mike Morton's argument that there are "no strings attached." But Trish Wood follows up with a series of further questions. Finding that MacMillan Bloedel still gives $100,000 a year to support Share, she asks, "Why would the forest industry fund you unless it was in their interest to do so?" Mike Morton has a good answer, again insisting that there are "no strings attached." But how convincing is his answer, given the presumption of bias raised by the question? One would have to think that the viewing audience is going to be pretty skeptical of Morton's claim that Share is independent of the logging industry in a way that makes its arguments not susceptible to quite a seriously compromising sort of bias that would question its credibility on the issue of logging and the environment.

10. How Bias Should Be Evaluated

In all the types of dialogue except the quarrel, there is a weighing of the strength of arguments on two sides of an issue, problem, or conflict of opinions that is unsettled and an expectation that a participant or an onlooker will weigh the arguments on both sides by the evidence. Even though a participant or an onlooker is an advocate for one side or the other, the presumption is that she will not be exclusively guided or dominated by that advocacy in coming to a decision on which arguments to which to commit. Only in the eristic dialogue is advocacy the exclusive driving force of commitment. In all the other types of dialogue, a participant is presumed to be open to committing to the conclusion of a good argument put forward by the opposed side (or is even obliged to do so, by the normative standards for the type of dialogue involved).

As participants in argumentation in one of these types of dialogue, we are all biased. That is normal and expected.[7] There is nothing bad about it, from a normative point of view of the evaluation of argumentation. However, this normal and expected bias becomes pathological, or a negative kind of bias, from this normative point of view, precisely when this presumption that one will commit to the conclusion of a good argument no matter which side it supports is violated.

In the Last Battleground case, the Share advocates did not deny that they had financial links with the forest industry or that they had something to gain by committing to or supporting the one side of the disputed issue. They freely admitted being advocates of a particular point of view. Thus, they admit that they have a bias or that there is a bias in their argumentation. What they deny is the charge that this is a negative or harmful type of bias.

One thing that is most important to see generally is that if one is accused of bias in an argument, in many cases the best defence is to admit bias, but to rebut the charge that it is of a negative or normatively objectionable type. This should be seen generally as an open avenue for reply to allegations of bias.

As onlookers or respondents to an argument, we will downgrade its credibility and our readiness to commit to its conclusion, to the extent we think the argument contains the negative kind of bias. This way of committing is reasonable because in many arguments in the different types of dialogues considered in chapter 2, the argument is so complex and the evidence so uncertain or unavailable that we have to decide partly on the basis of whether we can presume that the arguers on both sides are making sincere efforts to contribute to the dialogue. That is, they are not just pure advocates, engaging in a purely eristic contest, but intellectually honest and open-minded participants in the critical discussion or other type of dialogue in which they are supposedly engaged. If we think there is real evidence behind an argument, over and above pure advocacy, and that the arguer is supporting the argument, at least partly, on the basis of this evidence, we will upgrade our credibility in that argument and be more willing to take it seriously and to commit to the conclusion (as opposed to going for the conclusion of the other side).

Thus, bias is one factor in the evaluation of argumentation, but it is not the whole picture. We should evaluate arguments on the basis of the evidence given in the premises to support the conclusion. But if two opposed arguments are tied or evenly matched in a balance-of-considerations situation, which one should we choose? Here, bias comes in as a legitimate factor in judging argumentation. If an argument exhibits a negative bias, then it is reasonable to downgrade it, compared to the weight of commitment for the opposed argument on the other side, where this argument does not exhibit a negative bias.

So we could say that negative bias is closely associated with the eristic type of dialogue, even though the two things are not exactly equivalent. Eristic dialogue is about as close to pure advocacy as one can get in argumentation. However, we have maintained that quarreling is not, in itself, necessarily bad or negative, from a normative point of view as argumentation.

The negative bias, on the theory given here, is identified with the illicit shift from one of the other types of dialogue to the quarrel. Evaluating argumentation as containing negative bias therefore depends crucially on a contextual and normative judgment concerning the type of dialogue of which a given argument is supposed to be part. Only to the extent that such a presumption about the context of dialogue of a given argument is justified, can we justifiably judge that the argument contains a negative bias.

Notes

1. On issues of how to classify the various subspecies of *ad hominem* arguments, see Krabbe and Walton (1993).

2. See chapter 2, on the information-seeking type of dialogue.

3. Alter also refers to the famous case where incendiary devices were attached to a truck to make spectacular film footage of an explosion when another vehicle was smashed into the truck. This was done, without viewers knowing about the incendiary devices, on a program concerning claims that the fuel tank of the truck was hazardous.

4. This is a conditional presumption, however. News programs presumably have a primary function of giving information or "news," but in fact they are typically mixed in their dialogue typology.

5. See Walton (1992b, chapter 2).

6. Ibid.

7. See chapter 3, on bias not always being harmful. The idea of a participant (arguer) being biased, as opposed to her argument being biased, is taken up in chapter 10.

BIAS IN LEGAL AND SCIENTIFIC ARGUMENTS

Evaluation of scientific and legal arguments requires taking into account special conventions and assumptions that are in these structured, institutional frameworks, in addition to normative models of argument generally. In a legal trial, for example, there are specific rules governing evidence, relevance, and burden of proof. In scientific research, statistical methods and other guidelines governing the collecting of data and testing of hypotheses are relevant to judging when an argument is to be considered biased in a given case. In both law and scientific disciplines, the judgment of whether an argument is biased depends on special rules and normative requirements that are peculiar to a discipline or to a methodological point of view or structure. Hence any investigation of the kinds of bias involved in argumentation in these special contexts will take us beyond the normative frameworks developed so far.

Bias is a term frequently used in law to apply to judges, juries, and the testimony of witnesses. 'Bias' is also frequently applied to the collection, interpretation, and use of data in scientific research. Statistics is a special case in point, and logic textbooks often use the phrase *biased statistics* to refer to a widely recognized type of fallacy.

In both scientific and legal argumentation, there are several specific kinds of bias in argumentation that occur and are perceived to be problems, in the sense of being obstacles to good argumentation. But in both law and science there is also a more general and dialectical bias that can affect the structure of dialogue as a whole. These more holistic kinds of bias affect the dialectical structure of the argument.

Another possible area of future research already touched upon in chapter 5 is that of biased questions. A question is not an argument. So when it is judged that a question is biased, is it because that question is part of an argument or somehow functioned as argumentative? Or is it the question itself that is biased? In other words, are biased questions biased in a different way than arguments are?

These two problems are joined together when we look at cases of biased questions used in polling because this area relates to questions (and often to language) but falls under statistical methodology as well.

1. Bias in Legal Argument and Scientific Research

What constitutes bias in scientific research is quite different from what would be considered a biased argument in a court of law, for the type of dialogue is quite distinctively different in these two instances. In a North American court of law, the adversary legal system is based on a dialogue exchange where each of the two sides is supposed to present advocacy that is as strong and persuasive as possible for its own side. Rules of evidence constrain these arguments, but the arguments are supposed to be based on self-interested advocacy. Then a third party, a judge or jury, is supposed to decide which side's arguments are strong enough to fulfill the burden of proof set for a particular type of trial.

In legal argumentation, it is presumed that each side will advocate its own view and its own interests. Especially in litigation where a large sum of money is involved, it is assumed that each party will argue on a basis of his or her own self-interest.

The framework of dialogue for argument in academic or scientific research contrasts sharply with that of legal argument in a trial, when it comes to the concept of bias. Here the idea that a researcher would promote arguments based on his personal views or his own interests is a mark of the kind of bias that consciously should be resisted. The sharp contrast between the methods of argument used and approved of in legal argumentation as opposed to argumentation in academic research is well brought out in the list of key differences cited by Crossen (1994, pp. 193–194):

> The bald self-interest at the heart of litigation research is only one of the many ways it differs from the academic search for truth. A court constructs its view of the truth from the materials before it. If a witness says black is white, and no one contradicts it, then for purposes of the court, black is white. Legal adversaries stake out extreme positions, making consensus unlikely. In research, however, as in many other parts of life, consensus is an indicator—though an imperfect one—of truth.

The methods by which the two disciplines seek truth also differ. In uncorrupted research, the idea is to search for an unknown, probably hypothesized, truth; in law, it is to assemble facts to support a predetermined position. Or as the cynical lawyer in Frederick Busch's courtroom novel *Closing Arguments* said, "When we figure out what truth we're telling, then we'll work on how to tell someone that particular truth."

In law, if something happens once, it is a piece of evidence; in research, one piece of evidence is barely a start. While the law knowingly excludes evidence, its standard to establish a truth—a preponderance of the evidence, or probability greater than 50 percent—is less rigorous than ideal research. Full disclosure is built into the ethics of research; true science gives other researchers the chance to challenge a study by trying to replicate it. In law, lawyers have the right not to disclose adverse factual evidence.

The striking general contrasts brought out here suggest that if the inquiry could be the normative model of dialogue appropriate for scientific research, something quite different, perhaps a variant of the persuasion type of dialogue, is appropriate to model argumentation in a legal trial (at least, in the North American type of adversary system of law).

Some philosophers, notably Aristotle and Descartes, have argued that argumentation in academic and scientific research should take the form of an inquiry. This view is very popular with the scientists themselves, at least in their rhetoric to outsiders, when it comes to presenting their results. Descartes carried this a step further by even arguing that philosophy should take the form of an inquiry, using a Euclidean type of model. Spinoza also used a method of geometrical demonstration to present his arguments. However, in latter years many have disagreed with the foundational model of scientific argumentation and have seen scientific research as taking something much more like the form of a persuasion dialogue.

Also, scientific argumentation seems to go through several different stages. At the discovery stage, according to the kind of account favored by Peirce, there is speculative guesswork in abductive arguments. But at a later stage in argumentation, where results are tested and consolidated in a scientific discipline, the structure of the dialogue conforms much more naturally to that of the inquiry.

Another difficulty in determining bias in a given case of an argument in science is that bias, as we have seen, is defined and determined in particular cases partly by the special methodological norms and rules of each scientific discipline. Thus, which arguments in statistical reasoning are said to be biased and how that bias is to be evaluated (in a specific case) are, to a large extent, issues internal to the discipline of statistics.[1]

Even so, these questions are not wholly technical. They are partly philosophical or relate to the concept of bias that is general in all argumentation. So we think our dialectical concept of bias as one-sided advocacy can be of help as a research program to aid in the investigation of these questions.

Interpretation of the various legal notions of bias identified in this chapter also depends on how we see the philosophical foundations of legal disputation in a trial as a type of dialogue. It is a mixed type of dialogue, but it seems to have significant elements of a persuasion dialogue.[2] The opposing attorneys put forward advocacy arguments on both sides, and the judge or jury is supposed to decide, in accord with the legal requirements of burden of proof, which side has the winning argument and which side the losing one.

The lawyers are supposed to put forth biased arguments, in our sense, meaning that they each advocate their respective points of view. But the judge or the jury, whoever makes the decision on the outcome of the trial, is supposed to be "unbiased." This is not bias in argumentation, in our previously defined sense (see chapter 3), but it does seem to be related to it indirectly. The judge or jury is the referee or decision maker of the outcome and is supposed to judge on the weight of evidence presented in the arguments by the advocates on both sides. This judging function presumes that the judge or jury will pay attention to the arguments presented on both sides and will decide on a basis of weighing the legal evidence comparatively, without letting his or her personal preferences, financial interests, loyalties, and so on. be the basis for deciding. This is a kind of bias related to argumentation, but it is a kind of judging or refereeing type of role that is involved. This is different from being a direct participant in the argumentation. However, this kind of bias could be the same as our sense of bias in argumentation during the deliberation stage where the jury members are sequestered and argue among themselves to try to reach a unanimous decision.

2. Bias as Attributed to Witnesses

Another type of bias in legal argumentation has to do with cross-examination of witnesses in a trial. The witness type of bias is more similar to our basic dialectical concept of bias in argumentation. But the witness is not arguing, exactly. The function of the witness is to report the facts. The witness takes an oath to do so truthfully. So when we claim that the testimony of a witness is biased, it is not bias in argumentation that is (primarily) meant. What is referred to is a selective, untruthful, or distorted reporting of the facts by a witness.

If this interpretation is right, the interviewing of a witness could be seen as a kind of information-seeking dialogue. But the matter is more complex, because cross-examination of a witness tends to have a strongly adversarial character. Often this can seem to be more like a persuasion dialogue, or even an eristic dialogue, when the questioning of the cross-examining attorney shows advocacy.

Arguing against the testimony of a witness in cross-examination by showing that the testimony is biased is recognized in law as a legitimate type of argumentation in a trial. In law, this type of argumentation comes under the heading of "impeachment," defined by Degnan (1973, p. 908) as "the process of discrediting testimony by showing facts which tend to reflect upon the veracity of the witness and thus to authorize rejection in whole or in part of the testimony he has given." Here the law follows a kind of argumentation that is very common in everyday reasoning (as we saw in chapter 7) where one party attacks or questions the opinion vouched for by another by alleging that the other party's argument is biased.

Degnan (1973, p. 909) gives a number of different kinds of grounds that may be used to support the argument from bias in law.

> *Showing of Bias.*—Sympathy for one party or animosity for another may color testimony, wittingly or unwittingly. Hence family relationship, personal friendship and interest in the outcome of a case are open to inquiry. Hostile statements or actions by the witness in regard to one side may be shown. Greed and other personal interest may also affect testimony. One common example involves testimony in a criminal case from a witness who is himself in the hands of the law; wide inquiry is allowed to determine whether that testimony has been obtained or encouraged by suggestions of the prosecutor that leniency will follow cooperation in giving evidence. Payment received by an expert for testifying can be exposed because of its tendency to produce favorable testimony.

The case of expert testimony is especially interesting in connection with the argument from bias. In our system of law, expert witnesses are paid a fee to testify by the side that appoints them. Since both sides frequently use experts, who argue to opposed opinions in their testimony, commonly a trial turns into a "battle of the experts." In such cases, the attorney for the one side may attack the testimony of the expert witness of the other side on grounds of bias, because that expert has been paid by the other side to testify.

Graham (1977, p. 35) notes that advocacy of one side or the other by professional expert witnesses has "become a fact of life in the litigation process," and so prevalent that some expert witnesses make a living just from their court fees.[3] As a result, arguments by impeachment of the other side's expert witnesses on grounds of their having a financial interest have also become commonplace. Graham (1977, p. 50) outlines the various grounds used to support this kind of argument.

> How far may counsel proceed with cross-examination directed at establishing bias based upon financial interest? If cross-examination is directed at establishing bias through financial interest, it will generally be permitted if it is directed at establishing (1) financial interest in the case at hand by reason of remuneration for services, (2) continued employment by a party or (3) the fact of prior testimony for the same party or the same attorney. When it comes to questions directed toward establishing (1) the amount of previous compensation from the same party, (2) the relationship between the expert's income from testifying on behalf of a party or a category of party and total income of the expert, or (3) the mere fact of prior testimony most frequently on behalf of other persons or entities similarly situated, the cases indicate disagreement.

The basis of this type of negative argumentation is that the testimony of the expert can exhibit a negative type of bias that gives the audience, the jury, grounds for having reservations about it as a credible argument. The imputation is that the expert may be basing her opinion not just on the evidence in her field of expertise, but also partly on an interested advocacy for one side.

Imwinkelried (1982, pp. 290–296) has outlined several types of arguments that can be used by an attorney to attack the scientific expert witness who is testifying for the other side by arguing that the witness is biased. According to Imwinkelried (1982, p. 290) bias impeachment is one of the best "weight attacks," that is, arguments for decreasing the weight of plausibility of a proposition because the jurors can easily understand this type of attack (290). Suppose, for example (p. 297) that the witness is a medical doctor basing his testimony on the report of another physician. But suppose that the witness adopted only the findings favorable to the one attorney's case, and rejected or ignored the findings favorable to the case of the other side. Imwinkelried advises the cross-examining attorney, in such a case, to highlight the selectivity of the witness, and thereby suggest to the jury that the testimony of this expert witness is biased. Many different types of attacks on scientific evidence presented by an expert witness are described by Imwinkelried (p. 297).

McElhaney (1992, p. 62) describes this type of negative argumentation from a showing of bias as "powerful medicine" in a trial. He gives the advice to use it in "small doses" and avoid the common practice of most lawyers, who "keep pouring long after the tablespoon is already overflowing" (p. 62). He (p. 62) calls this "the powerful medicine rule": "It is better to put things together so the jurors feel they have figured it out for themselves than to try to pour the idea down their throats" (p. 62) This advice confirms the notion advanced in chapter 7 that bias can be a powerful type of argument when based on suspicions that may be difficult to refute.

In many cases of so-called "junk science," it is hard to tell whether highly paid expert scientific witnesses are "hired guns" or "true believers." For example, in recent years some leading geneticists and molecular biologists have appeared prominently as expert defence witnesses to argue against the new technique of DNA fingerprinting as evidence in court. Because they have made a good deal of income from these court appearances, some suspect these scientists of bias, on grounds of having a financial interest (Roberts 1992, p. 735).

> *Case* 8.1: The charge most frequently lobbed by prosecutors and officials at the Federal Bureau of Investigation against expert witnesses for the defense in DNA fingerprinting cases is that they are hired guns—scientists with questionable credentials who travel from courtroom to courtroom simply to make a buck. "It's a real scandal what these guys get paid. If you knew, it would make your head spin," says Rockne Harmon, an Alameda County prosecutor who spearheads a nationwide effort to defeat the courtroom critics of DNA. Adds James Kearney, head of the FBI's Forensic Science and Training Center in Quantico, Virginia: "There are some who are making a living out of this. We resent them."

One population geneticist complains that "the constant harping about hired guns" is just a tactic lawyers use "to discredit scientists who oppose them." Others have declined fees because "they knew it can be used to undermine their credibility" (Roberts 1992, p. 735). This type of case is only one of many different kinds of expert scientific testimony in the courts that has been very controversial in recent years because of the suspicion that expert witnesses are being used as "hired guns."

To contend with this problem, it has often been suggested that neutral scientific experts should be appointed by the courts. But this proposal has not yet been widely adopted, and critics (Howard 1991) have argued that it has many disadvantages.

Appeal to expert opinion is a distinctive type of argumentation in its own right,[4] and the argument from bias is used as a counterargument to attack the use of appeal to expert opinion in these legal cases. It too is, in principle, a reasonable type of presumptive argument that can be used to shift a burden of proof in a balance-of-considerations situation. In other instances, like the appeal to expert opinion, it can be used fallaciously. Such fallacious use of argumentation from bias to attack the argument of another party is frequently identified as *ad hominem* argument by textbooks. Waller (1988, pp. 107–113), for example, identifies a subtype of *ad hominem* argument called the "bias *ad hominem*" (p. 107). Fallacious appeals to expert opinion are classified under the heading of the "*argumentum ad verecundiam.*"[5] Use of personal-attack arguments as species of arguments from bias are studied at a deeper level in chapter 10.

3. Bias as Attributed to Judges and Juries

Several techniques are used in trials to try to identify bias in jurors or to minimize the effects of bias. According to Minow and Cate (1992, p. 59), these include change of venue (moving the trial), continuance (delaying the trial), *voir dire* (questioning potential jurors), jury instructions, and jury deliberations. Because of the current wide media coverage of events related to trials, one of the biggest problems has been to find jury members that are not "biased" in the sense of having some knowledge of the particulars of a case from media reports.

As Minow and Cate point out, however, many social scientists argue that these techniques are not effective in detecting or remedying bias in a trial. For example, the technique of *voir dire,* where judges or attorneys ask questions of potential jurors to detect bias, has been criticized (Minow and Cate 1992, p. 59).

> Existing research suggests that *voir dire* is ineffective as a means of identifying prejudice. Many critics charge that it fails to elicit

accurate or honest responses from potential jurors or members of the venire (the panel from which they are chosen). "Jurors do not speak out during *voir dire*, nor do they acknowledge their prejudices and preconceptions. Further, they occasionally lie when questioned in public." For instance, who is going to admit publicly to being a bigot? In addition, many attorneys and judges believe jurors use confessions of prejudice as a convenient method to avoid jury duty.

The kind of bias being searched for here seems to be more prejudice than dialectical bias in argumentation. But it may be related to the latter, because the attempt is to prevent the kind of bias that might occur in the jury's deliberations at a later stage of the trial.

Not as much attention appears to have been paid to the bias of judges. But one question that has arisen in Canada is whether the outspoken public pronouncements of a judge, expressing his or her personal or political point of view, should be taken as an indicator of a bias that could be harmful judicially. Some argue that judges should speak out in the media on their political views, even if the issue is controversial and the viewpoint provocative, but others feel that this increasing move away from the traditional silence of judges raises public worries about their impartiality (Fine, 1993, p. A1). One commentator (quoted in Fine 1993, p. A1) worried: "If judges take a stand one way or the other on the abortion issue, how could they possibly appear to be unbiased?" The evolving practice is for judges to speak out more freely, recently, on controversial issues.

A more worrisome type of indicator of bias is how judges apply the rules of evidence in given cases. This is tested by comparing how strictly or loosely the judge applied the rules in different cases, or even on different sides of the same case.

Landsman (1992, p. 639) cites the famous Sacco and Vanzetti case (1921) where two Italian immigrants were accused of murder, and robbery of a shoe company, in South Braintree, Massachusetts. The way the judge conducted this case, as compared to his conduct of another case, is summarized (below) from the account of Landsman (1992, pp. 639–646).

Case 8.2:   Carlos Goodridge, a salesman, claimed to have seen Sacco ride by in the robbers' getaway car. Goodridge was on probation, and was vulnerable to pressure to testify in a way that would support the prosecution case. Judge Thayer tightly constrained the rules of evidence by refusing to allow the defence to bring this out when cross-examining Goodridge in the trial. This starkly contrasted with the latitude permitted to the prosecution attorney during his cross-examination of Sacco and Vanzetti.

In this case, Landsman's criticism relates to the way the judge controlled the argumentation by interpreting the rules of evidence, more strictly or freely, to favor the argumentation of the one side over that of the other. Then this is not a bias in the argumentation *per se*, but a kind of external bias expressed in how a rule is applied to the participants' arguments. But this is a harmful bias on the argumentation in the trial, in respect to its contributing to a fair outcome by giving a balanced consideration of both sides.

This is a kind of dialectical bias, because it is part of the structure of dialogue, the framework of how the rules of evidence are applied, in the goal-directed framework of argumentation. But it is not so much a bias in the argumentation itself, in the sense of dialectical bias defined as the advocacy of one side in this book, as it is a bias in how the rules of the dialogue are applied to the argumentation of both sides by a third party referee (in this case, the judge), who is responsible for applying the rules to allow or disallow arguments in a given case.

Similarly, the kind of bias attributed to a jury is not straightforwardly a dialectical bias in argumentation, at least of the kind we have been analyzing previously. It is a bias in how jury members may decide a case. Screening by *voir dire* is an attempt to anticipate such a bias. This bias could occur in a jury member's argumentation at a later stage, however, when the jury is engaged in deliberations, after the trial.

4. Balance in a Fair Trial

The legal system is based on a set of rules that attempts to deal with or allow for various kinds of bias, in order to assure a defendant a fair trial, while at the same time prosecuting crimes and making decisions fairly. But such a system is always under political pressures by advocacy groups.

The most worrisome kind of harmful bias that affects legal argumentation is the kind where political pressure is brought to bear on the trial process itself, during periods of public panic and hysteria where some particular type of crime is demonized. A fair trial is based on a balance between the two sides—that of the accuser and that of the accused. But immense popular political pressure to prosecute certain types of crimes (or alleged crimes) at certain periods can result in an upset of this balance. The outcome can be a very harmful kind of bias affecting the arguments in a trial.

The central dialectical concept in our legal system is that of the fair trial. The basic idea is that there are supposed to be one-sided arguments on both sides, the defence and the prosecution. The procedure is supposed to be open and balanced, however, in the sense that both sides are allowed to collect and present evidence to mount the strongest possible case for their contentions. Also, the trial is judged by a third party (judge or jury) who can assess the weight of the arguments on both sides, and decide the outcome.

The outcome of the trial is based on burden of proof. In a criminal trial, the prosecution has the burden of proving that the accused is guilty beyond a reasonable doubt. The defense merely has to raise enough questions to show that there is a reasonable doubt that the accusation has been proved.

However, the trial system, as a way of deciding the outcome of proving guilt or not, is inherently fallible. Witnesses have been known to lie or be mistaken, for example. And the police may be under public pressure to make an arrest. It is known that some innocent persons inevitably will be convicted. But the structure of a fair trial is designed expressly to minimize this outcome and to reverse it, when it is found to occur. To achieve this purpose, the trial procedure must achieve a balance between the arguments of the two sides.

However, this balance can be affected when there is strong political pressure brought to bear on the court system to prosecute certain types of crimes very enthusiastically. In such a climate of public opinion, strong pressure is exerted on any trial for this type of crime to almost always consider the accused person guilty as charged. There may be such a stigma and fear attached to this particular type of accusation, during a certain period, that the defendant has very little credibility in trying to escape the "poisoning-the-well" effect of this type of accusation. And since law is very much a reflection of public opinions and attitudes and can be affected by the political views of the judges and juries, this kind of pressure can create a bias that pushes the balance strongly to one side, so that more weight is accorded to the claims of the accuser. In extreme cases, the defendant may be left with little or no room to put up any credible arguments.

The classic cases illustrating such a one-sided tribunal were the so-called witch hunts or witchcraft (sorcery) tribunals that took place in both Europe and North America. Another instance often cited were the McCarthy tribunals during the "Red menace" era in North America. These cases represent the degeneration of the balanced trial format into a one-sided political vehicle for enforcing a particular ideological view through pressure and intimidation. An investigation of this concept of the witch hunt is the subject of chapter 9.

5. Bias in Scientific Research

The term *bias* as applied to scientific research is used in two senses by Broad and Wade (1982). One refers to personal bias in the refereeing system and peer review process, when grants, journal articles, and so forth are evaluated by colleagues (p. 102). Recently, scientists have expressed worries that papers submitted to scientific journals are routinely rejected, based on the bias of reviewers (Begley 1992). The other meaning refers to bias in the interpretation of data. Under this heading are included (a) intentional bias or fraud, (b) unintentional bias, or "unconscious or dimly perceived finagling" (p. 85), and (c) the case of the scientist who "falls prey to dogma, and tries to promote doctrinaire beliefs, in the name of science." A fourth sense of the term *bias* used in science refers to a fault in experimental design or terminology that deceptively skews a result to one side. An example would be the bias in cancer research cited as a case of biased terminology in chapter 5.

Medical research has developed various methods of inquiry that help to deal with different kinds of potential biases in the collection of experimental data and the drawing of conclusions from data. For example, a report in the *Journal of the American Medical Association* (Forsyth et al., 1989) enumerated several types of bias that could be problems in explaining an association found between Reye's syndrome and previous use of aspirin. Reye's syndrome is an often fatal encephalopathy in children characterized by fatty infiltration of the liver and swelling of the kidneys and brain.

1. *Temporal Precedence Bias.*
    To avoid temporal precedence bias, investigators must demonstrate that aspirin use precedes rather than follows the earliest clinical manifestations of Reye's syndrome (p. 2518).

2. *Susceptibility Bias.*
    Susceptibility bias occurs if aspirin is prescribed preferentially to

children who have a particular cluster of severity of prodromal symptoms that may predispose them to Reye's syndrome (p. 2518).

3. *Recall Bias.*
Biased recall by the parent or guardian (or whoever provided care for the child) may produce a falsely high proportion of antecedent exposure to aspirin among case subjects compared with controls (p. 2518).

4. *Diagnostic Bias.*
Bias in diagnosis arises from the physician's initial suspicion that a child has Reye's syndrome, the decision to order tests, and referring of the patient to a care center. This could be affected by publicity about a relationship between aspirin and Reye's syndrome (p. 2518).

5. *Reporting Bias.*
This type of bias has to do with how cases are selected to be reported to the study. Particular surveillance physicians from certain hospitals were selected, and they were "telephoned every two weeks for routine inquiries about possible cases" (p. 2519).

In this study, there was a definite association found between Reye's syndrome and previous aspirin use, but the problem was that earlier methodological problems had overestimated it (p. 2524). Hence, to determine the medical significance of the association, the inquiry was redesigned in order to minimize or eliminate these five potential sources of bias.

In this kind of usage, 'bias' refers to failure to use general techniques appropriate for a scientific investigation, like randomization and control groups. However, at a more particular level, each field has its own techniques that are customarily used. Thus, *bias* has become, to a large extent, a technical scientific term that is defined and measured by the techniques used for collection, interpretation, and analysis of data by any particular scientific discipline at a given point in the development of that field.

These methods of inquiry are always changing and evolving. Hence, the identification and evaluation of bias in science is, to a significant extent, tied to the particular methods of that branch of science. This is relativization of bias to the particulars of a speech event framework in a given case.

Changes in the way scientific research is financed are leading to a situation where bias is more of a concern. According to Crossen (1994, p. 166), for example, biomedical research funding is increasingly funded by private industries that have a commercial interest in the outcome. For example, a good deal of research done on new drugs by physicians is funded by the pharmaceutical industry. Despite the use of scientific methods that are designed to prevent bias from distorting scientific research, subtle bias in biomedical research can intrude in many forms: (Crossen 1994, p. 167):

> Problems can arise in the labs of even the most conscientious and honest researchers. Biology is enormously complicated anyway, and like all research, biomedical studies begin with choices. Although biomedical research incorporates rigorous scientific rules and is often critically scrutinized by peers, the information can nevertheless be warped—by ending a study because the results are disappointing; changing rules—the protocol or analytic tools—midstudy; not trying to publish negative results; publicizing preliminary results even with final and less positive results in hand; skimming over or even not acknowledging drawbacks; and, especially, casting the results in the best light or, as scientists say, buffing them.

Concerns about the increasing prevalence of these various forms of bias in scientific research have been much more vocally expressed in recent years, because of the way science is practiced and funded.

One kind of bias in scientific drug data is the reluctance of scientists to publish findings that did not show any benefits of a drug or therapy manufactured by the company who funded the scientific research. A case is described in Altman (1997, p. B7).

Case 8.3: The thyroid drug case involved the Knoll Pharmaceutical Company of Mount Olive, N.J., the manufacturer of Synthroid, the third most widely prescribed drug in the United States. Knoll is a subsidiary of the BASF Group, a German manufacturer of chemicals, pharmaceuticals, cosmetics and electronics.

For several years Knoll had prohibited a team led by Dr. Betty J. Dong at the University of California at San Francisco from reporting a study showing that Synthroid was no more effective than less expensive generic versions of the drug.

> Dr. Dong signed a contract in 1987 giving Knoll's predecessor the right to veto any publication. The study was completed in 1990, but the findings were reported in *The Journal of the American Medical Association* on April 16 after Knoll relented.

The outcome of this kind of bias is that scientific journals present a much more positive picture of a new drug than the evidence really warrants. The Food and Drug Administration reported (Altman 1997, p. B7) that scientific journals provide "a skewed subset of information" and that consumers should have "a healthy skepticism" about reports of drug research in scientific journals.

There have been many changes in how scientific and other academic research has been funded in recent years. Research grants provided by government funding frequently target specific areas and problems for allocations of funds, based on essentially political judgments of what problems are deemed important for the interests of the country at a particular time or which advocacy groups have been vocal in the political arena at a particular time. Also, less and less research tends to be on theoretical and fundamental questions, and more and more funding is targeted to practical interdisciplinary projects that clearly have an immediate financial potential for benefiting the economy in the short term. These changes have been gradual, but they are cumulative and general.

According to John Ziman, a physicist and science policy observer, (Patel 1995, p. 7), these changes in the way science is practiced, over the past two decades, has led to a new research culture, called "postacademic science":

> Professor Ziman argued that in postacademic science, research is directed towards specific ends, and relates to problems which will not have been set by individuals themselves or even by the teams. The choice of problems to be worked on operates at the level of the bodies funding science: "All policy talk about foresight, priorities, accountability etcetera is really focused on 'problem choice.'"

In postacademic science these changes, according to Ziman (Patel 1995, p. 7) "could mean a decline in scientific objectivity." Bias is much more of a real danger in postacademic science because of the inherent conflict of interest in a scientific inquiry being conducted and paid for by those who primarily stand to gain or lose financially by the outcome of the research.

We have found then that in both science and law, 'bias' has various specific technical meanings, but there is also a systemic, dialectical type of bias that can affect the dialogue structure as a whole.

6. Biased Statistics

The word *bias* is used as a technical term in statistics, referring to the way of arguing from a representative sample. In sampling to a population in statistics, the sample chosen must not only be large enough to be meaningful, it must also be *representative,* in the sense that the distribution of items in the sample must correspond to the distribution in the population.[6] This kind of bias can be classified as bias in reasoning, of the kind studied by Evans (1989), as opposed to dialectical bias in argument. The bias is the failure of reasoning to meet standards of statistical inference.

For example, if an urn is filled with black and white marbles, and a handful is selected as a sample, in which the black and white marbles are counted, then we can use this to estimate the distribution of white and black marbles in the whole urn (the population). But this type of argument is defeated if there is any reason to think the distribution found in the sample is not representative of that of the population in the urn. For example, if it is known that there is a preponderance of black marbles at the top and the handful was taken from the top, then it would be a biased sample.

Many logic textbooks, for example, Salmon (1963, p. 57), define the *fallacy of biased statistics* as occurring where a statistical generalization is based on an unrepresentative sample.

> It is important not only to have a large enough number of instances, but also to avoid selecting them in a way which will prejudice the outcome. If inductive generalizations are to be reliable, they must be based upon representative samples. Unfortunately, we can never be sure that our samples are genuinely representative, but we can do our best to avoid unrepresentative ones. The *fallacy of biased statistics* consists of basing an inductive generalization upon a sample which is known to be unrepresentative or one which there is good reason to believe may be unrepresentative.

In Walton (1989a, p. 206) this same type of error of statistical reasoning is recognized, but it is called the "criticism" (as opposed to the "fallacy") of biased statistics" because it is sometimes a fault that can be corrected by improving an argument.

The classic case of the fallacy (or criticism) of biased statistics, given in many statistics textbooks, is cited by Salmon (1963, p. 58) and Baird (1992, p. 25). The version below can be found in Walton (1989a, p. 208).

> *Case* 8.4:   In 1936, the *Literary Digest* mailed out ten million ballots in a political poll to try to predict whether Franklin Roosevelt or Alfred Landon would win the upcoming election. According to the two million three hundred thousand ballots returned, it was predicted that Landon would win by a clear majority. The names for the poll were randomly selected from the telephone book, lists of the magazine's own subscribers, and lists of automobile owners.

In this case, when Roosevelt won with a 60 percent majority, it turned out that the poll was biased because it was selected from higher-income respondents (owners of cars and telephones, at that time), who tended to be Republicans. The poll was biased then, because of this association between income bracket and party preference. To prevent this kind of sampling error, statisticians take great care to try to pick a sample that is not known to be nonrepresentative, as a basis for drawing a statistical conclusion.

What is called "statistical bias" in sampling does not seem to be a species of dialectical bias in argumentation. It does not seem to be equatable, at least exactly, to the concept of bias we have defined in this book as advocacy in a context of dialogue. Instead, bias seems to be used in statistics as a technical term that refers to a specific type of failure of reasoning from a sample to a population in a way that meets the methodological requirements of correct reasoning in the discipline of statistics.

Baird (1992, p. 25) confirms this interpretation when he defines bias as a property of the method of sampling in statistics: "Bias is a property of the *method* of sampling. Occasionally, a *biased method may* produce a single sample that happens to represent well the whole population. But for the most part a biased method will yield samples that either systematically overestimate or systematically underestimate the average unemployment rate—or whatever is of interest." Thus the term *bias* in the field of statistics has a technical usage defined by the methods of reasoning in use. The field of statistics postulates particular methods and rules of correct statistical reasoning that specifically allow or approve certain inferences and exclude or condemn others as unacceptable (within statistics), in relation to the state of the art, at a given time.

However, this discipline-bound aspect of statistical standards governing polls and other sampling procedures does have a broader dialectical aspect. Many media polls fall short of statistical standards of argumentation, but would still be defended by their exponents as adequate for media purposes. While these polls would not satisfy standards of scientific inquiry, some would defend them as having some value as yielding information. Statisticians call these "SLOP polls," or self-selected opinion polls.

Although statisticians condemn SLOP polls as unscientific, many sociologists "say SLOPs are a valuable way to gauge opinion among a particular group of readers who may be biased but at least know something about the subject under discussion" (Gooderham 1994, p. D8). When the American Association for the Advancement of Science printed the results of a poll of this type, the scientific community divided on the question of whether its bias was of the harmful sort or not.

Case 8.5: Science magazine has solicited the views of its readership on two surveys over the last two years. One survey probed readers' opinions on the issue of how conflicts of interest should be handled in the scientific community. The other addressed the topic of whether there is a "female style" in science. Readers were asked to tick "yes," "no" or "not sure" boxes in response to a number of questions, then mail or fax their responses back to the publication.

The results of the questionnaire on conflicts of interest were not published, reserved solely for internal use by the magazine. Nevertheless, the use of such an "unscientific" survey ruffled more than a few feathers among the readers. But when the results of the questionnaire on female style in science—based on 200 reader responses—were published last summer, the complaints flowed in.

What concerned the statisticians was that the views of a very small number of respondents were being used to characterize the views of all members of the group. They say there is no way to draw conclusions from the responses of such a limited sample. The whole undertaking is unscientific, they say, and should be labeled as such. (Gooderham 1994, p. D8)

The statisticians' objection was that the technique used by the SLOP polls violated the statistical methods of selection used to eliminate bias.

The problem is (p. D8) that pseudo-scientific opinion polling, in which people answer 976 or 900 numbers, are proliferating in the media. While the statisticians argue, "No data is better than bad data," a features editor defended the other point of view, arguing, "There was so little literature on the issue of female style in science that it was better to summarize the findings of the SLOP than print nothing at all" (1994, p. D8). An argument that would have a negative bias as part of a scientific inquiry (at least in statistics) is here defended as having some value in an information-seeking type of dialogue (or, at any rate, some framework external to statistics as a field).

7. *Use of Statistics by Advocacy Groups*

A wider problem that has attracted a good deal of attention recently is the use of exaggerated and dubious statistical claims made by advocacy groups who want to influence public policy and argue that the end justifies the means, if the cause is worthy. In 1991, the Food Research and Action Center, an advocacy group, issued a news release that was widely reported in the media as saying that one out of eight American children under the age of twelve is hungry. According to Crossen (1994, p. 153), however, the study upon which these news reports were based contained several problems. The survey was a composite of seven different studies done by seven local advocacy groups. The survey did not attempt to ascertain food intake, and instead asked subjective questions such as "Did you ever rely on a limited number of foods to feed your children because you were running out of money to buy food for a meal?" The study was contradicted by the federal government's food consumption surveys, which measure food intake. Finally, the news reports biased the account even further, by changing the wording of the claims made.

Crossen also points out (p. 153) that most of the financing for this study came from a grant from Kraft General Foods Foundation—Kraft Foods is a beneficiary of government food subsidies. However, the most interesting aspect of the study is that when criticisms of its statistical claims were raised, people responded by saying that "the correctness of the data was less important than the study's worthy goals" (1994, p. 154). This type of defence against the charge of bias is based on the use of argumentation from consequences of a dubious sort. The argument is that if exaggerated biased statistical claims have good consequences, for example, helping lessen children's hunger, then any criticism of these claims (for example, on the grounds that they are biased) can be decisively refuted.

This style of argumentation, increasingly popular with advocacy groups for all sorts of causes, has a postmodernist feel to it. The idea seems to be that all arguments are biased anyway and having a bias for a cause that would help a victimized advocacy group is much better than having a bias for scientific research or for use of statistical methods of reasoning. Indeed, the idea seems to be that nobody has any real right to speak out against the arguments of this advocacy group whose cause is being supported because to criticize these arguments is to victimize these groups. The critic is held responsible for contributing to the death or suffering of the victims in this advocacy group.

In recent years, interest groups have learned that polls are a very powerful way to manipulate public opinion because they look very scientific and give an appearance of being based on hard empirical data. The figures for margin of error and other numerical tabulations accompanying polls give an aura of scientific accuracy to them. However, as Crossen (p. 104) points out, "much of polling—the asking and answering of questions—is soft science built on the shifting sands of human language and psychology." Because public opinion can change very rapidly, there is really no way of replicating a poll later to judge whether the first poll was accurate. The statisticians are well aware of the bias inherent in polls, but the public seems greatly impressed with their scientific validity.

8. Bias in Polling

Perceived bias is often a considerable problem in the use of polls—for example in political polls used to determine public opinion and to judge who is leading in an election campaign. Subtle differences in the wording and order of the questions asked can bias the outcome of the poll one way or another.

For example, in the 1992 election race between George Bush and Bill Clinton, polltakers were surprised at how small differences in the wording of questions made big differences in their results.

> *Case* 8.6:   Even subtle differences in how questions are worded, and in which questions precede the "Bush or Clinton?" query, can skew results. Some organizations identify the candidates by name only; most give party affiliation. If

> Clinton is identified as the Democrat, he might fare
> better in the cities of the Northeast and in union strong-
> holds, some of the last bastions of party loyalty. And if
> the horse-race question comes after a series on, say, the
> economy—asking whether the voter is better or worse
> off than he was four years ago, for instance—Bush fares
> worse. Since the ballot doesn't have an "Are you better
> off?" preface, such polls underestimate Bush's strength.
> (Begley, Fineman, and Church 1992, p. 39)

The problem here is not that the question is itself biased or illegitimate but that we draw conclusions from how respondents answered it without realizing that they were influenced by the wording of it in a way we did not anticipate or take into account.

Thus the meaning of 'bias,' when we say that this is a biased question or biased poll, is complex. For one thing, the bias is in the wording of the question, so it is a case of biased language in the sense discussed in chapter 6. But it is also a bias in a question. Furthermore, it is a bias in a poll, so it comes under the heading of "statistical methodology."

This issue is complicated by the fact that 'bias' is used in a specialized way in the context of statistics and scientific methodology generally. In this context, when we say that an argument or a question is biased, it seems to have a special meaning. It seems to mean that the question or the argument has skewed the collection of data in such a way that the poll or experiment is not what it seems. Instead of allowing the data to come in, in the normal way that would confirm or refute the hypothesis, a biased question or experiment somehow favors the one possible outcome unduly, or in a way that was not anticipated or foreseen, over the other. In this sense, a bias skews an investigation to one side unduly, where there should be a fair chance for the investigation to go one way or the other.

In this sense, we say that a poll is biased where there seems to be an open possibility for two outcomes that are roughly equal, or more or less balanced, but for some reason the poll is unduly weighted to the one outcome. For example, consider the question in the following poll.

Case 8.7:   Do you favor the banning of handguns in order to stop violent crime?

In this question, there is a bias because of the rider "in order to stop violent crime." Most people would give an affirmative answer to this question because most of us are strongly in favor of stopping violent crime. But if the results of the poll were taken to indicate that most people are in favor of banning handguns, this would be quite misleading. The comparable question "Do you favor or oppose the death penalty for persons convicted of murder?" was analyzed by Schuman and Presser (1981, p. 180) as lacking a proper balance.

What these examples suggest is that it is not so much the question itself that is biased but the use to which the question is put in argumentation. The question itself asks a complex question, which to be sure could be misinterpreted by the respondents to whom it is put. But it is not here that the bias aspect is to be found, at least completely. The bias emerges when an inference is drawn from the results of the poll, once the question has been asked. The aspect of bias depends on how the poll is interpreted, in context.

Schuman and Presser (1981) investigated statistical effects due to question wording in polls, called "response effects." One example cited in Moore (1992, pp. 343–344) concerned two identical questions, except that the phrase *assistance to the poor* was used in the one question in the same place where *welfare* was used in the other. A national survey showed that while only 19 percent of people said too little money was being spent on "welfare," 63 per cent said too little was being spent on "assistance to the poor" (p. 344). The difference, or so-called response effect, is 44 percent in this case. Since Schuman and Presser (1984) started examining response effects due to question wording, the study of this type of bias has become a flourishing field of study in the social sciences. Still, however, the public is not well informed about this kind of bias, and polls remain a source of biased and misleading conclusions.

The most significant problem in the use of these polls, from a point of view of informal logic is that frequently it is only the conclusion drawn (the interpreted results) of the poll that is announced. The actual question (with its subtleties of wording) used by the pollster to get that result is not even disclosed to the reader or user of the poll. Thus, if there is a bias, it is concealed, and the respondent to whom the outcome of the poll is addressed is given no chance to examine it for bias. This certainly is a misleading and harmful kind of bias, from a normative point of view of good argumentation.

9. Biased Questions

The phrase *biased question* is often used to indicate some sort of critical defect that should be related to the study of bias in argumentation. But a question is not an argument. Even so, questions play an important role in argumentation in dialogue exchanges of reasoning. Also, questions contain presuppositions that are often very influential in guiding an argument.[7] Hence, the problems are raised of what 'bias' means in 'biased question' and whether it means the same thing as what we have analyzed as bias in argumentation.

First, it is necessary to distinguish between loaded questions and biased questions. A question is *loaded* (Walton 1989a, p. 18) where the respondent in the dialogue is not committed to a presupposition of the question. A question is *aggressively loaded (argumentatively stacked)* where the answerer is committed to a proposition that is the negation of a presupposition of the question (Walton 1989a, p. 18). Such questions are often "loaded" in the same way Johnson and Blair (see chapter 5 above) define the fallacy of loaded term. A good example, from Engel (1982, p. 124) is the following case.

> *Case* 8.8:　What are our views on the token effort made by the government to deal with this monstrous oil crisis?

Whether a question is loaded depends on the context of dialogue in which it was used in a given case. But let us presume that the respondent in case 8.8 is not committed to the propositions that the government effort was "token" and that the oil crisis is "monstrous." Then the question in case 8.8 is a loaded question. It is an aggressively loaded question, if, in the given case, the respondent's position is actually opposed to one or both of these propositions.

The question in case 8.8 is also *complex* in the sense that it has more than one presupposition built into it. Hence Engel (p. 122) following the traditional treatment, classifies it as an instance of the fallacy of complex question.

The concept of a biased question is different from this because it is not tied directly to the commitments of the respondent. A *biased question* is one that subtly, or in a deceptive way, contains advocacy toward one of the possible answers to the question.

For example, the results of a verbal poll to seven respondents were printed in a column in *The Winnipeg Sun* (Andrews 1993).

> *Case* 8.9:　Is taxpayers' money being wasted on frivolous abstract art?

This question is deceptive because it looks like it is asking for an opinion—yes or no, one way or the other—on the question of whether or not the money being spent on abstract art is being wasted. That is, should we fund abstract art or not? This is what it may look like, superficially, but the terms *frivolous* and *wasted* definitely express advocacy for the thesis that the money spent on abstract art is being wasted. This is concealed or deceptive advocacy, because the general presumptions are that if something is frivolous, we should not spend money on it, and if we did, that money is probably being wasted. It is interesting that none of the seven respondents questioned the bias in the question. Several answered it directly, with responses such as "You bet it is" and "I think so" (Andrews 1993).

The question in case 8.9 was a yes-no question. The question in the following case is an either-or (disjunctive) question. According to *Newsweek* ("Perspectives," April 18, 1994, p. 17), it was asked of President Clinton by Rebecca Fairchild, a participant in a Charlotte, North Carolina, town meeting, questioning Clinton about his Whitewater investment deal.

> *Case* 8.10: Are you one of us middle-class people, or are you in with the villainous money-grabbing Republicans?

This question is not loaded because, presumably, the respondent, President Clinton, would have no objection to the Republicans being described in such a negative way. Or at any rate, it would not seem to go against his position as a Democrat. But the question is very definitely biased in the sense that the one answer is positively advocated, while the other is negatively advocated.

At any rate, we can see in this kind of case that a biased question does definitely advocate a particular proposition. Like an argument used in a persuasion dialogue, it does point toward a particular proposition as a conclusion, and its function seems to be to get the respondent's commitment to that proposition on record. Hence, it seems that the meaning of 'bias' in 'biased question' is similar to its meaning in the concept of a biased argument.

The use of biased questions in political opinion polling has even been given a name—according to Kesterton (1995, p. A24), it is called "push polling."

> *Case* 8.11: **Push polling:** A deceptive political telephone tactic that aims to sway, rather than survey, the opinions of voters. For example, people in Colorado last year were asked: "Please tell me if you would be more likely or less likely

> to vote for Roy Romer if you knew that Governor Romer appoints a parole board which has granted early release to an average of four convicted felons per day every day since Romer took office."

The word *push* here clearly expresses a concept of bias. The question itself is biased, but its use in a publicized poll as part of a political agenda also indicates the dialectical bias involved. What is presented as a finding of scientific research is in fact an interest-based political argument.

10. Postmodernist Law and Science

Our analysis has revealed that, to a certain degree, the postmodernist premise that legal and scientific arguments tend generally to contain bias is accurate.

The hiring of public relations firms by corporations to pay for and publicize scientific research that supports a product manufactured by the corporation has now become big business. Proctor (1995, pp. 104–110) cites many cases of such practices.

> When the Bureau of Alcohol, Tobacco and Firearms proposed a ban on whiskey bottles made from vinyl chloride, polymer industry officials hired Arthur D. Little to produce a report predicting staggering economic losses and unemployment from such legislation. When the nuclear reactor at Three Mile Island failed, its operator, Metropolitan Edison, expanded its public relations department to counter criticism of its handling of the incident. Union Carbide did likewise in the aftermath of the 1984 leak of methyl isocyanate that left more than 3,000 dead and 200,000 injured near the Indian city of Bhopal. (Proctor 1995, p. 103)

Hill and Knowlton, the largest public relations firm in the world, has made a specialty of the use of scientific research as a public relations tool.

> Hill and Knowlton was actually the first PR firm ever to establish an Environmental Health Unit; the move was made in anticipation of the establishment of OSHA and the EPA in 1970. The company had already helped the British asbestos industry polish its image (its London office had set up the Asbestos Information Council) and had been a key player in helping the Tobacco Institute get its mes-

sage out. By the end of the 1960s the firm was urging Johns-Manville, the asbestos giant, to establish a similar association: the net result was the creation of the Asbestos Information Association. (Proctor 1995, p. 103)

But the best known use of science for public relations is the Tobacco Institute, a research committee for "independent research" on issues of tobacco use and health, paid for by the tobacco industry. These practices have led people to question whether the system of scientific research as a framework contains biased argumentation.

In the legal system, cases of jury nullification—where the jury disregards the evidence in a trial and votes in favor of the defendant because he or she belongs to the same group as the jury members—are becoming more common. In some of these cases, juries argue that the legal system has been biased against their group in the past, so disregarding the evidence in this case can be justified as a protest against past injustices to their group. But once the step is taken to decide the outcome of a trial by making up your mind beforehand, instead of weighing the evidence on both sides, the trial itself has become a political tool for advocacy. It is understandable that once people see such practices in the legal system, the system itself is seen as containing biased argumentation.

The question to be asked is whether the inference can be drawn that since both systems contain biased argumentation we should feel free to reject them as expressing objective standards of rationality. Our conclusion is that this inference is not justified, and the tendency it appears to sanction—to exploit the established institutions of science and law to advance the interests of "worthy" advocacy groups—should be resisted. Our analysis indicates the dangers of harnessing statistics and other methods of scientific argumentation, by using them in a biased way to advance political interests.

In both legal argument and scientific research, there are certain specific types of bias recognized within either discipline. The methods of argumentation used in either discipline are designed to deal with these kinds of balance and to thereby preserve the balance necessary in either type of argumentation. However, in both cases, we also saw how there can be external pressures brought to bear on the system of dialogue as a whole. Both legal and scientific types of dialogue framework of argument can be exploited by advocacy groups for political reasons and for reasons of self-interest. This type of pressure on the system as a whole is a much greater danger and tends to be less well recognized by the practitioners—the lawyers, judges, and scientists—themselves. It is also difficult to evaluate, exclusively, by the normative models of dialogue studied in chapter 2, because both scientific research and the legal system have their own special rules and methods as working institutions.

Argumentation in scientific research is frequently evaluated, especially by those of a positivistic and foundationalist bent, in light of dialectical norms appropriate for the inquiry. Argumentation in a legal trial is frequently evaluated as being a sort of persuasion dialogue, where the best argument will reveal the truth or the basis of evidence behind the contested claims and their relative worth and value as plausible arguments. But neither of these normative theses is exactly right or at least complete because both of these types of argumentation are properly judged in relation to legal rules of evidence and scientific standards of evidence used in particular disciplines. So bias in such arguments and evaluations of whether a bias that has been detected is harmful or not are matters that should be judged by the norms appropriate for arguments in these special contexts.

Consequently, as shown in this chapter, there are scientific methods and legal criteria for detecting and evaluating scientific or legal bias in a given argument in a particular case. However, as shown in this chapter, interpretations of how to apply these norms can vary from time to time. At present, there are grounds for concern that postacademic science is tolerating more and more funding and problem setting by corporate interests, and that funding for academic research is driven more by explicitly political goals that promote the interests of advocacy groups. There are also grounds for concern that the legal system, driven more and more by political goals pushed ahead by powerful advocacy groups, is moving more and more to accepting the kind of "evidence" and argumentation that tilt too heavily to one side in the delicate balance between the side of the accuser and that of the accused.

Notes

1. See Evans (1989).
2. Feteris (1989) gives an analysis of legal argumentation in a trial as being based on the normative model of the critical discussion.
3. See Imwinkelried (1986) and Huber (1991).
4. See Walton (1989a, chapter 7).
5. Ibid.
6. See Baird (1992, chapter 2) on survey sampling.
7. See Walton (1989b).

THE WITCH HUNT AS A STRUCTURE OF ARGUMENTATION

The term *witch hunt* is coming to be used more and more frequently, to the extent that one wonders what this expression really means or should be taken to mean. For example, Coren (1994, p. A22), describes a sexual abuse case where a man's name was put on a child abuse register consequent upon his wife's accusation (during a custody dispute) that he had molested their daughter, despite no evidence of abuse being found. Coren comments (p. A22) that such cases "represent a contemporary Salem," adding that there exists an international computer network known as "witch hunt," contributed to by men fraudulently accused of this type of crime. Loftus (1995, p. 24) wonders why so many people are now being accused of child abuse based on dubious stories of "recovered memory." Pondering the many doubts expressed by people who find these cases bizarre and outrageous, she puts the question in the form, "Why is the cry of 'witch hunt' now so loud?" (p. 24). It seems widely evident that accusations, of a kind that are difficult or impossible to disprove, are being prosecuted both in the legal system and in various kinds of unofficial tribunals, in a type of procedure where there is a presumption of guilt. In these cases, there is such a stigma attached to the accusation and no serious penalty for making false accusations that the whole procedure is one-sided. Hence the procedure is described as a witch hunt, referring to historical tribunals where persons accused of being in league with the devil were burnt at the stake. But this vague reference to historical tribunals is meant by way of comparison—a metaphor. What exactly should we take 'witch hunt' to mean? Only if some clear criteria are formulated for what constitutes a witch hunt can we say, one way or the other, whether comments such as those of Coren and Loftus are justifiable.

One clue comes from the historical reference to the Salem witch-craft trials. Evidently, part of the meaning is derived from historical allusions to witchcraft trials. The other clue is the use of words such as *fraudulent,* suggesting that 'witch hunt' is a species of normative condemnation of the argumentation used to arrive at an outcome of 'guilty'—implying that such argumentation is logically defective, because it is part of an inquiry that is procedurally unfair, or somehow improper. In general, it seems that 'witch hunt' carries a negative normative load—it is used by someone accused (or someone commenting on the accusation) to say that he or she is being unfairly accused by a group who has set some kind of social framework, tribunal, method of inquiry, or procedure in place to secure conviction without properly justifying the accusation by arguments based on good (and adequate) evidence.

It is just this normative type of analysis of the witch hunt, as a normatively negative framework of argumentation, that is proposed below. A witch hunt will be defined as a normative framework, in which arguments are used, that has ten general identifying characteristics: (1) pressure of social forces, (2) stigmatization, (3) climate of fear, (4) resemblance to a fair trial, (5) use of simulated evidence, (6) simulated expert testimony, (7) nonfalsifiability characteristic of evidence, (8) reversal of polarity, (9) nonopenness, and (10) use of the loaded question. These ten conditions form a cluster of properties such that if a weighted number of them is present, the framework is that of a witchhunt. Some of the conditions carry somewhat more weight than others, as will be made evident below. For example, (8) is more essential than (10), but all the characteristics are important and have a place in identifying the normative structure of the witch hunt. Conditions (1), (2), and (3) are the initial conditions that make the accusation powerful and are the circumstances that make the witch hunt possible. Condition (4) gives the procedure apparent legitimacy by embedding the witch hunt in a socially recognized institution. Conditions (5), (6), and (7) describe the "evidence" brought forward to "prove" the accusation at the argumentation stage of the tribunal. And (8), (9), and (10) are the methods of argument used in the evaluation of the evidence in the procedure.

Characteristic (4) is especially important in understanding the normatively negative aspect of the witch hunt as a process of argumentation. The basic normative framework in which the arguments are to be evaluated is that of the *fair trial,* in which both sides have an adequate chance to bring forward their argumentation. The witch hunt is meant to resemble a fair trial but deviates in a systematic way from it. The witch hunt is classified as a *parasemotic structure* (from the Greek, *parasemos,* falsely struck, counterfeit), meaning that it derives its spurious legitimacy from its looking like a fair trial. The conclusions derived from these investigations are that the concept of a witch hunt is more than just a mythic concept and that it can be used as a legitimate normative tool in logic to critically evaluate arguments. The argumentation in a witch hunt is biased in the sense that the witch hunt is a one-sided tribunal that masquerades as a two-sided dialogue.

1. The Inquisition

The *inquisition* as an evolving social institution, according to Alphandery (1963, p. 377), was the ecclesiastical jurisdiction dealing with the "detection and punishment of heretics and all persons guilty of any offense against Catholic orthodoxy." Although primarily a phenomenon of medieval times, the inquisition as an institution had origins dating back to church procedures of the fourth century. The procedures characteristic of the inquisition are outlined in the general account given by Alphandery (1963, pp. 378–379). The procedure was secret, and its aim was not to detect particular offenses or acts, but tendencies (such as *heresy,* or being opposed to the church). The accused were arrested on a basis of suspicion, and were presumed to be guilty (p. 387). The accused had a right to demand a written account of his offenses, but the names of the witnesses against him were not made available (p. 378). The prosecution took place "in the utmost secrecy." Moral subterfuges and torture were allowed as ways of extracting confessions, and the procedure was not litigious in nature, meaning that the purpose of the process was not to provide an arena for the accused to argue his case. Instead, the procedure was more like what we would nowadays call an "interrogation" or perhaps a "re-education" (p. 379).

It is interesting to note that according to Peters (1988, p. 3), the inquisition as a "single all-powerful horrific tribunal, whose agents worked everywhere to thwart religious truth, intellectual freedom, and political liberty, until it was overthrown sometime in the nineteenth century" is a "myth" of "modern folklore" that exists only in polemic and fiction. Peters does not deny that the institutional tribunals employed by the clergy to protect their orthodox religious beliefs from the attacks of heretics actually existed. They did, but when we speak of the inquisition, which we often do, to condemn something or make a point in everyday conversation, we appeal to a kind of universalized mythic concept that has been transformed by literature and art into a symbol for something. But to understand the mythic concept, it is helpful to know what procedures the historical tribunes used to arrive at the conclusion that the accused party was guilty of heresy.

Some subtleties in the concept of evidence developed in the inquisition procedures are noted by Lea (1961). The crime sought out was purely a mental one, relating to the secret thoughts and opinions of the accused—a person might act in accord with orthodox religion, yet in "his secret heart" he might be a heretic (p. 184). Also, a heretic might be guilty even if he could not be brought to confession of his guilt, and hence instead of having to prove guilt, the tribunal could find different "grades of suspicion"—"violent," "vehement," and "light" (p. 204). A person could be judged to be guilty of heresy by the accusation (in some cases) of only one witness (p. 205). Resources for procuring unwilling confession included deceit and torture (p. 193). As a milder form of deceit, the examiner would ask loaded questions that assumed guilt, such as, "How often have you confessed as a heretic?" (p. 193). Thus the notion of evidence in the inquisition procedures was such that the accused was left little or no room to refute the charge by citing empirical evidence. In fact, the purpose of the tribunal was not really one of proving guilt or innocence. It could be better described as the goal of securing adherence to orthodox church opinions by rooting out heretics and converting them to these opinions or by eliminating the heretics who could not be converted.

2. Witchcraft Trials

In the fifteenth century, the inquisition became involved in tribunals where the charge was sorcery (witchcraft). In 1398, the theology faculty of the University of Paris declared that acts of sorcery accomplished by means of a pact with the devil were to be considered as heretical in nature. However, the number of cases of witchcraft brought before the inquisition was "insignificant," compared to the mass witchcraft trials that took place in Europe during the sixteenth and seventeenth centuries (Hamilton 1981, p. 95).

Trevor-Roper (1967 p. 91) described the European witch craze of the sixteenth and seventeenth centuries in Europe as a "new explosive force, constantly and fearfully expanding with the passage of time." The prosecution of witches was aided by "experts" who supplied the esoteric details (p. 97). Witches were old women who had secretly made a pact with the devil. But lenient judges, or those aiding witches, were described as "patrons of witches" (p. 96). This campaign against witches reached a "holocaust" by 1630, "in which lawyers, judges, clergy themselves join old women at the stake" (p. 97). Trevor-Roper suggests that the force behind the persecution of witches was "social pressure" (p. 110): the witch represented nonconformity and, in particular, heresy in the form of opposition to official religious views.

The Dominicans had theological experts on witchcraft who wrote "demonological manuals" outlining methods for determining guilt based on the witch's confessions. One such manual had the following epigraph on its title page: "To disbelieve in witchcraft is the greatest of heresies" (p. 117). Evidence used was of a kind that would be impossible to resist or rebut. Torture was sometimes used, and "signs of fear" or a person's being "old, ugly or smelly" were indications of guilt.

The Salem witchcraft trials in North America were actual legal proceedings. The height of these proceedings took place between June and September 1692, when fourteen women and five men were hanged as witches in Salem, Massachusetts, and one man was tortured to death (Shapiro 1992, p. 64). Reverend Samuel Parris was the minister of Salem at the time.

> *Case* 9.1: During the winter of 1691–92, a few girls, mostly teenagers, started gathering in Parris's kitchen. There they listened to stories, perhaps voodoo tales, told by his West Indian slave Tituba; they also tried to discern their future husbands by fortune telling—dropping an egg white into a glass and seeing what shape it took. For girls raised in Puritanism, which demanded life-long discipline and self-control, these sessions with Tituba represented a rare and risky bit of indulgence in pure fancy. Too risky, perhaps. Suddenly one after another of the girls was seized with fits. Their families were bewildered: the girls raved and fell into convulsions; one of them ran around on all fours and barked. Dr. William Griggs was called in and made his diagnosis: the "evil hand" was upon them.
>
> Fits identified as satanic possession had broken out among adolescent girls at earlier times in New England. Often their distress was traced to local women who, it was said, had entered into a compact with the Devil and

> were now recruiting new witches by tormenting the in-
> nocent until they succumbed. So the adults in Salem
> Village began pressing the girls with questions: "Who
> torments you? Who torments you?" Finally they named
> three women—Tituba, Sarah Good and Sarah
> Osborne—all of them easily recognizable as Satan's
> handmaidens. Tituba was seen as a shameless pagan,
> Good was a poor beggar given to muttering angrily as
> she went from house to house and Osborne was known
> to have lived with her second husband before they were
> married. The three were arrested and jailed, but the
> girls' torments did not cease. On the contrary, fits were
> spreading like smallpox; dozens more girls and young
> women went into violent contortions, flailing, kicking
> and uttering names. Shapiro (1992, p. 65).

While they were testifying, the girls went into shrieking fits, and at any sign that the jury might be willing to find the defendant innocent, these fits increased in volume. This performance kept pressure on the proceedings, and the wailing ceased only when the defendant confessed (Shapiro 1992, p. 64).

Witchcraft, the crime of which the defendants were accused, was defined (as noted above, in the European context) as a contract between the witch and the devil. The evidence of this crime was called "spectral evidence," referring to the shape or "specter" of the devil, as he took the shape of the witch. Spectral evidence is characterized by Boyer and Nissenbaum (1977, p. 19) as "ticklish" because so much of it took place in the mind of the witch and because it was based on visions or other-worldly experience that was visible only to the person testifying. The witness would report that the accused person "appeared devilish." According to Boyer and Nissenbaum (p. 20), this kind of testimony "possessed a superficial resemblance to firm empirical evidence" but "remained impossible to verify, since only the person experiencing the vision could see it."

The problem of falsification inherent in this kind of evidence has the consequence that the accused party is not effectively able to mount a defence against the accusation because evidence to refute or falsify the charge is not really open or available. The reason is that what can be observed as evidence relevant to the charge is available only to the accuser and the accused, and the credibility of the latter is discounted from the outset because this person is in league with the devil and would be expected to lie and engage in subterfuges anyway.

The above historical sketch gives one some insight into the derivation of the mythic concept of a witch hunt, and an intuitive idea of its main features. How could this concept be clarified and analyzed systematically so that it could be useful as a tool for the critical analysis of arguments? The first step is that the main identifying characteristics of the concept need to be clearly expressed in a form that is amenable to analysis as a pragmatic structure.

3. Initial Conditions

A circumstance that is very important in defining and understanding the witch hunt and seeing how it functions as a kind of framework of argument is the "hysteria" or wave of popular opinions and feelings that initiates and propels the witch hunt. Witch hunts occur only at certain times and in certain social conditions, where powerful social and political forces have an impact on the legal system. Some describe this as "hysteria." But what it really amounts to is political pressure being exerted on the legal system or on the currently accepted ways of making determinations of criminal guilt, by powerful forces that have ideological backing of a kind that could be called "zealous." Thus, the tribunal or trial becomes a tool for display of public, visible punishment for selected persons (apparently) opposed to the ideology advocated by the zealots and thereby to make public morality come more in line with the cause of the zealots.

The set of circumstances that gives rise to the witch hunt is a pressure of social forces causing conflicts and a changing climate of opinion, where a new ideology is on the upswing. Originally, the inquisition was a method devised by the growing church to accelerate the process of gaining converts and forcing their conversion and allegiance to the religious viewpoint of the church. The Salem outbreak occurred during a time when Massachusetts was politically adrift and there were ideological clashes between the thriving merchants and the Puritan farmers (Watson 1992, p. 121). In both instances, the religious ideology was used to target individuals who were not members of the group ideology and who were designated as offenders who were in league with those identified as the most evil and vilified persons one could imagine, from the point of view of the ideology of the group.

Then a key characteristic of the witch hunt is that the accused is under suspicion for having committed some type of offense that is regarded or portrayed as particularly disgusting, at a particular period and in a particular climate of opinion then popular. Hence, his or her reputation is badly damaged merely by the accusation.

A second characteristic of the witch hunt in the initial conditions is the stigmatization of the accused party by accusing him or her of a particular type of crime that is seen as particularly horrible, so that the charge of having committed this offense tends (at the outset) to destroy his or her credibility. Thus, the accused party cannot effectively mount a credible argument in order to defend him or herself against the charge. This aspect of the witch hunt is often called (interestingly) "demonization" because the accusation implies that the accused party is a "devil," that is, an evil, deceitful person who can never take part in a sincere and honest discussion. In logic, this type of personal-attack argument is known as the *argumentum ad hominem* (see for example, Walton, 1989a, chapter 6). For example, in the McCarthy era, the accused was said to be a "Communist sympathizer," and in the climate of the time this allegation meant he or she was a bad and dangerous person who could not be trusted to tell the truth and was probably a spy or member of a Communist "cell."

This characteristic of stigmatization is achieved by tailoring the charge to some category of malfeasance that is particularly "taboo" during a particular social and historical period so that even the accusation sounds so repellent that it destroys the reputation of the accused party. During an era characterized by dominant religious ideology, the accusation of being a witch was the worst possible one to stigmatize a person because such a person was said to be in league with the devil, and the devil was the very personification of evil and cunning deception. Anyone in league with the devil would be expected to lie and engage in subtle deceptions and evil seductions in her arguments. The implication is that such a person must not be trusted. Any arguments she might use to defend herself must therefore automatically be discounted as worthless.

In the *abusive ad hominem* argument, the proponent argues that the respondent has a bad character, generally, or, more specifically, a bad character for veracity, and then uses this allegation to try to get the audience to conclude that the respondent lacks credibility and therefore to conclude that his argument should not be accepted as plausible (believable, credible). This type of argument is (generally, but not always) allowed in a trial in cross-examination of a witness.

The circumstantial type of *ad hominem* argument is also a very common and powerfully effective form of political attack on an opponent's credibility or integrity on an issue (Walton 1989a, chap. 6). But it is primarily the abusive type and a third subtype of *ad hominem* attack that are used to undermine the credibility of the person accused in a witch hunt.

The third subtype is the *bias ad hominem argument,* where the proponent claims that the respondent has a bias on the issue being discussed (often on the grounds that the respondent has a financial stake or something else to gain in the outcome) and that therefore he is not credible, and therefore his argument should not be accepted as credible (or as credible as it would be without the bias). A standard textbook example is the following case:

> *Case* 9.2:   Bill Gates has argued at length that Microsoft Corporation does not have a monopoly on computer disc operating systems. But Gates is chief executive officer of Microsoft, and he desperately wants to avoid antitrust action against his company. Therefore, we should ignore Gates's arguments. (Hurley 1994, p. 121)

The idea here is not that Gates' argument is totally worthless but that we judge it to be less credible once we are told that he is CEO of Microsoft. Therefore, the conclusion in the example above, using the word *ignore* is too strong.

In the literature on *ad hominem* arguments there are differences of opinion on how to evaluate such arguments, and differences of opinion on how to classify the subtypes. Hurley (p. 121), for example, classifies the Gates case above under the circumstantial category, as opposed to the bias category. For more on these questions of classification of the subtypes, see Krabbe and Walton (1993).

In the witch hunt, the abusive type of *ad hominem* against the accused party is built right into the structure of the procedure. For only certain types of charges are alleged—those that have a stigma attached, during a particular historical epoch and in a particular social setting and climate of opinion—so the accused is demonized from the outset of the proceedings. Since the accused is in league with the devil and represents the devil's interests, naturally he is going to lie and to conceal his demonic nature. And therefore he will be devious and hypocritical in his arguments. Then the proposed approach is not to listen to his arguments, but only to get him to "confess" and to adopt the new values by "re-educating' him and other offenders.

A climate of fear is a third important characteristic of the initial conditions of the witch hunt. First, the witch hunt is based on and propelled by fear of the stigmatized individuals who are the objects of the hunt. Witches are portrayed, for example, as both repellent and dangerous. But, second, the whole procedure of the witch hunt is suffused with fear. Everyone who could be accused is terrified because they know that the targeting is relatively random and even an innocent person can be accused. But also, they know that once they are accused, and caught up in the tribunal process, the consequences are horrific (for anyone whose reputation matters to him) and the outcome is certain to be bad. Thus, a climate of (well-founded) fear is characteristic of the whole process of the witch hunt.

It is exactly with respect to this climate of fear that Trevor-Roper (1967, p. 128) saw the European witch craze of the sixteenth and seventeenth centuries as being comparable to the McCarthy tribunals of the 1950s in the United States.

> *Case* 9.3:　The McCarthyite experience of the United States in the 1950s was exactly comparable: social fear, the fear of a different kind of society, was given intellectual form as a heretical ideology and suspect individuals were then persecuted by reference to that heresy. In the same way, in the fourteenth and fifteenth centuries, the hatred felt for unassimilable societies was intellectualized as a new heresy and politically suspect individuals were brought to judgment by reference to it. The great sorcery trials in France and England at that time—the trials of the Templars and Joan of Arc, of the Duchess of Gloucester and the Duchess of Bedford—were political exploitations of a social fear and a social ideology, whose origins were to be found at a deeper level and in another field. The difference was that whereas McCarthyism in America lasted only a few years (although it may yet recur), the European witch-craze had a far longer history.

This aspect of fear and panic was especially noted on by Rovere (1959, pp. 16–17) who recalled his experience in 1953 that "the very thought of Joe McCarthy" could "shiver the White House timbers":

> *Case* 9.4:　I remember once, in about the middle of that year, calling upon one of the President's assistants, a man who seemed to me then, as he does today, to be well above the average in courage and candor. I had gone in search of enlightenment on a number of things, most of them as unrelated to McCarthy as it was possible for anything to be in those days. We had a friendly enough talk and

> toward the end of it I brought up Topic A—and of course offered the customary assurances that I would not make use of anything he said in such a way as to embarrass him or make his life more difficult than it already was. At the mention of McCarthy, his whole manner and expression changed; though he did not move from his chair or put his palms together he assumed, figuratively, and on his face quite literally a supplicating mien. I have no record of the exact words he used, but I have a painfully vivid memory of them. "Don't ask me," he said. "For God's sake, please don't ask me to discuss this. Not now. I'll help you as much as I possibly can, I'll talk about anything else you want. Anything. Just don't press me on this. Don't even ask me why I don't want to talk about it. Maybe someday we can talk it all over, but not now. Accept my word that my reasons are good." I have not before or since seen a grown man in a responsible position behave in such a fashion.

It is this climate of fear that presses the witch hunt ahead and suppresses the normal opposition to it that would be voiced by the victims of it, or by anyone who disagrees with the advocacy it represents.

There are three connected factors in the circumstances that make the witch hunt possible. One is a dominant or rising advocacy group in a position to punish both its victims and any of its opponents in a social climate of opinion in a particular historical epoch that makes it possible for this advocacy group to base its tribunal on conflicting but changing public opinion. Another is the stigmatizing of perceived offenders of the values advocated by the ideology. A third is the exploiting of underlying fears and emotions, whipping them up to marshal social forces toward a particular line of action.

4. Parasemotic Structure

The fourth characteristic of a witch hunt is that it is meant to resemble a fair trial. The witch hunt derives whatever force it has to convince an audience from taking it to represent a genuine, truth-seeking, fair trial, or taking it to be like a fair trial in key respects. To make the witch hunt function credibly, the trappings of a trial, or of some sort of official tribunal, must be present. Of course, if the proceeding really is a witch hunt, these outward features of the trial will be phony or simulated. But it is precisely this element of phoniness or deception that makes the witch hunt what it is.

For example, the McCarthy tribunals were not real (i.e., legally constituted) trials. They were Senate hearings. But they were televised, and the image conveyed was that of a trial. McCarthy was seated at a desk, and witnesses of various kinds were called forth to appear, while McCarthy questioned them and read from papers that appeared to have the form of evidence. According to Chase (1956, p. 164), these tribunals looked like a "Hollywood version" of a trial, when viewed on television, but, in reality, the accusations made were based on little or no real evidence.

But it is not just the outer trappings of a trial that are most important or even the official sanction of the tribunal as being a legal trial. What is important is that there be a pretense or simulation that factual or verifiable evidence of some sort is being collected and then evaluated by examining and evaluating the reasons for and against the charge. The perception conveyed is that some third party, a judge or jury, who is not committed (at the outset) to either side, is evaluating the evidence on both sides.

What general requirements can be cited to justify the fair trial as an institution to which reasonable people could agree, taking the criminal trial as the case in point, for purposes of discussion? One requirement would be that the crime or type of act subject to prosecution, should be generally agreed to be something that should be prosecuted. Another requirement is that the question of whether this alleged act was committed in a given case should be subject to an open examination of relevant evidence on both sides and the issue decided by a third, neutral party on the basis of this evidence. This second requirement is procedural and pragmatic in nature. It has to do with what is considered to be evidence, and how that body of evidence is used to reach the conclusion of whether or not the accused party committed the crime.

As set out here, the concept of the 'fair trial' is an abstract normative structure that provides an ideal model of a type of dialogue exchange in which arguments can be evaluated as strong or weak, correct or incorrect, reasonable or fallacious, insofar as they contribute to the goals of the dialogue or not. In this sense, the concept of the fair trial does not vary from culture to culture, or from one historical epoch to another. But the parasemotic concept of resemblance to a fair trial does vary in its application to different actual cases and historico-social contexts. For it is social recognition of the institution of the witch hunt, in a given case, as being similar to a fair trial, that gives the procedure its apparent legitimacy. In other words, the seeming legitimacy or parasemotic aspect of the witch hunt as resembling a fair trial is dependent on cultural and historical factors of what appears legitimate at a given time.

In this regard, the witch hunts of the 1500s are parasemotic in relation to the people who endured them, participated in them, and observed them, in that period because those trials must simulate a fair trial of the 1500s, which would have differed markedly from modern fair trials in Western society. For one thing, fair trials of the 1500s would have included torture.

The McCarthy tribunals in Washington in the 1950s were socially sanctioned, in that not only were they not illegal, but they were activities of socially recognized institutions. However, their activities were considered unfair by many then, and are definitely considered unfair now, by popular and educated opinion.

So we need to be sensitive to these differences in historical and cultural contexts in understanding how the witch hunt gets its apparent legitimacy by acting as a counterfeit, in relation to the perceptions of the time, of a fair trial. But from an abstract normative point of view, we can criticize the argumentation in a witch hunt framework as failing to meet certain standards of correctness as arguments, on the grounds that they systematically deviate from the general normative requirements of a fair trial.

5. Evidence

An important characteristic of a witch hunt is the nature of the "evidence" itself. This evidence may look scientific, it may be reported by witnesses, and these witnesses may be said to be experts in some field of supposed scientific knowledge. But this resemblance to evidence is really a sham. What is characteristic of the argumentation used in a witch hunt is that it is not verifiable (and, in particular, not falsifiable) by appeal to empirical findings or generally accepted scientific findings of some established field of expert inquiry. For example, in the witchcraft trials, the "spectral" evidence was visible only to certain people. So if an ordinary person failed to see it in a particular case, this failure would not count as evidence against its existence in that case. The point is that the evidence is inaccessible to anyone on the side of the defence, who might try to deny it. Such evidence is not real evidence, in the sense of the term appropriate for a fair trial or a scientific investigation. It is only taken to be evidence because of its ideological colorization and stigmatization and its perceived resemblance to some kind of legitimate and widely accepted evidence.

In courts of law 'evidence' is used in a narrow sense to mean anything that meets the requirements of the rules of evidence. For example, the Federal Rules of Evidence apply in the United States. In fact, a good deal of the evidence actually used in a criminal trial tends to be testimonial in nature, even though objects (like a pistol) and documents are admitted. For expert testimony is now prevalent in courts. A ballistics expert, may be needed for example, to testify about what a pistol was probably used to do, or an accountant, to interpret a tax document.

In our present legal system, expert testimony is presumed to be based on scientific evidence. For example, a qualified expert on DNA testing may be called in to testify on the question of whether an accused person's blood has the same DNA as that of blood found at the scene of the crime. According to the Frye Rule (which has been broadened by the new Federal Rules of Evidence, however) a scientific technique or theory used in expert testimony must have gained "general acceptance" in a scientific field of knowledge (Giannelli 1981, p. 13). As more and more psychologists and psychiatrists have been brought in as expert witnesses in criminal cases, however, there has been some worry expressed that the courts are relying on expert testimony too much, in a way that tends to usurp the jury's function of deciding guilt (Imwinkelried 1991).

In the inquisition, as described by Lea (1961, p. 807) so-called committees of experts (theologians) were used in trials. Here the problem is that the function of providing expert testimony has been perverted by using these experts, who are not really experts in a scientific field of knowledge, but who have a strong professional bias toward convicting the accused party of a particular type of offense. These experts are really advocates for a particular ideology or partisan interest group that is socially powerful.

In a trial where there is no verifiable or falsifiable evidence and everything turns on what the accuser claims versus what the accused claims, the outcome depends on the credibility of the two parties. But credibility is subjective. The issue becomes one of whom you believe. A trial sometimes can be fought out on this basis.

Even so, it seems to be an assumption that evidence generally should be verifiable or falsifiable in principle, by appeal to some observable or checkable facts, so that in cross-examination it can be challenged or refuted by appealing to other evidence.

Hence, another very important distinction between the fair trial and the witch hunt relates to the falsifiability of evidence. In a legal trial, legal rules of evidence define what is or is not evidence. For example, witness testimony or expert testimony is admitted, under the right conditions and subject to cross-examination, as evidence. In order to be evidence in a trial, as well, there needs to be a verifiability (or falsifiability) requirement similar to scientific requirements on evidence. If something is evidence, it should be open to verification or falsification by being judged in relation to observations and accepted scientific facts and theories (Huber 1991). In other words, evidence should be subject to checking and to falsification if it can be shown to be inconsistent with the facts or with what is known to be true. Evidence that is private or subjective to only one party and cannot be checked by referring to observable facts or reproducible findings must be treated with special care. Is it really "evidence" if no one except the accuser or the accused can ever falsify or verify it by facts that can be reproduced, tested, or checked by other parties?

6. Nonopenness

One important characteristic of a fair trial is the requirement that the judge or jury, who decides the outcome, must not have made up its mind on that outcome before all of the evidence has been presented. That is, the judge or jury must be sufficiently unbiased, at the beginning stage, that she or they can be swung one way or the other by evidence produced during the argumentation stage of the trial. Otherwise, the trial is pointless, from a normative perspective of judging the case on the balance of all the relevant evidence presented.

The opposite quality is characteristic of the witch hunt. The judge or jury (the deciding party) in a witch hunt has already determined that the accused party (once designated as the accused) is guilty before the argumentation stage and evidence evaluation stages of the trial have taken place. So the whole effort of the trial, once started, is focused on reaffirming the presumption of guilt, and no effort is made to collect or present evidence that might tend to indicate that the accused party is not guilty. Instead, the procedure is designed to shield off this possibility or prevent it from arising.

One of the most important characteristics of the critical discussion as a type of talk exchange is the willingness of a proponent to admit or concede that her argument was wrong or inadequate to justify its conclusion, should evidence be given by the respondent to reveal such an inadequacy (van Eemeren and Grootendorst 1984, p. 160). This willing-ness to admit defeat is an important characteristic that distinguishes the critical discussion from the quarrel or eristic type of dialogue (Walton 1989a, p. 4).

This quality of openness in a critical discussion is contrasted with the attitude of an arguer in the eristic type of dialogue. In this type of talk exchange, the proponent of an argument is never open to defeat (Wal-ton 1995). Should convincing arguments that present evidence against his point of view be presented by an opponent, he will always try to brush them aside or use personal attack or whatever means in order not to admit that his argument was wrong.

The opposite of this quality of openness in a critical discussion is the notion of the "closed mind" associated with quarrelsome and dogma-tic argumentation. Advocacy or partisan argumentation that supports one's own point of view as strongly as possible is not a bad thing in a critical discussion. In fact, it is normal and expected and is vitally impor-tant for the success of the critical discussion. But if such advocacy is pressed ahead too strongly, so that it becomes a dogmatic and quarrel-some refusal to even consider any opposed viewpoint, the result is an obstruction to the critical discussion and is likewise an obstruction to a fair trial.

It is crucial in a critical discussion that advocacy be fully and openly expressed on both sides, so that the originating conflict of opinions can be resolved by a balance of the evidence on both sides. This balancing of the evidence on both sides of a disputed case is also the key requirement of a fair trial.

7. Reversal of Polarity

The problem with the fair trial as an instrument for the proving of guilt is that it is imperfect and fallible in drawing a conclusion, based on the known evidence in a given case. From time to time, parties who are not guilty are convicted even in a fair trial. One problem is that witnesses lie, often because it is in their best interests to do so. Yet the trial could be procedurally fair, on the basis of the given evidence.

So, to justify the trial as an institution, we have requirements of burden of proof that are meant to make it more difficult to convict accused persons who are not guilty and keep the number of such convic-tions to a tolerable proportion (Morton and Hutchison 1987, p.7). The tool for this purpose in the criminal trial is to require proof beyond a reasonable doubt. The burden is on the prosecution to prove that the accused party is guilty. The defence has only to cast doubt on this claim by raising enough questions against it. By the initial stigmatization, however, this burden of proof is reversed in the witch hunt. Such a reversal of burden of proof is called "reversal of polarity" because it is a constant pull that affects a whole procedure.

Another characteristic of the witch hunt is the reversal of polarity in the normal burden of proof appropriate for a fair trial. In a fair criminal trial, a high burden of proof is on the accuser, to prove that the defendant is guilty of the allegation beyond reasonable doubt. The burden of proof is allocated in this asymmetrical way, upon the accuser, in order to minimize the mischief of innocent persons being convicted by false or frivolous accusations.

This allocation of burden of proof is reversed in the witch hunt, giving the whole procedure a reversed polarity. The weight of proving his own innocence falls heavily on to the side of the accused. The accused party must struggle to collect and present evidence to show that he or she is not guilty. Unless he or she can present overwhelming evidence that he or she is not guilty, the outcome is a finding of guilt. In effect, there is a polarization of the burden of proof. It is supposed to be allocated one way, but during the whole sequence of argumentation, its effect keeps pulling the argumentation the other way, so that the defendant has to struggle against it.

The logic of the argument in such a polarized framework is that of the traditional *argumentum ad ignorantiam* or argument from ignorance, of the following form: proposition *A* is not known (proved) to be true (false), therefore *A* is false (true). This form of argument defines the burden of proof in a criminal trial and in such an instance is a reasonable argument. But, notoriously, *ad ignorantiam* arguments can be used fallaciously, especially in cases where falsifiability of evidence is a problem, as noted by Copi (1982, p. 101): "This fallacy often arises in connection with such matters as psychic phenomena, telepathy, and the like, where there is no clear-cut evidence either for or against." It is interesting in connection with the subject of witch hunts that Copi (p. 112) uses the following example, in an exercise, as an instance of the *ad ignorantiam* fallacy.

> *Case 9.5*   On the Senate floor in 1950, Joe McCarthy announced that he had penetrated "Truman's iron curtain of secrecy." He had 81 case histories of persons whom he considered to be Communists in the State Department. Of Case 40, he said, "I do not have much information on

> this except the general statement of the agency that there is nothing in the files to disprove his Communist connections."

According to the pragmatic analysis of the *ad ignorantiam* fallacy given in Walton (1995), it is the normative framework of dialogue in which this type of argument is used that is a main factor in accounting for whether or not it is fallacious in a given case.

It is precisely in the witch hunt context, where the burden of proof appropriate for a fair criminal trial is reversed, that the *ad ignorantiam* fallacy is fallacious yet at the same time so terribly effective as a sophistical tactic. Even the suspicion of guilt raised by the accuser is enough to press forward the *ad ignorantiam* argument: if the accused party cannot prove that he or she is not guilty, then he or she must be guilty. The parasemotic framework of the witch hunt makes the argument seem legitimate when, in reality, from the point of view of a fair trial, it is not.

8. Use of Loaded Questions

Another important characteristic of the witch hunt is the technique of questioning used in the sequence of dialogue exchanges between the prosecutor and the accused. Instead of questions being asked in a normal sequence that would be appropriate for a critical discussion, a loaded question technique is used. This technique is characteristic of the type of dialogue called the "interrogation." The use of loaded questions as a sophistical tactic used in argumentation has been studied in Walton (1989a, pp. 27–43; 1991b). A *loaded* question may be defined (Walton 1989, p. 31) as a question containing a proposition (as presupposition) to which the respondent is not committed, in the given context of dialogue in a case (see also chapter 8). The idea is that if the respondent gives a direct affirmative answer to the question, he or she will become committed to this proposition contained within the question. For example, the question "Did you burn the book that contained the incriminating evidence against you?" contains the proposition (as a presupposition) that the book referred to contained incriminating evidence against the respondent.

Normally, in a critical discussion, questions in a sequence are asked in a certain appropriate order in the dialogue. For example, a sequence might consist of the following ordering of questions.

Q1:   Did you burn a book?

Q2:   Did the book contain evidence?

Q3:   Was that evidence incriminating against you?

This sequence allows the respondent to give a definite "yes" answer to *Q1*, to give a qualified answer to *Q2*, or perhaps to indicate a lack of certainty, and to then give a "no" or "I didn't think so, at the time," answer to *Q3*. These refinements and clarifications are not so easy to make if the respondent has to give one simple answer to the original loaded question, "Did you burn a book that contained incriminating evidence against you?" The asking of this question (in context) puts pressure on the respondent.

The use of loaded questions is characteristic of interrogation. Instead of asking a respondent, "Did you hide a weapon?" or even "Where did you hide the weapon?" an interrogator may put the question "Did you hide the gun in the well or the field?" The use of this loaded, complex (disjunctive) question puts pressure on the respondent. The tactic is to try to trap the respondent into some guilt-implying concession. In particular, the question is loaded, and either direct answer, of the two alternatives, implies guilt on the part of the respondent.

9. The Sequence of Argumentation in the Witch Hunt

Broadly speaking, what characterizes the witch hunt as a parasemotic and pathological framework of argumentation is that the sequence of argumentation is (comparatively) compressed and distorted. Instead of the sequence going forward in the prescribed and appropriate way in a critical discussion, where the arguments on both sides are given a consideration that is balanced and probing, the structure of the dialogue puts the argumentation in it under distorting pressure at every stage. For example, in Shapiro's description of the Salem trial, the wailing and convulsions of the girls put terrific pressure on all participants to push ahead to a confession. Similarly, all the other elements of fear, use of loaded questions, stigmatization, and so forth are both methods for applying this pressure and are themselves the indicators of how the sequence of argumentation is distorted and compressed. For example, instead of a properly linked sequence of questions and answers, loaded questions are used that compress the argument sequence, distorting toward the presumption of guilt, instead of yielding question-reply sequences that are balanced and probing.

A fair trial should exhibit question-reply sequences of connected argumentation comparable to that of a probing critical discussion that looks into all the relevant evidence on both sides. Then at the concluding stage, a decision should be arrived at by using the principle of burden of proof agreed upon at the opening stage. We know what such a connected sequence of argumentation should look like in a fair trial. It has a certain quality of controlled argument and coherent openness to questioning and rebuttal. What is crucial is that the judging party is guided by a weighing of the body of falsifiable evidence that is presented and evaluated during the trial.

The witch hunt, by comparison, exhibits a pressurized sequence of argumentation that is steamrollered ahead by the compressive forces of the argument on the one side. The initial presumption is that the accused party is guilty, so all the argumentation used in the trial is supportive of this outcome. The other side is only given a sham hearing, and every time it puts an argument forward, that argument is immediately discounted or pushed down, overwhelmed by the pressure on the other side.

What is normatively defective in the argumentation is not visible exclusively in any particular argument (taken as a local set of premises and conclusions) by itself. The problem lies in how the sequences of arguments are tied together within the structure of the comprehensive dialogue structure. The defect is a pragmatic one of how an argument is situated in a context—it is in the procedure itself. Even a very good argument by the defence—"good" in the sense of being based on appropriate, falsifiable, and relevant evidence—has no chance of going anywhere. It cannot contribute to the goal of supporting one side of the conflict of opinions that is supposed to be resolved by the dialogue because it is buried in the overwhelming onslaught of the argumentation pressed ahead by the other side. Even a good argument against guilt has no real chance because the procedure itself is so heavily and relentlessly stacked against it.

To test whether or not the expression *witch hunt* is appropriate to characterize the argumentation in a given case is to reconstruct the sequences of questions and replies in which the argument was embedded (in the text of discourse given in the case). This sequence is called a "profile of dialogue" (Walton 1989b, p. 67) in that it represents an outline or sketch of a sequence of connected moves as part of a context provided by a larger framework of dialogue (procedure). The profile then has to be evaluated in light of the broader context of dialogue of which it is a part. The ten characteristics of the witch hunt cited above are to be evaluated by comparing the actual sequence of dialogue in the given case to an abstract profile of dialogue that represents the kind of question-reply sequence that would be appropriate for the argumentation in a fair trial. The more the argumentation in the given case exhibits more of the ten characteristics and deviates from (or even subverts) the profiles of dialogue characteristic of the fair trial, the more evidence one has for characterizing the given case as a witch hunt.

10. Judging Cases

With regard to the kinds of cases cited by Coren (1994) and Loftus (1995), the reader can evaluate each case on its merits and judge the extent to which the argumentation in that case conforms to the characteristics of a witch hunt. There is a vast array of materials from which to choose, involving a wave of trials and tribunals that makes the Salem witchcraft trials look like a small and relatively minor localized incident by comparison. Good places to start are the account of the McMartin Preschool trial given in Eberle and Eberle (1993) and accounts of the comparable Martensville trial (see Roberts 1994). The sequence of argumentation in these trials has the classic pattern of many similar trials in North America in recent years—the pushing forward of false allegations of satanic-ritual abuse based on questionable argumentation tactics of inexperienced police officers and interviewing of suggestible children by aggressive questioning techniques of social workers and therapists.

Another prominent characteristic of the kinds of evidence used in such cases is the questionable verifiability of the claims. Sexual-abuse claims based on recovered memory are highly problematic or even impossible to verify subsequently on a basis of reproducible evidence. Although recovered memories have gained increased acceptance by psychotherapists, there has been considerable controversy about the validity of such interviews between therapists and patients as scientific evidence (Loftus and Rosenwald 1993).

At any rate, there is an abundant mass of case material in recent court cases for the reader who wants to apply the parasemotic structure of the witch hunt to evaluating current practices of argumentation. But just as the argumentation in the Salem trials proved to be more clearly evaluated in historical perspective, some time after the events occurred, so too will the argumentation used in the current cases come to be more clearly evaluated once the social pressures surrounding it have abated.

The problem in recognizing and evaluating the witch hunt type of bias is that enthusiastic advocates of a cause of ideology see their goals as representing what is right and good, and therefore they see anyone who is opposed to them, or even anyone who does not accept their viewpoint as evil or as a "problem" to be "fixed." During the witchcraft trials, the Christians saw their views as representing what is right and good. The all-important thing for them was to convert nonbelievers, so that their souls could be "saved." So anyone who opposed their views had to be evil or representatives of the devil because they were opposed to what is good and right.

It is very difficult for the enthusiastic advocates of the popular viewpoint to accept the idea that any other viewpoint could be anything other than evil. So producing more converts and fighting anyone opposed to the new view seems to be permissible by any means. Use of force, threats, or one-sided tribunals and interrogations appears to be permissible, because it is for a good end. So it is hard for those caught up in such an ideology to see their argumentation as biased or to see that bias as something that could be harmful in any way. If a critic comes along, a kind of Socratic gadfly, that person who sees the bias and speaks up about it is likely to be punished.

Ordinarily, bias of the witch hunt type is not that visible during a historical period when it actually occurs, and it can be very dangerous for any individual who tries to identify or question it in any way. So it is a difficult type of bias to determine precisely. It is not limited to just a single argument, and the evidence for it needs to take into account global factors in the type of dialogue. Even so, this type of bias is important, because the concept of a fair trial is the basis of not only our own legal system but any legal system that stands a chance of being successful.

Chapter Ten
EXTENDING THE THEORY

So far, the dialectical theory of bias has viewed judgments about whether persons are biased or not as outside the scope of the theory. The dialectical concept of bias has been restricted in its application to arguments. But in some cases it would be useful to model arguments where the person is attacked as biased—for example in cases of the *ad hominem* type. So is there any way that the dialectical theory of bias could be extended so it could be used to evaluate this sort of case?

The extension proposed in this chapter is based on defining the participants in a dialogue as agents, in a sense of this term now widely used in the field of computer science called "multi-agent systems" (Wooldridge and Jennings 1995). According to this extended view of dialogue, the participants in a dialogue are capable of taking the other party's moves and goals into account when they argue with each other. And it will be shown how each of them can take the credibility of the other as an agent into account, in reacting to and evaluating that other participant's arguments.

1. Summary of the Dialectical Theory

The new dialectical theory of bias sees bias as a property of arguments. To apply the theory to a particular case—a text of discourse that contains an argument—one must not only identify the argument itself but also draw up some account of how this argument was used for some purpose in the given case. The presumption is that the context of use of the argument in the given case is that of one of the types of dialogue identified in chapter 2, or some mixed type of dialogue that is a combination of two of the basic types. Also, other special features of the context of dialogue may

259

have to be taken into account, if the case is a legal argument in a trial, for example, or a political argument in a parliamentary or congressional debate (where special rules of procedure apply). To judge whether a given argument exhibits a bias of the dialectical kind, one must evaluate the argument in relation to how it was used as part of the type of dialogue in which the participants in the argument were supposedly engaging. Of course, bias is harmless, in many cases. But the kind of case where bias is a problem, from a dialectical point of view, is that where the argumentation is supposed to be two-sided, when, in reality, the argument is one-sided. And how exactly is bias determined in a given case? It is the indicators of bias described in chapter 4 that function as the evidence to be used in evaluating any case where a criticism of bias has been put forward. So that is how the dialectical theory of bias generally works and how it is to be applied to specific cases.

The exception to the general rule is the kind of case discussed in chapter 9, where the bias is systematically built into the structure of the dialogue. In this kind of case, the so-called witch hunt type of case, the whole framework of dialogue is made to look like that of a fair trial, while, in reality, the dialogue is a one-sided pressing ahead for a pre-ordained outcome.

In this kind of case, the bias resides in the parasemotic structure of the dialogue—its calculated appearance of being a fair trial. To determine bias in this kind of case, the analysis of the case needs to be more elaborate and carefully documented by the ten criteria for the witch hunt presented in chapter 9.

The new theory makes bias a property of arguments. But in one particularly important way, the new theory is limited because it does not enable us to judge whether an arguer—that is, the person or the participant in the dialogue—is biased. This limitation can be a problem, particularly with *ad hominem* arguments and arguments based on appeals to expert opinion because the concept of attacking the person as biased plays an important role in how we evaluate argumentation. For example, if an argument is based on an appeal to expert opinion, and if the expert is attacked as being biased, by means of an *ad hominem* argument, then that expert's credibility will be lowered. And the outcome will be that the appeal to expert opinion will be given less weight as a plausible argument. So the bias of the arguer and the bias of the argument are connected, in the way that argumentation is commonly evaluated.

But how could the concept of a biased argument be extended, in the new dialectical theory, to take into account the judgment that the arguer is biased? This problem seems to be insoluble, however, in the current state of the art of formal dialectical systems because there is no part of the dialogue structure that would allow for systematic assessment of the internal states of an arguer as a participant in dialogue.

2. The State of Formal Dialectic

In the formal structures of dialectic developed in Hamblin (1970; 1971), Mackenzie (1981; 1990), and Barth and Krabbe (1982), very little is said about the participants themselves or internal properties of them as entities. Only in the comments of Grice (1975) on how the participants in a conversation need to follow collaborative rules of politeness is there found any suggestion that the participants should have qualities such as honesty, sincerity, or trustworthiness.

In the Hamblin structure of formal dialectic (Hamblin 1970, chapter 8), very little is said about the internal makeup of the two participants who take turns moving in the dialogue. They are called "speakers," and they have to make moves in a dialogue that is governed by rules (p. 257). Each speaker keeps a store of statements representing her previous commitments (p. 257). According to the dialogue rules, after one speaker makes a certain type of move, the other must reply by choosing an option among the set of legitimate replies for that kind of move allowed by the rules. Presumably then these speakers have to have the capability to recognize a move made by the other party as being of a certain type, and they have to be aware of the rules, so that they can recognize what sort of reply is appropriate. They also need to be aware of their previous commitments, as well as those of the other party, and to be able to recognize an instance where some newly asserted proposition is inconsistent with previous commitments.

Hamblin (1970) says very little about the goal of the dialogue as a whole. His discussion of various possible alternative rules (pp. 269–276) suggests that the two participants are arguing against each other in a kind of competitive fashion. But we do not get any really firm idea of what the purpose is generally or whether there is a single purpose. It appears that there can be a multiplicity of different types of dialogue. Also, nothing appears to be said about the individual goals of the participants.

In Walton and Krabbe (1995), much more of a specific nature is said about different types of dialogue. Each type of dialogue cited has a specific goal stated. But, once again, very little is said about the participants themselves. Nevertheless, an important distinction is made between the goal of each type of dialogue as a whole and the goal of each participant who takes part in that type of dialogue. In the list of the different types of dialogue given (p. 66), a main goal is given for each type of dialogue and a participant's aim is defined for each type. For example, in a persuasion dialogue, the goal of the dialogue is said to be to resolve the conflict of opinion by verbal means, while the participant's aim is said to be to persuade the other party to accept a particular thesis (proposition) as true. Here then, at least something positive is said about the participant. Other than being a repository for commitments, a participant must also have a goal—an individual goal, as distinguished from the collective goal of the dialogue. Then what is implied is that a participant in a dialogue must be a goal-directed entity.

But still not much is said about the internal makeup of the participant or "speaker" in the dialogue. What seems to be important are the moves made by the participant, especially the assertions she makes and the arguments she puts forward and how these fit in with her prior commitments and the moves she makes now in the dialogue. It seems that the propositions and how they are ordered in the sequence of dialogue are primarily important in allowing the dialogue structure to function as a tool for evaluating argumentation.

But in the remarks of Grice (1975) on conversational principles there are some suggestions about the properties of the participant needed to sustain a collaborative conversation. According to this account, participants need to be sincere and honest in making their contributions to a conversational exchange, by following maxims of politeness. But Grice's remarks on the logic of conversation offer no formal dialectical theory of how these properties of the participant in a conversation can be precisely defined.

So the current state of dialectical systems offers no way of giving any analysis of the properties of a participant that would be helpful to extend the new dialectical theory of bias. But there is a new development in computer science, in the multi-agent system, that does appear to offer some useful resources for this application.

3. Multi-Agent Systems

New developments in computer science are based on seeing a robot or a software system as not just a passive device that follows rules or programs but as an autonomous agent that can not only seek out information[1] but also carry out tasks based on this information. These robots—or "softbots" in the case of software systems—may even need to engage in dialogue with other robots, in order to carry out their tasks.

In multi-agent systems in computer science, the idea of two so-called agents engaging in argumentation with each other has become an important topic for research. Two examples, cited by Wooldridge and Jennings (1995, p. 115) indicate the source of this concern.

> *Case* 10.1: When an air-traffic control system fails, two computerized air-traffic control systems in adjacent countries negotiate to track and deal with affected flights.

> *Case* 10.2: When you log on to your computer, your personalized digital assistant (PDA) sorts out your list of E-mail messages in order of importance, scans through new articles in your field, draws attention to one new article that describes work close to your own, and obtains a technical report for you, after an electronic discussion with other PDA's.

The new agent architectures being developed in AI (Artificial Intelligence) are software models that define how agents reason together for some communicative purpose. *Agent theory* uses mathematical formalisms to represent reasoning about the properties of agents (Wooldridge and Jennings 1995, p. 115).

Franklin and Graesser (1996) cite several agent characteristics that have been used in AI research.

1. Agents carry out "autonomous execution" of actions (p. 22).
2. Agents perform "domain oriented reasoning" (p. 22).
3. An agent can "perceive its environment through sensors" (p. 22).
4. An agent can act on its environment to realize goals (p. 22).
5. An agent can employ knowledge of another agent's goals in carrying out a set of operations (p. 22).
6. An agent can engage in dialogues with another agent (p. 23).

This last characteristic is important, for, as pointed out by Jennings and Wooldridge (1995, p. 364), since agents are autonomous, it has proved to be a problem in AI to predict how agents will react to moves made by other agents. Hence, the problem is one of effectively managing cases where one agent needs to depend on another, where the two of them need to solve a problem so that a "deadlock" in the system does not occur. In order to solve these problems in devising software that is useful for practical purposes, agent theory needs "a sophisticated means of dealing with incomplete and conflicting viewpoints" (Jennings and Wooldridge 1995, p. 365). Then the need is for agents to reason together in a dialogue exchange. But in a dialogue, how, more exactly, should the concept of an agent be defined?

Wooldridge and Jennings (1995, pp. 116–117) distinguish between two usages of the term *agent,* a stronger and a weaker use. According to the weaker notion, an agent is a computer system that has the following four properties (p. 116).

1. *Autonomy:* the agent has control over its actions and internal states.
2. *Social Ability:* an agent can interact linguistically with other agents.
3. *Reactivity:* an agent perceives its environment and reacts to changes in it.
4. *Pro-activeness:* an agent can take the initiative in its goal-directed actions, so that it is not just responding to these changes in its environment.

According to the stronger notion, an agent has the following four properties (p. 117):

1. *Mobility:* an agent can move around an electronic network.
2. *Veracity:* an agent will not knowingly communicate false information.
3. *Benevolence:* an agent will do what is asked and not have conflicting goals.
4. *Rationality:* an agent will act in order to achieve its goals and not prevent its goals from being achieved (in line with its beliefs about these matters).

In a multi-agent system, the agent is seen as more than a repository of commitments or beliefs. An agent is an entity that not only has goals but that can carry out actions. In dialectical contexts, these actions will be speech acts—communicative messages sent out to another agent as moves in a dialogue.

The suggestion then is to add the concept of an agent to formal dialectic. But how far should we go? The weaker notion of an agent seems to relate more to bias. But before getting to that point, it is best to consider briefly the stronger notion of an agent.

4. The Stronger and Weaker Notions of an Agent

One reason why it is helpful to think of a participant in a dialogue as being an agent is that for us to understand how the argumentation in a dialogue is really working and to evaluate the moves in it as argumentation, not only must a participant have rules that govern her conduct in the dialogue globally but she also must be able to see a move made by the other party in the dialogue and to recognize this move—to grasp it as a move so that she can then react to it at the next move. To do this, a participant has to be more than just a commitment store. She has to grasp something in her environment as input, to be aware of it, to recognize it as a certain type of thing, and then to react to it appropriately at the next move (or at least be capable of doing that). Both agents have to have this capacity for there to be a real dialogue between them.[2]

How do the two agents interact with each other in sequences of verbal argumentation in a dialogue exchange? How it works is that one agent not only sees the move the other has made and can recognize that move as being a certain type of move, like a question or an argument, once he has made it. But she can also recognize if that move is inappropriate at that particular point in the dialogue. And if it is inappropriate, then she will try to explain or guess why. Was the agent trying to deceive her or to intentionally opt out of the dialogue, or was he simply making a mistake? For in order to repair the flaw and help the dialogue go along constructively, making a guess at the nature of the fault may be helpful.

Grice (1975) very astutely observed that some apparent mistakes in conversational exchanges can be diagnosed as intentional violations of the collaborative rules of dialogue, as opposed to being mistakes. To react in this way to the prior move of a respondent, a proponent must be able to have proactive expectations about how the respondent would normally move. For example (Grice 1975, p. 72), suppose that one person at a tea party asks a question that is socially embarrassing, and the other person replies with something irrelevant such as "The weather has been nice this summer, hasn't it?" This irrelevant reply is not a mistake. The second person is suggesting that the subject should be changed because the question was a "social gaffe" and a conversation about it should not be continued. The inappropriateness of the unexpected reply should suggest something—a secondary message—to the first person.

A lot of everyday argumentation is only comprehensible as argumentation of a kind that can be evaluated as logical or illogical because each party in a dialogue has expectations of how the other party should normally react to a certain move at a particular point in an argument exchange. These expectations will be built up in a systematic way during the course of a dialogue, as one participant begins to get a grasp of how the other party tends to argue. And certainly these expectations of how a speech partner will tend to argue, based on his past performances in a dialogue, are an important part of building up an argumentation strategy, in a persuasion dialogue, for example.

Much of the strategy of argumentation, in the persuasion dialogue in particular, is based not only on the other party's commitments but also on proactively guessing how the other party is likely to respond to certain kinds of arguments, based on how he has responded in the prior sequence of dialogue (to the extent this is known). In short, it seems that thinking of the participants in a dialogue as agents is a useful extension of formal dialectic, at least insofar as the stronger notion of agency is concerned.

But it is the weaker notion of agent and particularly properties such as veracity and benevolence that are of interest with respect to the question of bias. In a persuasion dialogue, we expect a participant to be open to new evidence and to take a two-sided approach, instead of only pushing ahead in an aggressive one-sided way. In other words, an arguer is expected to exhibit qualities of balance and openness. And these qualities are important to the success of the dialogue. But why are they important?

The answer is that in all of the types of dialogue described in chapter 2 (except the eristic type), to make the dialogue productive, there is an assumption that both parties will collaborate by following certain principles of cooperativeness of the kind cited by Grice (1975). In all five basic types of dialogue there is a presumption that both participants will be two-sided in their argumentation, meaning that they will judge the worth of an argument as a contribution to the dialogue based not just on self-interest or on how it supports their own thesis but on what the real support or lack of support for the argument is, based on the evidence on both sides. Anyone who violates this presumption is not contributing to the dialogue. In fact, what they are doing may be an obstacle to its productive progress. So the weak notion of agency does matter. It matters in judging how an argument has or has not been used for some constructive purpose in a goal-directed communicative exchange. What properties do matter? Veracity and benevolence are important.

5. Characteristics of a Credible Arguer

The assumption behind the kinds of criticisms of dialectical bias studied in the various cases in previous chapters is based on the principle that in a type of dialogue such as a critical discussion, if an argument is judged to be biased, then the other party to whom that argument was directed in the dialogue will attach less weight to the argument, meaning that he will judge it to be less persuasive as an argument. The presumption is that each participant will generally presume that the other participant is cooperatively and honestly following the collaborative rules of the dialogue, and therefore each party will grant the other a certain degree of trust that he or she is following the rules and paying attention to and fairly considering the evidence on its merits. But this trust can be broken very easily, and, in the experience of everyday argumentation, it often is. So arguers will be alert to any indications of bias. Once trust appears to have broken, there is an assumption that the other party may not be reliable, may have a hidden agenda, may be engaging in deception, and so forth. Once such evidence appears, what is called the "credibility" of an arguer is impugned or challenged, with the result that the initial assumption of collaborative honesty is cast into doubt.

According to the account in Walton (1996b, pp. 244–245), there are five positive characteristics of a credible arguer in a critical discussion. All of these five qualities can be thought of as characteristics that are part of the weaker notion of an agent as a participant in a critical discussion (and in other types of dialogue as well).

1. *Flexibility of Commitment.*
   An arguer must stick to a proposition she has committed herself to, but must also be ready to retract her commitment to it (in the right circumstances).

2. *Empathy.*
   An arguer must be willing to consider the other party's point of view accurately, perceptively, and fairly.

3. *Open-mindedness.*
   An arguer must be willing to consider the arguments of the opposed party and weigh them on their merits, instead of reflexively rejecting them out of hand (just because they are opposed to her point of view). Part of this characteristic is what Johnstone (1981, p. 309) describes as an ethical duty of rhetoric requiring an arguer to protect a space for future arguments on an issue.

4. *Critical Doubt.*
   An arguer must be able to suspend her acceptance of a proposition. This attitude is typified by utterances such as, 'Why should I

accept this?'. Not only must this attitude apply to propositions accepted or proposed by the other side. An arguer must be willing to give up her own argument or proposal (concede defeat), if this argument or proposal is shown to be weak or refuted.

5. *Evidence Reactivity.*
An arguer must adjust her commitments, or acceptance of arguments, based on considerations that are clearly admissible (in a dialogue) as relevance evidence.

These five characteristics are all good qualities of a participant in a dialogue such as a critical discussion. In fact, the absence of any one of them is a hindrance to the progress of a critical discussion. And failure of a participant to exhibit any one of these qualities would be an indicator that the participant is biased. These characteristics have already been studied in a different format in chapter 4, as indicators of bias in an argument. Now they can be identified, as well, as positive qualities that an agent needs in order to argue in a constructive and collaborative fashion in a persuasion dialogue and in other types of dialogue.

What needs to be done now to extend the dialectical theory of bias is to examine how such positive characteristics of a credible arguer are requirements of the other types of dialogue, such as negotiation and deliberation. But this is not a task that will be carried out here. It is left as a problem for further studies in the dialectical theory of bias.

6. The Credibility Function

How do the five characteristics of a credible arguer play a role in critical judgments of bias, according to the new dialectical theory? So far, the concept of an agent has been added to the structure of formal dialectic, so that a participant in a dialogue is thought of as an agent who interacts verbally in argumentation with another agent. But how is the agent connected to the argument and to the concept of bias?

The answer is implicit in observations already made. If an agent shows evidence of having failed to exhibit one or more of the five characteristics, then her credibility will be reduced. Credibility is the quality an agent is presumed to have, on the grounds that she has exhibited these five qualities in a dialogue and, what is more important, has not showed any evidence of not having them.

What happens if a participant in a critical discussion shows evidence of having failed to exhibit one or more of these five characteristics is that her credibility will be reduced. As a result of this credibility reduction, the weight assigned to this participant's argumentation will be reduced.

But how can such a mechanism for evaluating argumentation be built into the structure of formal dialectic? The answer is that there needs to be a connection between the agent and the argument that the agent has put forward as a participant in a dialogue with another agent. What is needed is a credibility function that takes an evaluation of an agent onto an evaluation of that agent's argument.

How the credibility function works is that it takes as an input value a credibility rating of a participant in a dialogue and takes as an output value a plausibility weighting of the participant's argument that she has put forward. If the credibility rating goes down, then the plausibility weighting will go down proportionately. If the credibility rating goes up, the plausibility weighting will go up proportionately. For example, suppose that new information comes in that the proponent of an argument is an expert in a domain of knowledge into which the argument she has put forward falls. Then her credibility will go up, and as a result, the plausibility accorded to her argument will go up. But then suppose that it is found out that this expert has something financially to gain by supporting this particular argument. Then her credibility rating will go down, and her argument will be found to be less plausible, in the sense of being less persuasive in proving the thesis at issue in the dialogue. What we see here is that the arguer has a credibility rating, and this credibility rating will affect how her argument is judged or weighed as persuasive or not, by another party who is supposed to accept that argument.

The credibility function does not determine what an arguer's initial credibility is. It only takes that initial credibility rating and then adjusts it upward or downward, depending on many factors. But one of the most important factors is bias. If an arguer is found to be biased, in the negative or harmful sense, meaning that her arguments are one-sided in a context of dialogue where they are supposed to be two-sided, then her credibility rating will be lowered. For example, if an arguer is taking part in a critical discussion of an issue, but then she always bases her arguments on one-sided eristic dialogue and interest-based bargaining, it will become apparent that she is biased. In a critical discussion there is a presumption that an arguer will abide by the collaborative rules of the dialogue and will consider the arguments on both sides of the contested issue, not always favoring the one side for reasons of self-interest. If there is evidence that an arguer is not taking a balanced, two-sided approach that is giving the evidence on the other side its due consideration, her credibility will be lowered. In a critical discussion, each side will give the other side a certain weight or presumption of credibility. There is an expectation that how she weighs an argument is based on how she takes into account the real weight of plausibility of the arguments on both sides of a disputable point. But if the indicators show she is biased, this initial credibility will be withdrawn or adjusted downward.

7. Agent and Argument Bias

In a critical discussion, it is normal to expect a reasonable amount of what Kienpointner and Kindt (1997, p. 574) call "local bias," or bias during specific parts of the argumentative exchange. For we expect an arguer in a critical discussion to support her own viewpoint as an advocate and to challenge and criticize the opposed viewpoint. Not only is this kind of advocacy or localized partisanship normal, but it is a required aspect of a successful critical discussion. But if a global bias is detected in the arguer's global argumentation in the dialogue—especially if it is a universal pattern—where the arguer always supports her own side and dismisses or attacks arguments on the other side, even when these arguments are plausible and do make a good point that needs to be conceded, then there is evidence of the harmful kind of bias. And it is exactly in this kind of case that it is judged that the arguer, the person herself, is biased, over and above any single or local argument of hers that is judged to be biased.

Where the participant as agent comes in is in a global perspective, as the evidence mounts from a lengthy sequence of argumentation that there is a pattern of recurring bias in a person's arguments. Using this global evidence of biased arguments, the conclusion is drawn that the arguer herself (the participant as agent) is biased. From there, the credibility function transfers from this judgment about the agent to a lowering of credibility for that agent's subsequent arguments in a dialogue.

Generally then, in the new dialectical theory of bias, there are two different ways of making a criticism of bias. One way is to allege that an argument is biased. The other way is to allege that the arguer is biased. The second way is a more diffuse kind of criticism that is more difficult to prove and also has more personal overtones. It really is a kind of personal attack or *ad hominem* argument to criticize a proponent's argument by claiming that the proponent is biased as a person. The best way to handle criticisms of bias is to regard the second kind of bias criticism as a more tricky and difficult kind of criticism to prove and to deal with generally.

For these reasons, it is better to regard the first way as the fundamental type of bias criticism, and generally, in an argument, it is better to keep criticisms of bias at this level. However, in some cases, concentrating on the bias of the arguer, as opposed to the bias of the argument, is a useful and even necessary move to make and is a common form of argument.

A case in point would be a negotiation where it might appear that someone is on your side but where in fact this person is being paid by the other side (Edwards 1997).

> *Case* 10.3: In a class action lawsuit by many home buyers against a real estate firm, the buyers argued that when they bought their homes, they thought their real estate was working for them. In fact, the agents had all been working for the sellers. As a result of this case, which was decided in favor of the home buyers, Oregon passed a new law saying that real estate agents must disclose their relationship at "the first substantive contact" with a buyer or seller.

The problem here is that most home buyers think that a real estate agent represents their interests, but, in fact, they are usually paid by the seller. It could be a big mistake to share your excitement and offer strategies to your real estate agent, if you do not know that it is the agent's fiduciary responsibility to reveal this information to the owner of the house (Golden, 1997).

To handle such cases, the dialectical theory of bias needs to be extended to take characteristics of a participant in a dialogue as an agent into account. In this kind of case, the critic of an argument cannot evaluate the argument without taking the trustworthiness and credibility of the arguer into account. So the arguer needs to be thought of as an agent, a participant in a dialogue who needs to be counted on to have the characteristics of a credible arguer, in order for the dialogue to progress constructively toward its goal. If that agent exhibits the harmful type of bias, the resulting loss of credibility will affect how his argument should be evaluated.

8. Why Should Bias Matter?

Taking the credibility of an arguer into account in the logical evaluation of arguments is a difficult step for some to take. Indeed, many will insist that bias is not a matter to be judged by methods of logic. "What does bias matter anyway?" a critic might say, when confronting the dialectical theory of bias. Such a critic may argue, "Dialectical bias doesn't really matter anyway, because an argument should be judged only on whether or not the premises support the conclusion." The critic's remark (rightly) brings out the thesis that dialectical bias is a contextual matter of how an argument was supposedly used for some communicative purpose. But is the conclusion drawn from this insight justified? Is it really true that bias does not matter? Why is a criticism of bias of any importance for logic? Why should it be taken into account at all in assessing the worth of an argument? And, of course, postmodernists will say that everyone is inevitably biased by their own self-interest and group affiliations anyway and ask why pointing out such a bias should not itself be regarded as just another bias.

At least part of the answer to the question of why bias should matter resides in the need to have collaborative principles of conversation for argumentation to be productive. In practice, if an arguer is shown to be biased by the indicators described in chapters 4 and 5, then her argument will not be found to be as credible as a contribution to a critical discussion as it was before. The reason is that there is a presumption that a participant in a critical discussion is not biased. And if there are indicators that she is biased, her credibility will be "damaged," that is , reduced. Bias matters because the evidence of it indicates that the arguer has been shown to fail to have one or more of the five characteristics of a credible participant in a critical discussion. This finding suggests, in turn, that the participant is not contributing to the critical discussion in a constructive way and that this failure is a problem. But why, exactly, is it a problem?

The assumption that a participant can be relied on to take into account both the arguments for and those against her position is vital to the success of a critical discussion. Otherwise, it cannot be said that the conflict of opinions has been resolved by rational argumentation, as opposed to having been resolved by an eristic struggle or a clash where one party's interests were represented by threats or appeals to self-interest. If there is evidence that this assumption is not met, the credibility accorded to the arguer will be reduced.

The same is true of other types of dialogue such as deliberation, negotiation, and inquiry. If there is evidence that one party is only pretending to co-operate, while all the time using arguments that are not the kind needed to contribute to the goal Tof the dialogue, then the other party needs to take notice of this failure and take appropriate action to get the argument back on track.

But one might still reply, Why do we need these conventions of dialogue at all? Why not forget about trust, rules of procedure, and maxims of polite conversation? Why not judge each argument on its merits alone and not get involved in personal matters of the qualities of an agent at all? Doesn't this involvement introduce an *ad hominem* element that is a bad direction to take? The answer to this question is Yes, it does introduce an *ad hominem* element, and yes it is better not to take this step if you can avoid it, but in some kinds of cases, you cannot avoid it.

9. Three Ways of Evaluating an Argument

There are three ways of evaluating an argument, and going to each new way involves a broadening of perspective. The first way is to look at the argument to see if the premises support the conclusion. One can evaluate the argument as deductively valid, as inductively strong, as having presumptive weight, and so forth. This way looks at the propositions in the argument and the reasoning that joins the premises to the conclusion. The second way is to evaluate how the argument was used in a context of dialogue to make a contribution to the type of dialogue of which it was supposed to be part. This pragmatic way of evaluating an argument is a broader perspective because you have to look at the argument as a local sequence in a broader context of dialogue. The third way is to examine the arguer, the agent, or the proponent who had put the argument forward and then to evaluate the argument in light of the credibility of that arguer. This third way is even broader because it involves making a general judgment about an agent, based on that agent's performance in a dialogue or in other dialogues, and facts that may be known about that agent. In many cases, we do not need to move to this third way, and what is important is to evaluate the argument on its own merits, regardless of the qualities of the agent who put that argument forward.

When is it useful or necessary to take the step of evaluating an argument in this third way? Typically, such a step is useful when we lack direct access to the facts ourselves or do not have a complete basis for evaluating an argument in the first way or perhaps even the second. Then we have to look at the person who stands behind the argument and work on assumptions about this person as an agent who is a participant in a dialogue with us.

> *Case* 10.4: Suppose your financial adviser is giving you advice about which investments she thinks are best for you. You are not an expert, on investments, and you do not have direct access to all the facts you need to make a wise decision in such a deliberation. So you have to depend on the expert and you assume that she is giving you balanced advice, based on the evidence of which stocks are the best investments at the present. As an expert, she has a certain credibility. As long as that credibility is not questioned or challenged, perhaps by some evidence of bias, you will continue to give her a certain degree of credibility. But if it should become known to you that she has profited financially from certain investments you have made, or if there is some other indicator of bias, her credibility will be open to question.

Each case will have to be examined on its merits. But if she has a persistent track record of this sort of advice, you may conclude that she is biased in a certain way. So here you would be moving to the third way of evaluating argumentation. Because you have judged that this person is biased, you will accord her less credibility as a proponent who is giving you balanced advice on your investments. And that judgment is a reasonable one, in the circumstances, precisely because you lack the financial information and expertise necessary for you to make up your own mind, independently of having to rely on someones else's advice.

It is precisely in this type of lack-of-knowledge situation that the third way of evaluating an argument is useful and necessary.[3] Generally, to evaluate an argument, all three ways may need to be taken into account. The perceived bias of the arguer may be one small factor to be balanced against what is known about the evidential strength of the argument, apart from the characteristics of the agent who advocated it.[4]

The problem still remains that some readers will see this third way of evaluating arguments as a kind of postmodern view. And, in a way, it is.

10. Postmodernism and Bias

The traditional positivistic view that was the conventional wisdom of the first half of the twentieth century saw science as being the only kind of thinking worth taking seriously. Scientific research was "objective," and all else was "subjective." To support this viewpoint, the model of reasoning advocated was that of deductive and inductive logic, coupled with a strong kind of empiricism that held collecting "hard evidence" as the way to resolve any issue. The postmodern view that has now taken over as the popular wisdom is the direct opposite of the positivistic view. According to the postmodern view, there is no such thing as objective knowledge, and science is just another point of view, based on "models" of reality that are invented by the scientists to suit their needs for calculation and other instrumental purposes.

According to the positivistic view, deductive and inductive reasoning is all that really matters. An argument is either valid (or inductively strong) or not, and that is all that matters. Matters of the context of dialogue of an argument are subjective. There is no way of objectively determining such matters, so they are of no importance.

The postmodern view agrees that matters of the context of use of an argument are subjective but draws the opposite conclusion. The postmodern view takes the subjective approach to the limit, claiming that even science itself is a kind of subjective viewpoint.

The dialectical viewpoint is midway between these two polarized views. The dialectical view agrees with the postmodern view in that it judges arguments in relation to different contexts of dialogue. Unlike the positivistic view, the dialectical view does not see an argument as objectively valid or invalid (inductively strong or weak), period. The dialectical view claims that one must judge an argument from a contextual and communicate point of view. It could be a good (correct) argument in one context of dialogue and a fallacious (incorrect) argument in another context of dialogue. In this respect the new dialectical viewpoint is postmodern.

But where the new dialectical theory of bias is not postmodern is that it does not imply the conclusion that all arguments are biased and that therefore there are no standards of rationality by which arguments can be judged by an external critic. Instead, the new dialectical theory of bias actually gives objective standards that can be used to determine whether an argument in a given case is biased and to evaluate whether that bias is harmful or not, from a critical point of view.

Neither the positivists nor the postmodernists will like the new dialectical theory of bias. The positivists, who favor deductive (and/or) inductive logic as the only objective standard for evaluating arguments, will see the dialectical approach as too contextual. The postmodernists, on the other side, will see the new dialectical theory as an even worse restriction on their freedom to say whatever they want than deductive logic was. They see any kind of systematic method of evaluating arguments as being an oppressive restriction on their rights to express views that promote their own interests as individuals or as members of groups who need to speak out.

Unfortunately, philosophy in the late twentieth century has become strangled and marginalized as a useful discipline that has anything to offer to anyone not already in the grip of its tribal ideologies. Although much good work is now being done in applied areas, such as medical ethics and business ethics, there is no methodology for evaluating the argumentation used. Deductive (and inductive) logic is of limited use, by itself. And the only alternative seems to be the postmodern approach, which makes a venting of personal feelings the best to which philosophy can aspire as a discipline. There is no method for criticizing arguments or the kind so badly needed for philosophy to be taken seriously as a discipline that has anything to contribute to those outside the field.

What is needed is for those not already dogmatically committed to the programs of positivism and postmodernism to take a look at the new dialectical theory of bias as offering a way of critically evaluating argumentation by objective and useful criteria that can be used to facilitate arguments in communicative exchanges such as negotiation and persuasion dialogue. Yes, the dialectical method is critical—if an argument exhibits evidence of the harmful kind of bias, that determination is a kind of strike against it, a way of judging the argument to be faulty or deserving of criticism. And yes, such a critical viewpoint is just one point of view. But it is a viewpoint that is vitally important for philosophy and for all other academic disciplines as well, including its application to argumentation in law and science.

In short then, the new dialectical theory of bias is, in some sense, a postmodernistic view because it judges arguments in many different contexts of dialogue. But it is opposed to postmodernism in that it sees each type of dialogue as having a goal-directed structure with rules and requirements for correct argumentation.

Notes

1. For a good introduction to the theory of intelligent agents in AI, see Russell and Norvig (1995, chapter 2).

2. Failure to grasp the other's message by one party in a dialogue, due to factors such as ambiguity or lack of clarity does seem to be important in relation to fallacies such as equivocation.

3. Reasoning under uncertainty is an important subject of research in AI. For an introduction to principles-of-uncertainty reasoning, see Russell and Norvig (1995, chapter 5).

4. In defeasible reasoning, a conclusion is tentatively accepted as plausible, subject to qualifications that may lead to its nonacceptance at a later point in a discussion. On defeasible reasoning, see Pollock (1987; 1991).

Bibliography

Alphandery, Paul D. "The Inquisition." *Encyclopaedia Britannica,* vol. 12, 1963, 377–383.

Alter, Jonathan. "The Incendiary Aftershocks." *Newsweek,* March 15, 1993, p. 65.

Altman, Laurence K. "Experts See Bias in Drug Data." *The New York Times,* April 29, 1997, B7 and B12.

Andrews, Kirsten. "Sound Off." *The Winnipeg Sun,* July 17, 1993, 8.

Aristotle. *Nicomachean Ethics.* In *The Works of Aristotle Translated into English,* ed. W. D. Ross, Oxford: Oxford University Press, 1928.

———. *Rhetoric.* Trans. John Henry Freese. Loeb Classical Library, Cambridge, Mass.: Harvard University Press, 1937.

———. *On Sophistical Refutations.* Trans. E. S. Forster. Loeb Classical Library, Cambridge, Mass.: Harvard University Press, 1939.

———. *Posterior Analytics.* Trans. Hugh Tredennic. Loeb Classical Library, 1939, Cambridge, Mass.: Harvard University Press, 1939.

Arnauld, Antoine. *The Port-Royal Logic* (translation of *La Logique, ou L'Art de Penser,* 1662). Trans. Thomas Spencer Baynes. Edinburgh: Oliver and Boyd, 1865.

Bacon, Francis. *The Advancement of Learning* (1605). In vol. 3 of *Works,* ed. Spelling, Ellis and Heath, London, 1858–74.

———. *Novum Organum* (1620). New York: P. F. Collier & Son, 1902.

Baird, Davis. *Inductive Logic: Probability and Statistics.* Englewood Cliffs: Prentice Hall, 1992.

Barth, Else M., and Erik C. W. Krabbe. *From Axiom to Dialogue.* New York: De Gruyter, 1982.

Beardsley, Monroe C. *Practical Logic.* New York: Prentice-Hall, 1950.

———. *Thinking Straight.* 3rd ed. Englewood Cliffs: Prentice-Hall, 1966.

Begley, Sharon. "Is Science Censored?" *Newsweek,* September 14, 1992, 63.

Begley, Sharon. Howard Fineman and Vernon Church, "The Science of Polling," *Newsweek,* September 28, 1992, 38–39.

Bentham, Jeremy. "The Book of Fallacies" (1824). In *A Bentham Reader,* ed. Mary Peter Mack. New York: Pegasus, 1969, 331–358.

———. *Bentham's Handbook of Political Fallacies* (1824), ed. Harold A. Larrabee. New York: Thomas Y. Crowell, 1971.

Blair, J. Anthony. "What is Bias?" *Selected Issued in Logic and Communication*. Ed. Trudy Govier. Belmont, California: Wadsworth, 1988, 93–103.

Blyth, John W. *A Modern Introduction to Logic*. Boston: Houghton Mifflin, 1957.

Boyer, Paul, and Stephen Nissenbaum. *The Salem Witchcraft Papers*. Vol. 1. New York: Da Capo, 1977.

Brinton, Alan. "Seeing the Word through Our Own Eyes: The Doctrine of Logical Prejudices." *Philosophy and Rhetoric* 28, 1995, 316–332.

Broad, William, and Nicholas Wade. *Betrayers of the Truth: Fraud and Deceit in the Halls of Science*. New York: Simon and Schuster, 1982.

Carney, James D. and Richard Scheer. *Fundamentals of Logic*. 2nd ed. New York: Macmillan, 1974.

Carson, Rachel. *Silent Spring*. Boston: Houghton Mifflin, 1962.

Castelfranchi, Cristiano. "Commitments: From Individual Intentions to Groups and Organizations." *Proceedings: First International Conference on Multi-Agent Systems*, Menlo Park: AAI Press, 1995.

Cernetig, Miro. "Loggers Stage Massive Protest." *The Globe and Mail*, March 22, 1994, A1 and A8.

Chase, Stuart. *Guides to Straight Thinking*. New York: Harper and Row, 1956.

Copi, Irving M. *Introduction to Logic*. 6th ed. New York: Macmillan, 1982.

Copi, Irving M. *Introduction to Logic*. 7th ed. New York: Macmillan, 1986.

Copi, Irving M., and Carl Cohen. *Introduction to Logic*. 8th ed. New York: Macmillan, 1990.

Copi, Irving M., and Keith Burgess-Jackson, *Informal Logic*. 2nd ed. New York: Macmillan, 1992.

Coren, Michael. "Fifth Column." *The Globe and Mail*, April 27, 1994, A22.

Creighton, James Edwin. *An Introductory Logic*. New York: Macmillan, 1909.

Crossen, Cynthia. *Tainted Truth: The Manipulation of Fact in America*. New York: Simon & Schuster, 1994.

Damer, T. Edward. *Attacking Faulty Reasoning*. Belmont, California: Wadsworth, 1980.

Davis, Wayne A. *An Introduction to Logic*. Englewood Cliffs: Prentice-Hall, 1986.

Degnan, Ronan E. 1973. 'Evidence.' *Encyclopaedia Britannica*, vol. 8. 15th ed.

Donohue, William A. "Development of a Model of Rule Use in Negotiation Interaction." *Communication Monographs* 48, 1981, 106–120.

Eberle, Paul, and Shirley Eberle. *The Abuse of Innocence: The McMartin Pre-school Trial*. Buffalo: Prometheus, 1993.

Edwards, Marcia. "Who's on Your Side in Home Deal?" *The Register-Guardian*, Eugene, Oregon, April 26, 1997, 4E.

Ehninger, Douglas. *Influence, Belief and Argument*. Glenview, Illinois: Scott, Foresman, 1974.

Engel, S. Morris. *With Good Reason*. 2nd ed. New York: St. Martin's Press, 1982.

Evans, J. D. G. *Aristotle's Concept of Dialectic.* Cambridge: Cambridge University Press, 1977.

Evans, Jonathan St. B. T. *Bias in Human Reasoning: Causes and Consequences.* Hillsdale, New Jersey: Lawrence Erlbaum Associates, 1989.

Fearnside, W. Ward and William B. Holther. *Fallacy: The Counterfeit of Argument,* Englewood Cliffs, N. J. Prentice-Hall, 1959.

Feteris, Eveline. "Discussieregels in het Recht: Een Pragma-dialectische Analyse van het Burgerlijk Proces en het Strafproces." Ph.D. Dissertation, University of Amsterdam, 1989.

"The Fifth Estate: The Last Battleground." CBC Transcript, October 12, 1993 [six pages].

Fine, Sean. "More Judges Dare to Break Silence Away from the Bench." *The Globe and Mail,* November 13, 1993, A1–A2.

Alec Fisher, "Critical Study of Paul's *Critical Thinking, Informal Logic*" 13, 1991a, 113–123.

———. "Testing Fairmindedness." *Informal Logic* 13, 1991b, 31–35.

Forsyth, Brian W., Ralph I. Horwitz, Denise Acampora, Eugene D. Shapiro, Catherine M. Viscoli, Alvan R. Feinstein, Rochelle Henner, Nancy B. Holabird, Beth A. Jones, Artemis D. E. Karabelas, Michael S. Kramer, Michele Miclette, and James A. Wells, "New Epidemiologic Evidence Confirming That Bias Does Not Explain the Aspirin/Reye's Syndrome." *Journal of the American Medical Association* 261, 1989, 2517–2524.

Franklin, Stan, and Art Graesser. "Is It an Agent, or Just a Program?: A Taxonomy for Autonomous Agents." In *Intelligent Agents III: Agent Theories, Architectures and Languages,* ed. Jorg P. Muller, Michael J. Wooldridge and Nicholas R. Jennings. Berlin: Springer, 1996, 21–35.

Freeman, James B. *Thinking Logically.* Englewood Cliffs: Prentice Hall, 1988.

Frye, Albert M. and Albert W. Levi. *Rational Belief: An Introduction to Logic.* New York: Greenwood Press, 1969.

Garver, Eugene. "Point of View, Bias and Insight." *Metaphilosophy* 24, 1993, 47–60.

Giannelli, Paul C. "General Acceptance of Scientific Tests: Frye and Beyond." In *Scientific and Expert Evidence,* 2nd ed., ed. Edward J. Imwinkelried. Practising Law Institute, 1981, 11–35.

Golden, Caron. "Sometimes Home Buyers Need Their Own Agents." *The Register-Guardian,* Eugene, Oregon, May 3, 1997, 5E.

Goldman, Ari L. "Religion Notes." *The New York Times National,* April 24, 1993, L11.

Gooderham, Mary. "When Reading Media Polls, It's *Caveat Emptor* as Usual—and Pass the Salt." *The Globe and Mail,* Feb. 26, 1994, D8.

Graham, Michael H. "Impeaching the Professional Expert Witness by a Showing of Financial Interest." *Indiana Law Journal* 53, 1977, 35–53.

Grice, H. Paul. "Logic and Conversation." In *The Logic of Grammar,* ed. Donald Davidson and Gilbert Harman. Encino: Dickenson, 1975, 64–75.

Hamblin, Charles L. *Fallacies.* London: Methuen, 1970. Reprinted by Vale Press, Newport News, Virginia, 1993.

———. "Mathematical Models of Dialogue." *Theoria* 37, 1971, 130–155.

Hamilton, Bernard. *The Medieval Inquisition.* New York: Holmes and Meier, 1981.

Hibben, John Grier. *Logic: Deductive and Inductive.* New York: Scribner's, 1906.

Howard, M. N. "The Neutral Expert: A Plausible Threat to Justice." *The Criminal Law Review,* Feb. 1, 1991, 98–105.

Huber, Peter. *Galileo's Revenge: Junk Science in the Courtroom.* New York: Basic Books, 1991.

Huppé, Bernard F. and Jack Kaminsky. *Logic and Language.* New York: Knopf, 1957.

Hurley, Patrick J. *A Concise Introduction to Logic.* 4th ed. Belmont: Wadsworth, 1991 [5th ed., 1994].

Imwinkelried, Edward J. *The Methods of Attacking Scientific Evidence.* Charlottesville, Virginia: The Michie Co., 1982.

———. "Science Takes the Stand: The Growing Misuse of Expert Testimony." *The Sciences* 26, 1986, 20–25.

Jacobs, Scott, Sally Jackson, James Hallmark, Barbara Hall, and Susan A. Stearns. "Ideal Argument in the Real World: Making Do in Mediation." *Proceedings of the Fifth SCA/AFA Conference on Argumentation,* ed. Joseph W. Wenzel, Annandale, Virginia, Speech Communication Association, 1987, 291–298.

Jennings, Nicholas R., and Michael Wooldridge. "Applying Agent Technology." *Applied Artificial Intelligence* 9, 1995, 357–369.

Johnson, Ralph H. "Hamblin on the Standard Treatment." *Philosophy and Rhetoric,* 23, 1990, 153–167.

Johnson, Ralph H., and J. Anthony Blair. *Logical Self-Defense.* 2nd ed. Toronto: McGraw-Hill Ryerson, 1983.

Johnstone, Henry W., Jr. "Toward an Ethics of Rhetoric." *Communication* 6, 1981, 305–314.

Kahane, Howard. *Logic and Contemporary Rhetoric.* 6th ed. Belmont, California: Wadsworth, 1992.

Kant, Immanuel. *Kant's Introduction to Logic* (first published in 1800) *and his Essay on the Mistaken Subtility of the Four Figures.* trans. Thomas K. Abbott. London: Longmans, Green & Co., 1885.

Kesterton, Michael. "Social Studies." *The Globe and Mail,* June 8, 1995, A24.

Kienpointner, Manfred and Walther Kindt. "On the Problem of Bias in Political Argumentation." *Journal of Pragmatics* 27, 1997, 555–585.

Kostash, Myrna. "Whose Body? Whose Self?" in *Ethical Issues,* ed. Eldon Soifer. Toronto: Broadview Press, 1992, 379–386.

Krabbe, Erik C. W. and Douglas N. Walton, "It's All Very Well for You to Talk:

Situationally Disqualifying *Ad Hominem* Attacks." *Informal Logic* 15, 1993, 79–93.

Landsman, Stephan. "Who Needs Evidence Rules, Anyway?" *Loyola of Los Angeles Law Review* 25, 1992, 635–648.

Lea, Henry Charles. *A History of the Inquisition of the Middle Ages.* Abridged version. New York: Macmillan, 1961.

Lee, Charles S. "Books of Their Own." *Newsweek,* November 1, 1993, p. 69.

Leo, John. "The Journalistically Challenged." *U.S. News and World Report,* August 3, 1992, 18.

Little, J. Frederick, Leo A. Groarke, and Christopher W. Tindale. *Good Reasoning Matters.* Toronto: McClelland and Stewart, 1989.

Little, Winston W., W. Harold Wilson, and W. Edgar Moore. *Applied Logic.* Boston: Houghton Mifflin, 1955.

Loftus, Elizabeth. "Remembering Dangerously." *Skeptical Inquirer* 19, 1995, 20–29.

Loftus, Elizabeth F., and Laura A. Rosenwald. "Buried Memories: Shattered Lives." *ABA Journal* 79, 1993, 70–73.

Macdonald, Sally. "Armed Situation Impacts Severely, Linguistics-Wise." *Seattle Times.* Reprinted in *Winnipeg Free Press,* November 23, 1991, 42.

Mackenzie, Jim. "Why Do We Number Theorems?" *Australasian Journal of Philosophy* 58, 1980, 135–149.

———. "The Dialectics of Logic." *Logique et Analyse* 94, 1981, 159–177.

———. "Four Dialogue Systems." *Studia Logica* 49, 1990, 567–583.

MAL and NS. "Buzzwords." *The Progressive* 54 (July), 1990, 21.

Mander, A.E. *Clearer Thinking.* London: Watts & Co., 1936.

McElhaney, James W. "An Impeachment Checklist." *American Bar Association Journal* 78, 1992, 62–63.

Michalos, Alex C. *Improving Your Reasoning.* Englewood Cliffs: Prentice-Hall, 1970.

Minow, Newton H., and Fred H. Cate. "The Search for Justice—Is Impartiality Really Possible?" *USA Today,* January, 1992, 58–60.

Moore, David W. *The Superpollsters.* New York: Four Walls Eight Windows, 1992.

Morabia, Alfredo, and Phillipe Flandre. "Misclassification Bias Related to Definition of Menopausal Status in Case-Control Studies of Breast Cancer." *International Journal of Epidemiology* 21, 1992, 222–228.

Morton, James C., and Scott C. Hutchison. *The Presumption of Innocence.* Toronto: Carswell, 1987.

Mourant, John A. *Formal Logic.* New York: Macmillan, 1963.

Newman, Jay. *Fanatics and Hypocrites,* Buffalo: Prometheus Books, 1986.

Patel, Kam. "Science Losing Its Cutting Edge." *The Times Higher Education Supplement,* July 7, 1995, 7.

Paul, Richard. *Critical Thinking.* Rohnert Park, California: Center for Critical Thinking, Sonoma State University, 1990.

Paul, R., A. J. A. Binker, and M. Charbonneau. *Critical Thinking Handbook K-3.* Sonoma State University, Center for Critical Thinking and Moral Critique, 1986.

Paul, R., E. Glaser, and B. Bowen. "Critical Thinking Appraisal: Fairmindedness Subtest." Sonoma State University, Center for Critical Thinking and Moral Critique (unpublished, but available from Richard Paul, Sonoma State University, Rohnert Park, CA 94928).

Perelman, Chaim, and Lucie Olbrechts-Tyteca. *The New Rhetoric.* Trans. John Wilkinson and Purcell Weaver. Notre Dame: University of Notre Dame Press, 1969.

Perkins, David. "Informal Reasoning." In *Automated Practical Reasoning and Argumentation,* ed. Dov M. Gabbay and Hans Jürgen Olbach, Dagstuhl-Seminar, Report 70, 1993, 6–7.

Peters, Edward. *Inquisition.* New York: The Free Press, 1988.

Pollock, John. "Defeasible Reasoning." *Cognitive Science* 11, 1987, 481–518.

———. 'A Theory of Defeasible Reasoning.' *International Journal of Intelligent Systems.* 6, 1991, 33–54.

Proctor, Robert N. *Cancer Wars.* New York: Basic Books, 1995.

Purtill, Richard L. *Logical Thinking.* New York: Harper and Row, 1972.

Rescher, Nicholas. *Introduction to Logic.* New York: St. Martin's Press, 1964.

Research Profile. "Economist Examines the Environment." *In Edition* 18, 1992, 2.

Roberts, David. "The Martensville Horror." *The Globe and Mail,* February 19, 1994, D1–D3.

Roberts, Leslie. "Science in Court: A Culture Clash." *Science* 257, 1992, 732–736.

Robinson, Richard. *Definition.* Oxford: Clarendon Press, 1950.

———. *Plato's Earlier Dialectic.* Oxford: Clarendon Press, 1953.

Rovere, Richard H. *Senator Joe McCarthy.* New York: Harcourt Brace, 1959.

Ruby, Lionel. *Logic: An Introduction.* Chicago: J. B. Lippincott Co., 1950.

Russell, Stuart and Peter Norvig. *Artificial Intelligence: A Modern Approach.* Upper Saddle River, N.J.: Prentice Hall, 1995.

Salmon, Wesley C. *Logic.* Englewood Cliffs: Prentice-Hall, 1963.

Sandholm, Tuomas, and Victor Lesser. "Issues in Automated Negotiation and Electronic Commerce: Extending the Contract Net Framework." *Proceedings: First International Conference on Multi-Agent Systems,* ed. Victor Lesser. Menlo Park: AAAI Press, 1995, 328–335.

Schiappa, Edward. "Arguing about Definitions." *Argumentation* 7, 1993, 403–417.

Schopenhauer, Arthur. "The Art of Controversy" (1851). In *Essays from the Parerga and Paralipomena.* Trans. T. Bailey Saunders. London: Allen and Unwin, 1951.

Schuetz, Janice. "Corporate Advocacy as Argumentation." In *Perspectives on Argumentation,* ed. Robert Trapp and Janice Schuetz. Prospect Heights, Illinois: Waveland Press, 1990, 272–284.

Schuman, Howard, and Stanley Presser. *Questions and Answers in Attitude Surveys.* New York: Academic Press, 1981.

Scriven, Michael. *Reasoning.* Point Reyes, California: Edgepress, 1976.

Shapiro, Laura. "The Lesson of Salem." *Newsweek,* August 31, 1992, 64–66.

Simons, Herbert W., and Michael Billig. "Editors' Introduction: In Search of a Postmodern Rhetoric of Criticism." *Argumentation* 9, 1995, 1–4.

Smith, Anna Marie. "What Is Pornography?" *Feminist Review* 43, 1993, 71–87.

Soccio, Douglas J. and Vincent E. Barry, *Practical Logic.* Fort Worth: Harcourt Brace Jovanovich, 1992.

Stevenson, Charles L. *Ethics and Language.* New Haven: Yale University Press, 1944.

Thouless, Robert H. *Straight and Crooked Thinking.* London: The English University Press, 1936.

Trevor-Roper, H. R. *Religion: The Reformation and Social Change.* London: Macmillan, 1967.

"20/20," September 20, 1990, Show #1039, "It's Really a Commercial." Journal Graphics (transcript), 1990.

van Eemeren, Frans H., and Rob Grootendorst. *Speech Acts in Argumentative Discussions.* Dordrecht: Foris, 1984.

———. "Fallacies in Pragma-Dialectical Perspective." *Argumentation* 1, 1987, 283–301.

———. *Argumentation, Communication and Fallacies.* Hillsdale, N.J.: Lawrence Erlbaum, 1992.

———. "The History of the *Argumentum ad Hominem* since the Seventeenth Century." In *Empirical Logic and Public Debate,* ed. Erik C. W. Krabbe, Renée José Dalitz, and Pier A. Smit. Amsterdam: Editions Rodopi, 1993.

Waller, Bruce N. *Critical Thinking: Consider the Verdict.* Englewood Cliffs: Prentice Hall, 1988.

———. "Advocacy and Fallacy." *The International Journal of Applied Philosophy* 6, 1991, 47–51.

Walton, Douglas N. *Logical Dialogue–Games and Fallacies.* Lanham, University Press of America, 1984.

Walton, Douglas N. *Arguer's Position.* Westport, Connecticut: Greenwood Press, 1985.

———. *Question-Reply Argumentation.* New York: Greenwood Press, 1989b.

———. *Informal Logic.* Cambridge: Cambridge University Press, 1989a.

———. *Begging the Question.* New York: Greenwood Press, 1991.

———. *Practical Reasoning.* Savage, Maryland: Rowman and Littlefield, 1990c.

———. "Ignoring Qualifications (*Secundum Quid*) as a Subfallacy of Hasty Generalization." *Logique et Analyse.* 129–130, 1990b, 113–154.

———. "What Is Reasoning? What Is an Argument?" *Journal of Philosophy* 87, 1990d, 399–419.

———. "Hamblin on the Standard Treatment of Fallacies." *Philosophy and Rhetoric* 24, 1991c, 353–361.

———. "Bias, Critical Doubt and Fallacies." *Argumentation and Advocacy* 28, 1991a, 1–22.

———. "Critical Faults and Fallacies of Questioning." *Journal of Pragmatics* 15, 1991b, 337–366.

———. "Questionable Questions in Question Period: Prospects for an Informal Logic of Parliamentary Discourse." In the *Proceedings of the Conference "Logic and Politics,"* ed. E. M. Barth and E. C. W. Krabbe, published by the Royal Netherlands Academy of Arts and Sciences, Amsterdam, North-Holland, 1992a, 87–95.

———. *Plausible Argument in Everyday Conversation.* Albany, New York: State University of New York Press, 1992b.

———. *The Place of Emotion in Argument.* University Park: Penn State Press, 1992c.

———. "Types of Dialogue, Dialectical Shifts and Fallacies." In *Argumentation Illuminated,* ed. Frans H. van Eemeren, Rob Grootendorst, J. Anthony Blair, and Charles A. Willard. Amsterdam: SICSAT, 1992d, 133–147.

———. *A Pragmatic Theory of Fallacy.* Tuscaloosa: Alabama, University of Alabama Press, 1995.

———. *Arguments from Ignorance.* University Park: Penn State Press, 1995.

———. *Argument Structure: A Pragmatic Theory.* Toronto: University of Toronto Press, 1996a.

———. *Fallacies Arising from Ambiguity.* Dordrecht: Kluwer, 1996b.

Walton, Douglas N. and Erik C. W. Krabbe. *Commitment in Dialogue.* Albany: State University of New York Press, 1995.

Walton, Douglas, and Alan Brinton, eds. *Historical Foundations of Informal Logic,* Aldershot, England: Ashgate, 1997.

Walton, R. E., and R. B. McKersie. *A Behavioral Theory of Labor Negotiations.* New York: McGraw-Hill, 1965.

Watson, Bruce. "Salem's Darkest Hour: Did the Devil Make Them Do It?" *Smithsonian* 23, 1992, 117–131.

Watts, Isaac. *Logick: Or, the Right Use of Reason in the Inquiry After Truth.* 15th ed. London, printed for J. Buckland et al., 1972.

Wooldridge, Michael, and Nicholas R. Jennings. "Intelligent Agents: Theory and Practice." *The Knowledge Engineering Review* 10, 1995, 115–152.

York, Geoffrey. "The Evolution of Lloyd Axworthy." *The Globe and Mail,* April 5, 1994, pp. A1, A2, and A5.

Zeller, Eduard. *Outlines of the History of Greek Philosophy.* 13th ed. Trans. L. R. Palmer, revised by Wilhelm Nestle. New York: Harcourt, Brace & Co., 1931.

INDEX

characteristics, 243–5, 251–3, 256
defined, 238
determining circumstances, 247
hysteria, 243
new use of term, 237
parasemotic framework of, 254
pressurized sequence of argumentation, 256

Wooldridge, Michael, 263–4

Z
zero point of view (*see also* neutrality), 64, 66–67, 74–75, 85
zero-sum game, 36